£3

Robert Louis Stevenson

PAUL BINDING

Robert Louis Stevenson

Illustrated by
ROBIN JACQUES

London
OXFORD UNIVERSITY PRESS
1974

Oxford University Press, Ely House, London W. 1

GLASGOW NEW YORK TORONTO MELBOURNE WELLINGTON
CAPE TOWN IBADAN NAIROBI DAR ES SALAAM LUSAKA ADDIS ABABA
DELHI BOMBAY CALCUTTA MADRAS KARACHI LAHORE DACCA
KUALA LUMPUR SINGAPORE HONG KONG TOKYO

ISBN 0 19 273133 5

© Paul Binding 1974
First published 1974

ACKNOWLEDGEMENT

The extract from *Critical Kit-Kats* by Edmund Gosse
is reprinted by kind permission of the publishers,
William Heinemann Ltd.

Printed in Great Britain by T. & A. Constable Ltd., Edinburgh

For
KERSTIN BAER

'I have come so far; and the sights and thoughts of my youth pursue me; and I see like a vision the youth of my father, and of his father, and the whole stream of lives flowing down there far in the north, with the sound of laughter and tears, to cast me out in the end, as by a sudden freshet, on these ultimate islands. And I admire and bow my head before the romance of destiny.'

ROBERT LOUIS STEVENSON
SAMOA 1892

Chapter 1

Climb to the top of the small craggy hill which stands at the east end of central Edinburgh. This is the Calton Hill and can be distinguished by the sham Greek temple that crowns it. Of all places from which to view Edinburgh and its surroundings, 'this Calton Hill', said Robert Louis Stevenson, 'is perhaps the best'. He certainly was in a position to know; born in Edinburgh on 13 November 1850, he grew to manhood there, and though ill-health in later years compelled him to live far away from it, the city never ceased to be a source of creative inspiration to him:

'Writing as I do in a strange quarter of the world, and a late day of my age, I can still behold the profile of her towers and chimneys, and the long trail of her smoke against the sunset; I can still hear those strains of martial music that she goes to bed with. . . .' In those years of exile there would come flooding back into his mind memories of 'the august airs of the Castle on its rock, nocturnal passages of lights and trees, the sudden song of the blackbird in a suburban lane, rosy and dusky winter sunsets, the uninhabited splendours of the early dawn, the building up of the city on a misty day, house above house, spire above spire, until it was received into a sky of softly glowing clouds, and seemed to pass on and upwards, by fresh grades and rises, city beyond city, a New Jerusalem, bodily scaling heaven. . . .'

The ascent of Calton Hill is made by a flight of steps cut in the rock. On the way up, you will pass a memorial to Robert Burns, and perhaps be reminded of one of the great Scottish poet's most tender verses, the song of a young man who has to leave behind his Edinburgh sweetheart and is shortly to embark on a boat leaving from the Port of Leith, which can splendidly be seen from the top of the hill:

> Go fetch to me a pint o' wine,
>   And fill it in a silver tassie,
> That I may drink, before I go,
>   A service to my bonie lassie;
> The boat rocks at the Pier o' Leith,
>   Fu' loud the wind blaws frae the Ferry,
> The ship rides by the Berwick-law,
>   And I maun leave my bonie Mary.

Directly below the hill lies the Canongate Kirkyard where another Scottish poet, Robert Fergusson, lies buried. On his own walk up to the Calton Hill, Stevenson would have been more likely to have been thinking of Fergusson than of Burns. Fergusson's life was short, intense, debauched and tragic; he died insane at the age of twenty-four. Born one hundred years after the poet, Stevenson used to wonder, in troubled moments of his youth when he too was up against the conventionality of upper-middle-class Edinburgh society, whether he might not be a reincarnation of Rab Fergusson.

How romantic Edinburgh and the countryside around it look from the top of the hill! No wonder Stevenson grew up to be a writer of romances, whose books awaken and appeal to our own deepest romantic instincts. To the North lies the Firth of Forth, with the hills of the Kingdom of Fife beyond; ships can be seen in the docks of the Port of Leith, and farther along the coast, dropped into the cold waters of the Forth, is the lump-like islet known as the Bass Rock. Then look to the South. 'There,' wrote Stevenson in his description of the Calton Hill view in *Edinburgh: Picturesque Notes*, 'is Holyrood Palace, with its Gothic frontal and ruined abbey, and the red sentry pacing smartly to and fro before the door like a mechanical figure in a panorama. By way of an outpost, you can single out the little peak-roofed lodge, over which Rizzio's murderers made their escape and where Queen Mary herself [Mary Queen of Scots], according to gossip, bathed in white wine to entertain her loveliness. Behind and overhead, lie the Queen's Park, from Muschat's Cairn to Dumbiedykes, St. Margaret's Loch, and the long wall of Salisbury Crags: and thence, by knoll and rocky bulwark and precipitous slope, the eye rises to the top of Arthur's Seat, a hill for magnitude, a mountain in virtue of its bold design. This upon your left. Upon the right, the roofs and spires of the Old Town climb one above another to where the citadel prints its broad bulk and jagged crown of bastions on the western sky. Perhaps it is now one in the afternoon; and at the same instant of time . . . a puff of smoke followed by a report bursts from the half-moon battery at the Castle. This is the time-gun by which people set their watches, as far as the sea coast or in hill farms upon the Pentlands. To complete the view, the eye enfilades Princes Street, black with traffic, and has a broad look over the valley between the Old Town and the New: here, full of railway trains and stepped over by the high North Bridge upon its many columns, and there, green with trees and gardens.'

Stevenson always delighted in the numerous historical associations of Edinburgh. But today, in addition to these, one thinks of the associations with Stevenson's own stories. Out of the Firth of Forth sailed David Balfour, kidnapped on board an ill-crewed ship bound for the West Indies. On the Bass Rock he was held prisoner; amid the dark tenements and wynds of the Old Town he sought helpers, evaded enemies and first met the beautiful Catriona. From the Castle, St. Ives made his daring escape, while in the New Town lived one of Stevenson's heroes who most resembles himself—John Nicholson in *The Misadventures of John Nicholson.*

You have to look to the North-West to study the New Town properly—that beautiful sequence of wide streets and spacious squares, most of which are filled with gardens. The New Town of Edinburgh was laid out according to designs of the Adam Brothers in the period 1770-1820 and is perhaps the earliest example of its kind of careful town planning. It was here that so many of the distinguished men who made Edinburgh the cultural centre it was in the late eighteenth century lived—it was here, like so many members of the prosperous professional classes, that the Stevensons had their home. For when Louis was seven years old, his father, Thomas Stevenson, a successful engineer, moved his family to No. 17 Heriot Row, a terrace of elegant but solid-looking houses, parallel to Queen Street, one of the New Town's principal thoroughfares. The Stevensons remained in that house for almost thirty years.

Had one been walking past these houses in Heriot Row in the early hours of the morning in, say, the year 1858, one might, looking up at No. 17, have seen a pale face against the window. It would have belonged to a small boy wrapped up in a blanket and, behind him, holding him up, would have been his nurse. It is fitting to begin the story of Louis Stevenson's life with such a picture, since perhaps the most distinguishing feature of his childhood was that it was marred by a terrible amount of illness. He had inherited from his mother a severe chest weakness, which remained with him all his life; during these early years it was at night that he suffered the most intensely. Persistent coughing prevented sleep and nothing took his mind off his pain more than being lifted up by his nurse, Cummy, to the window, to look into 'the blue night starred with street-lamps' and to see whether lighted windows could be spied in Queen Street itself. Louis and Cummy would wonder if 'there also, there were children that could not sleep, and if the lighted oblongs were signs of those that waited like us for the morning'.

The particular aspect of the morning the small boy so tensely waited for was the arrival of the carts: 'It was my custom, as the hours dragged on, to repeat the question "When will the carts come in?" and repeat it again and again until at last those sounds arose in the street . . . The road before our house is a great thoroughfare for early carts. I knew not, and I never have known, what they carry, whence they come, or whither they go. But I know that, long ere dawn, and for hours together, they stream continuously past, with the same rolling and jerking of wheels, and the same clink of horses' feet. It was not for nothing that they made the burthen of my wishes all night through. They are really the first throbbings of life, the harbingers of day; and it pleases you as much to hear them as it must please a shipwrecked seaman once again to grasp a hand of flesh and blood after years of miserable solitude.' (One thinks of Ben Gunn, marooned on Treasure Island, united with other men again.) The carts coming he knew not whence and bound he knew not

4

whither must have early aroused in Louis the feeling for mysterious ventures and journeys which are so marked a feature of his books. But so too must the tales his father told him.

These also took place at night. Sickness often produces disturbing dreams, and those nights on which Louis was actually able to sleep were often made dreadful by nightmares from which he would waken screaming and trembling. These dreams 'were sometimes very strange', Stevenson later remembered. 'I dreamed I was to swallow the world: and the terror of the fancy arose from the complete conception I had of the hugeness and populousness of our sphere.' His screams would bring his father on to the scene, and Thomas Stevenson would, to comfort him, tell him stories. And what stories they were! Stories of ships, roadside inns, highwaymen, old sailors, robbers. These stories inevitably bring to mind Stevenson's own ones. Later on, Stevenson was able to send himself to sleep with tales of his own. He particularly liked relating to himself the doings of a highwayman called Jerry Abershaw. In his adult years he often expressed a wish to write a story about this character, but he never did.

Bad dreams, broken sleep, insomnia-ridden nights, the constant battling against pain—these are not pleasant experiences for a small boy and they played a dominating role, indeed a determining one, in Stevenson's childhood. They are partly responsible for the adult Stevenson having such a lively sense of horror and terror. *The Body-Snatcher* and *Dr. Jekyll and Mr. Hyde*—the story for which actually came to him in a dream—are among the most frightening tales in our language. But being ill and having the night hours to get through were not unqualified misfortunes. They developed the boy's imagination and love of stories to a degree that perhaps wouldn't have been reached had he enjoyed the best of health. And, as everyone remembers, there are times in one's childhood when having to spend a day in bed with one's thoughts and possessions for company, can bring one considerable delight. Stevenson tried to express this feeling himself, in childish language, in one of the poems in *A Child's Garden of Verses*:

> When I was sick and lay a-bed,
> I had two pillows at my head,
> And all my toys beside me lay
> To keep me happy all the day.

And sometimes for an hour or so
I watched my leaden soldiers go,
With different uniforms and drills,
Among the bed-clothes, through the hills;

And sometimes sent my ships in fleets
All up and down among the sheets;
Or brought my trees and houses out,
And planted cities all about.

I was the giant great and still
That sits upon the pillow-hill,
And sees before him, dale and plain,
The pleasant land of counterpane.

Louis Stevenson was a very excitable, imaginative and highly strung little boy, and being an only child increased these qualities. He gave signs of his unusual mind early on; given a strong religious upbringing, he was worried at the age of only three by the fact that sheep and horses did not know about God. 'I think,' he said, 'somebody might read the Bible to them.' At the age of six, he crooned himself to sleep with what he called his Songstries. Songstries were odd chants based on religious stories which he must have heard from his nurse and from his grand-father, the minister, at the Manse at Colinton. Hiding behind the door of his son's room, Thomas Stevenson noted down one of them—strange lines indeed for a six-year-old:

Had not an angel got the pride of man,
No evil thought, no hardened heart would have been seen,
No hell to go to, but a heaven so pure,
      That Angel was the Devil.
Had not that angel got the pride, there would have been no need
For Jesus Christ to die upon the Cross.

A favourite game of Louis' was to play at churches. He insisted on playing this game at the house of a friend, Walter Blaikie. Walter's mother entered the room, and found Louis blasphem-ously dressed up as a minister in a black cloak and a white paper dog-collar, preaching a sermon from a platform constructed out of turned-over chairs. Mrs. Blaikie was shocked and furious and ripped the collar from Louis' neck.

Louis showed his lively imagination in the games he played by himself and in those he played with other children. He sent himself in his fancy on fantastic voyages to remote and wondrous islands; climbing a tree and looking out over the surrounding gardens or watching the sun set as he lay in bed would stimulate him to dreams of exotic travel. From the very earliest age he adored reading, particularly tales of adventure and far-away places, and possessed a remarkable faculty for really *dwelling* in the world of the stories. Homely things pleased him too. How he loved on a winter's evening to gaze into the flames of the fire and see armies and curious cities there! He knew the names of all the flowers he was likely to see on his urban walks. And he rejoiced in an object that stood outside his own home door— a street light. He would point it out in his youth and young manhood to visitors, and later he wrote one of his most often quoted verses to celebrate it and the man who came to light it:

My tea is nearly ready and the sun has left the sky;
It's time to take the window to see Leerie going by;
For every night at teatime and before you take your seat,
With lantern and with ladder he comes posting up the street.

Now Tom would be a driver and Maria go to sea,
And my papa's a banker and as rich as he can be;
But I, when I am stronger and can choose what I'm to do,
O Leerie, I'll go round at night and light the lamps with you!

For we are very lucky, with a lamp before the door,
And Leerie stops to light it as he lights so many more;
And O! before you hurry by with ladder and with light,
O Leerie, see a little child and nod to him to-night!

Though Louis' father was not a banker but an engineer, Louis must have had the ambition he records in the poem.

In the games he played with other children, Louis was generally the leader, principally because of these remarkable powers of invention. The scene of these games was most often the home of his mother's father, Dr. Balfour, the Manse at Colinton; Louis' mother was one of thirteen, and so the house was usually full of cousins—many of them roughly Louis' age. Louis used to be sent to the Manse to convalesce after bouts of illness, and his times there he looked back on afterwards as perhaps the happiest of his childhood. Organizing games revealed once more his highly excitable temperament, for by the end of the day he was often 'exhausted to death'. One day of such happiness was often followed by 'two or three in bed with a fever'. But it must have been worth it. From the games and the sense of adventure they involved came much of the stuff that thrills us in his later books, and in essays and poems Stevenson was able to capture the child's world of play and make-believe almost better than any other writer.

Stevenson seems to have remembered the Manse always in an early summer setting: 'It was a place in that time like no other,' he wrote later in one of his earliest essays, '. . . with the smell of water rising from all round, with an added tang of paper-mills; the sound of water everywhere, and the sound of mills—the wheel and the dam singing their alternate strain; the birds on every bush and from every corner of the overhanging woods pealing out their notes until the air throbbed with them; and in the midst of this, the manse.' In the laurel bushes Louis would hide pretending to be a huntsman—once, his imagination got the upper hand and he claimed he actually could see a herd of antelope coming down upon the lawn. Then there was the exciting discovery of a secret passage and doorway, an enterprise dear to every child. The passage-way was through a dense clump of evergreens, the door was hidden in the wall at the end, and it gave out on to a mysterious spot by the river, above which the woods rose like a wall into the sky. 'I wish', wrote Stevenson later, 'I could give you an idea of this place, of the gloom, of the black slow water, of the strange wet smell, of the draggled vegetation on the far side whither the current took everything, and of the incomparably fine, rich yellow sand, without a grit in the whole of it, and moving below your feet with scarcely more resistance than a liquid. . . . I remember climbing down one day to a place where we discovered an island of treacherous material. O the great discovery! On we leapt in a moment; but on feeling the wet, sluicy island flatten out into a level with the river, and the brown water gathering about our feet, we were off it again as quickly.' Perhaps his fascination with islands dated from that experience.

In later years he would often hear the sound of the water-mills in his imagination, and return, in lyrical contentment, to the Colinton days. He liked to think of the millwheels still turning and churning, preserving as they did so past joys.

Over the borders, a sin without pardon,
    Breaking the branches and crawling below,
Out through the breach in the wall of the garden,
    Down by the banks of the river, we go.

Here is the mill with the humming of thunder,
    Here is the weir with the wonder of foam,
Here is the sluice with the race running under—
    Marvellous places, though handy to home!

Sounds of the village grow stiller and stiller,
    Stiller the note of the birds on the hill;
Dusty and dim are the eyes of the miller,
    Deaf are his ears with the moil of the mill.

Years may go by, and the wheel in the river
    Wheel as it wheels for us, children, today,
Wheel and keep roaring and foaming for ever
    Long after all of the boys are away.

Home from the Indies and home from the ocean,
    Heroes and soldiers we all shall come home;
Still we shall find the old mill wheel in motion,
    Turning and churning that river to foam.

You with the bean that I gave when we quarrelled,
    I with your marble of Saturday last,
Honoured and old and all gaily apparelled,
    Here we shall meet and remember the past.

Readers of Stevenson's novel *The Black Arrow* will remember the somewhat sinister incident of the live eye in the tapestry. This must have had its origin in a curious adventure that befell

B

young Louis and Henrietta and Willie, two of his cousins. The churchyard near the Manse had always been a source of mystery to the children who were ever mindful of the 'spunkies' (ghosts) and went by it, half-fearing, half-hoping to see one of these supernatural beings. Then one evening, as dusk was falling, they saw looking out from a hole in the churchyard wall, at the point where it adjoined the back of the stable, a burning eye. The children were both fascinated and horrified, and in whispers discussed what on earth it could be. They came to the conclusion that it was either the eye of a bird of ill-omen or a dead man sitting up in his coffin, watching them. (This fitted in with the actual position of the graves themselves.) The cousins got hold of a wheelbarrow and drew it up beside the wall; one after the other they climbed upon it and peered through the hole. And having accomplished this fearful feat, they took to their heels and ran all the way home as fast as they could.

By a coincidence, not only was Mrs. Stevenson one of thirteen, but Thomas Stevenson also. One of the cousins on his father's side, Bob, was to become one of Louis' closest and dearest companions in later years; from all accounts he was a remarkable and fascinating character. Their friendship began when Louis was five and Bob eight. Looking back on him, Louis thought his cousin, 'an imaginative child who had lived in a dream with his sisters, his parents, and the *Arabian Nights*, and more unfitted for the world, as was shown in the event, than an angel fresh from heaven'. The friendship greatly developed Louis' own imagination; even ordinary mealtimes with Bob were fun:

'When my cousin and I took our porridge of a morning, we had a device to enliven the course of the meal. He ate his with sugar, and explained it to be a country continually buried under snow. I took mine with milk, and explained it to be a country suffering gradual inundation. You can imagine us exchanging bulletins; how here was an island still unsubmerged, here a valley not yet covered with snow; what inventions were made; how his population lived in cabins on perches and travelled on stilts, and how mine was always in boats; how the interest grew furious, as the last corner of safe ground was cut off on all sides and grew smaller every moment.'

These were not the only imaginary countries the boys had together. There was Nosingtonia (Bob's) and there was Encyclopaedia (Louis'). Endless maps were drawn of these countries, histories concocted, wars strategized and fought. This last occupation was not to die with childhood: Stevenson was a life-long amateur student of military campaigns—his knowledge of them was exhaustive. And even in adult life he was very keen on playing with toy soldiers. Another game played with Bob was that of toy theatres, a hobby that lasted until his fifteenth year and which, one imagines, meant far more to Louis than to his cousin.

Perhaps the partiality to the model theatre is the first real indication of Louis' being destined to become a writer. As a matter of fact, he had resolved to become one ever since the age of six when his Uncle David had awarded him a prize for winning a competition (for which his other cousins entered) with a very dramatic account of the life of Moses. But the Toy Theatre was truly a passion with him and later the subject of an amusing and nostalgic essay, 'A Penny Plain and Twopence Coloured'. From a shop in the now rather grim and tatty Leith Walk, Louis bought the scenery, the pasteboard figures and the scenarios for such riproaring melodramas as *The Old Oak Chest, The Wood Daemon* and *Three-Fingered Jack, the Terror of Jamaica*. His skill at working out plays for the little theatre must have been excellent practice for the later construction of tense plots. And the pastime developed his romantic tastes. He responded to the kind of story the Toy Theatre specialized in with every fibre of his being. He never grew out of his love for benighted woods pregnant with ominous events, inns where significant encounters took place, highwaymen and pirates. Stevenson himself places his debt to Skelt's (the makers of the Toy Theatre equipment) even more highly:

'Out of the art I seem to have learned the very spirit of my life's enjoyment; met there the shadows of the characters I was to read about and love in a later future ... acquired a gallery of scenes and characters with which I might enact all novels and romances.'

Another significant influence on his later story-telling powers was his nurse Cummy. Her real name was Alison Cunningham. She came to look after Louis when he was only eighteen months old—she survived her charge by twenty years. Her devotion to Louis and to the Stevenson family with whom she lived as a respected member, was intense; she is alleged to have declined an offer of marriage to go on caring for 'her boy'. She was a great teller of stories, and her telling was dramatic in the extreme —with flourishes and gestures and changes of voice and theatrical facial expressions. Cummy was a woman of intense piety and her stories were generally of a religious nature; she was particularly fond of reading aloud the work of Presbyterian divines. Among the books she delighted in reading to little Louis were such appealing-sounding titles as *A Cloud of Witnesses*, *The Saint's Everlasting Rest*, Foxe's *Book of Martyrs* and *The Remains of Robert Murray McCheyne*. Protestant tract-stories are both thrilling and frightening, with their sense of the nearness of this life to the next, the perpetual awful shadow of God, and the ever-ready traps awaiting one in daily life laid by the Evil One himself. Cummy belonged to an extreme Calvinist sect which had broken away from the established Church of Scotland to which Louis' parents belonged. Her heroes were the seventeenth-century Covenanters who came to dominate Louis' own imagination throughout his life—his first real literary work, *The Pentland Rising*, written when he was sixteen, deals with their last days. More will be said about the Covenanters later; here one must merely say that, believing as they did in the idea of Election (in God's having predestined certain souls for salvation, others for damnation), and seeing that Scotland was the part of Britain where these Calvinist ideas flourished, they became convinced that the Scots were the chosen race of God—a view not shared, of course, by all their countrymen—and that it was their sacred duty to see their ideals and beliefs held and practised, not only all over Scotland, but in England as well. Their bravery when the governments of both countries decided that they must be put down was astonishing and moving, and someone interested in the 'Men of the Moss Hags', as they came to be known, cannot do better than wander round the stunningly dramatic Greyfriars Kirkyard in Edinburgh, look at the tombs erected to the Covenanter martyrs and read the sad inscriptions engraved on them, monuments to a faith fanatically held to the death. In the nineteenth century there was a revival of certain of the religious doctrines that the Covenanters held dear, and Cummy used to love to point out to her boy those hollows in the near-by Pentland Hills where they had held their secret, doomed meetings before being slaughtered so brutally. All this fed the child's idealistic tendencies, and, as we own much fine writing to it, we should be grateful. But there was much that was wrong with Cummy's upbringing of Louis, much that went to form the dark shadow which cast itself over his whole emotional and imaginative life, even to the end.

One must not make a mistake about Cummy—she was a warm, deeply affectionate person, to whom Louis remained devoted all his life. He never ceased to correspond with her, and even tried to make arrangements for her to come out to Samoa to visit him in his years of compulsory exile. *A Child's Garden of Verses* is, appropriately, dedicated to her. Indeed, the dedicatory verses are so fulsome that they are rather embarrassing to a modern reader. Louis speaks of Cummy as:

> My second Mother, my first Wife,
> The angel of my infant life.

But a narrow-minded intolerant religious creed, preoccupied with sin, guilt, damnation and election, even if learnt from a kind and sensible person, is not a healthy influence on a small boy. It was damaging to Louis and set up tensions and conflicts he never overcame. In a private paper written when he was thirty and thought himself to be dying—he was in California at the time—he poured out his true feelings on this matter.

'I would not only lie awake to weep for Jesus, which I have done many a time, but I would fear to trust myself to slumber lest I was not accepted and should slip, ere I awoke, into eternal ruin. I remember repeatedly . . . waking from a dream of Hell, clinging to the horizontal bar of the bed, with my knees and chin together, my soul shaken, my body convulsed with agony. It is not a pleasant subject. I piped and snivelled over the Bible, with an earnestness that had been talked into me. I would say nothing without adding "If I am spared", as though to disarm fate by a show of submission; and some of this feeling still remains upon me in my thirtieth year . . .

'Had I died in these years,' he goes on to say, and it must be remembered that he was often near to doing so, 'I fancy I might perhaps have featured in a tract. I have been sometimes led to wonder if all the young saints of whom I have read and meditated with enthusiasm in my early periods, suffered from their bio-graphers the same sort of kindly violence, or had idealized themselves by the same simply necessary suppressions, that would have fitted myself and my career for that gallery of worthies.'

His Christian instruction made him feel that he had an obliga-tion to practise kindness to the outcasts of humanity he might come across—old Annie Torrence, for instance, who helped do the washing. She was an 'inhuman, bearded spectre, with a human heart in spite of all; who made it her business to be kind to me and show off before me, singing, "It's all round my hat for a twelve month and a day" with witch-like steps and gestures, backing to and fro before me, the horrified and fascinated child. Out of my dreams, I have never feared so cordially any other phenomenon as this of Annie Torrence and her song; for I thought the song to be hers and to commemorate some romance of her so-long departed youth. Yet I know I was ever consciously busy in my own small and troubled soul, to bear a good face before this dismal entertainment and conceal from the old woman the disastrous effect she was producing.' This attitude towards human oddity was to have significant development.

Louis' delicate health and position as an only child meant that he was the subject of undivided affection and solicitousness. The affection he was given meant that, throughout his life, he responded to this quality and returned it: he was to be a devoted husband, the most understanding of fathers to his stepson. But the attention he was accorded did not have totally desirable results; not only did it develop in him an accustomedness to being the centre of interest that was to bear a lifelong inability to resign from the emotional limelight, but, in the form of the constant concern with his moral state, it left him with a neurotic relationship with the idea of virtue. Even in the charming re-capturings of childhood in *A Child's Garden of Verses*, we can see an almost unhealthy preoccupation with whether he was being a 'good boy' or not. His over-protected existence must have irked him; too often did he dutifully accompany Cummy or his parents on walks round Edinburgh while rough town boys bawled out after him: 'Hauf a laddie, hauf a lassie, hauf a yellow yike'—unpleasant words to hear about oneself!

And in looking back over his life, Stevenson found himself

bitterly critical of the yoke of religion that had been placed from such an early age round his neck:

'I have touched already on the cruelty of bringing a child among the awful shadows of man's life; but it must not be forgotten, it is also unwise, and a good way to defeat the educator's purpose. The idea of sin, attached to particular actions absolutely, far from repelling, soon exerts an attraction on young minds. Probably few over-pious children have not been tempted, some-time or other and by way of dire experiment, to deny God in set terms. The horror of the act, performed in solitude, under the blue sky; the smallness of the voice uttered in the stillness of noon; the panic flight from the scene of the bravado: all these will not have been forgotten.'

Stevenson may have had in mind while writing this passage a childish experiment he once made to raise the Devil. But surely what he is generally saying here makes sense—there is nothing like dwelling on the wickedness of something to make it have an unhealthy fascination. Histrionic denunciations against popery, drink, cards, and so on, are not sensible ways of approaching the subjects and are much more likely to provoke a counter-reaction than to convince the person they are addressed to of the rightness of the views, as many other examples than Stevenson's will testify. Throughout his life Stevenson always longed to be good, and this is a tribute to the strength and natural virtue of his personality. But he had to struggle to realize that there are many other ways of being good than those of the tract child in the Puritanical Sabbath story. Certainly the ideas first of Cummy, and later, as we shall see, of his father, produced a great deal of suffering in both the boy and the man Louis.

Chapter 2

As we have seen, Louis was a much-loved boy—loved by his nurse and by his parents. What kind of people were Mr. and Mrs. Stevenson? What were their backgrounds?

Margaret Stevenson (1829-1897) came from a distinguished professional-class family, members of which had been lawyers and ministers for many generations. Their name was Balfour, the surname Stevenson later gave to his favourite hero, David, of *Kidnapped* and *Catriona*. David Balfour was meant to be an imaginary past member of his mother's family and from what we know of it, it is not hard to envisage him as one: high-minded, tender-hearted, firmly convinced of the truth of his religion (we remember that when he arrives for the first time in Edinburgh he looks forward greatly to hearing the sermons of the leading divines), unflinching in his sense of right and wrong, and possessing a capacity for serious study and intense application—at the end of *Catriona* a successful legal career awaits him. Farther back in time, the Balfours present a more romantic aspect. Balfour ancestors had been Covenanters; one indeed had fought at the

Battle of Bothwell Brig for the cause. The family links up remotely with that of the Gordons, who produced Lord Byron, and less remotely with the Elliots, who connected themselves with the Scotts of whom Walter Scott was the most distinguished member. Here, then, Stevenson could feel roots with the proud, passionate and hard-headed families of the Border. It is interesting to note that when he drew a Border family—as he does wonderfully in *Weir of Hermiston*—he called them Elliot.

Margaret Balfour Stevenson was by all accounts a delightful woman, possessed of a singular sweetness of nature. She was tall, graceful in her movements and exceedingly fair. She was also delicate in health; indeed, as we have seen, it was from her that Louis inherited his lung condition. By temperament she was sunny of disposition, with a liveliness of humour that Louis inherited. Together they would share many jokes and both delighted in amused observation of other people; this pre-dilection seems to have flowered best when Mr. Stevenson was not at hand. From Margaret, too, Louis inherited his love of literature and his taste for what a contemporary of his, Lord Guthrie, called 'pauky Scottish stories'. (Lord Guthrie, indeed, became deeply attached to Mrs. Stevenson. 'She had an air of distinction and refinement,' he wrote later, 'her bearing in repose was detached and serene . . . hers [was] the beauty of a mind and soul which had heard the voice "Be of good cheer, I have overcome the world".')

In contrast to his gentle wife, Thomas Stevenson (1818-1887) had a complex and difficult personality, as much so as his famous son. And the family he came from were remarkable too, a family of lighthouse engineers:

'We rose out of obscurity in a clap. My father and Uncle David made the third generation, one Smith and two Stevensons, of direct descendants who had been engineers to the Board of Northern Lights; there is scarce a deep sea light from the Isle of Man north about to Berwick, but one of my blood designed it; and I have often thought that to find a family to compare with ours in the promise of immortal memory, we must go back to the Egyptian Pharaohs:—upon so many reefs and forelands that not very elegant name of Stevenson is engraved with a pen of iron upon granite. My name is as well known as that of the Duke of Argyle among the fishers, the skippers, the seamen, and the masons of my native land. Whenever I smell salt water, I know I am not far from one of the works of my ancestors. The Bell Rock stands monument for my grandfather; the Skerry Vohr for my Uncle Alan; and when the lights come out at sundown along the shores of Scotland, I am proud to think they burn more brightly for the genius of my father.'

In the last years of his life, Stevenson was at work on a history of his family, *Records of a Family of Engineers*, something which, alas, was never completed.

A certain romance hangs about the name of Alan Stevenson, Louis' great-grandfather. Alan and his elder brother, Hugh, were heads of a business complex with considerable interests in the West Indies. In Louis' home there was an oil painting of a ship, said to have belonged to these Stevenson brothers. It was 'the only memorial of my great-grandsire, Alan. It was on this ship that he sailed on his last adventure and it used to be told me in my childhood how the brothers pursued him [a dishonest agent of theirs] from one island to another in an open boat, were exposed to the pernicious dews of the tropics, and simultaneously struck down.' The story, Stevenson later thought, had probably become somewhat exaggerated over the years, but one can see the effect it must have had on the imagination of the future author of *Treasure Island*.

The man who died so picturesque a death left behind him a widow and a son, Robert. Jean Stevenson was a 'woman of strong sense . . . and a pious disposition. . . . Like so many other widowed Scotswomen, she vowed her son should wag his head in a pulpit.' However, nothing became of her ambition. She herself married again, to Thomas Smith, a man of formidable character and enterprise. August 1786 was the date of his chief advancement, when, 'having designed a system of oil lights to take the place of the primitive coal fires before in use, he was dubbed engineer to the newly-formed Board of Northern Lighthouses'. Not only were his fortunes bettered by the appointment, but he was introduced to a new and wider field for the exercise of his abilities, and a new way of life highly agreeable to his active constitution. He seems to have rejoiced in the long journeys, and to have combined them with the practice of field sports. 'A tall, stout man coming ashore with his gun over his arm—so he was described to my father—the only description that has come down to me—by a lightkeeper old in the service.' When Jean and Thomas Smith married, Robert Stevenson was an impressionable boy of fifteen. His mother's re-marriage completely changed his existence, for, as to his career, he turned his back on his mother's plans of the Church and entered his stepfather's engineering business, and, as to his private life, he was to marry his stepsister, also called Jean, 'fervent in piety, unwearied in kind deeds', a very similar person indeed to his own mother to whom he was devoted.

To be an engineer in the late eighteenth century was to embark on an exciting and challenging career, for the field was an unexplored one. The pioneering aspect of the profession greatly appealed to the young Robert Stevenson. There was a very strong romantic vein in his temperament and the life he had to lead catered for it, though it also involved him in considerable intellectual labours demanding much patience. But 'the seas into which his labours carried [him] were still scarce charted, the coasts still dark; his way on shore was often far beyond the convenience of any road, the isles in which he must sojourn were still partly savage. He must toss much in boats; he must often adventure on horseback by the dubious bridle-track through unfrequented wildernesses; he must sometimes plant his lighthouse in the very camp of wreckers; and he was continually enforced to the vicissitudes of out-door life. The joy of my grandfather in this career was strong as the love of woman. It lasted through youth and manhood, it burned strong in age, and at the approach of death his last yearning was to renew these loved experiences.'

The relationship between Jean and Thomas Smith and that between Jean and Robert Stevenson have marked similarities to each other. The women were quiet, religious, unworldly, a little timid, the men adventurous, somewhat worldly, romantic, industrious and ambitious. In his last and greatest novel, *Weir of Hermiston*, Louis was to portray such a relationship when he wrote of the married life of Archie's parents, the Lord Justice-Clerk and his wife, Jean Rutherford.

Louis' father, Thomas, was born in 1818, one of Robert's thirteen children. Some sides of Thomas' boyhood certainly sound appealing:

'No. 1 Baxter's Place, my grandfather's house, must have been a paradise for boys. It was of great size with an infinity of cellars below, and of garrets, apple-lofts, etc. above; and it had a long garden, which ran down to the foot of the Calton Hill, with an orchard that yearly filled the apple-loft, and a building at the foot frequently besieged and defended by the boys, where a poor golden eagle, trophy of some of my grandfather's Hebridean voyages, pined and screamed itself to death. Its front was Leith Walk with its traffic; at one side a very deserted lane, with the office door, a carpenter's shop, and the like; and behind, the big, open slopes of the Calton Hill, within, there was the seemingly rather awful rule of the old gentleman, tempered, I fancy, by the mild and devout mother with her "Keep me's". There was a coming and going of odd, out-of-the-way characters, skippers, light-keepers, masons, and fore-men of all sorts, whom my grandfather, in his patriarchal fashion, liked to have about the house, and who were a never-failing delight to the boys.' (As indeed they were to Louis, for do we not meet such characters in the pages of his books?)

Thomas Stevenson was a dreamy and impetuous youth who found school an intolerable burden—he delighted in playing truant from any form of regular instruction. On the other hand, when he joined his father's engineering concern, he applied himself to his studies with tremendous assiduity and intensity, and indeed became of all the Stevensons the most successful in his profession—both in his largeness of vision and in his actual achievement. His contribution to optics as applied to lighthouse engineering has been of lasting value. He was in demand for giving engineering evidence for Government commissions and Parliamentary committees. In 1884 his eminence in the scientific field was recognized by his being elected President of the Royal Society of Edinburgh.

Nor was science the only domain in which he excelled. Thomas Stevenson was a devout member of the Church of Scotland, and wrote several respected works on Christian doctrine. His son tells us that he valued his works justifying the Christian faith above his other achievements.

But the wild-boy side of him never disappeared. Stevenson himself was surprised at the enormous enthusiasm with which his father greeted the opening chapters of *Treasure Island*, and learnt that his father nightly sent himself to sleep with adventure-stories of his own devising—similar to those he had told to Louis on those awful nights of sickness. He was an ardent lover of the countryside, and therefore a keen walker—he was an incorrigible browser round old bookshops and stalls, and he made 'romantic acquaintance with every dog that passed'. All who knew him paid tribute to his being a wonderful talker, lively, enthusiastic, well-informed, humorous. At the same time there were difficult elements in his temperament. Some of these we will deal with later, when the relationship between Thomas and Louis was so strained. He suffered from what would now be termed a depressive temperament. Moods of deep gloom alternated with high spirits; fears of death and a rather morbid sense of his own unworthiness were followed by periods of stubborn certainty of the righteousness of his own views. '. . . his affections and emotions, passionate as these were, and liable to passionate ups and downs, found the most eloquent expression both in words and gestures. Love, anger and indignation shone through him and broke forth in imagery, like what we read of Southern races.'

Not an easy father to have, and in his years of adolescent rebellion Louis was to find him difficult indeed. But for a boy he had decided advantages. Not many fathers 'bravely encourage' their sons to neglect their lessons, and it would be pleasant to be able to say, as Louis could, that one's father 'never so much as asked me my place in school'. The stories he had to tell of his forebears inspired Louis' imagination, and we can find elements of his family history turning up again and again in his books.

Though the seeds of later tensions were there, in those early years, the home Thomas and Margaret Stevenson created for their son was essentially a secure and loving place. One of the most beautiful of the 'Songs of Travel' pays tribute to this. Written to an old Scotch air, 'Wandering Willie', it is used at a dramatic point in Stevenson's novel *The Master of Ballantrae* to suggest the tenderness that dwells deep inside its wicked and tormented villain. The singer is looking back over the vanished years of childhood and at the home that exists no more:

Home was home then, my dear, full of kindly faces,
　　Home was home then, my dear, happy for the child,
Fire and the windows bright glittered on the moorland;
　　Song, tuneful song, built a palace in the wild.

Now, when day dawns on the brow of the moorland,
    Lone stands the house, and the chimney-stone is cold,
Lone let it stand, now the friends are all departed,
    The kind hearts, the true hearts, that loved the place of old.

The house in the poem has a country setting, but the emotions are those of Stevenson thinking of his life at 17 Heriot Row.

Chapter 3

'The thin, elfin lad with the brilliant eyes' was how a boyhood contemporary saw Louis. Another wrote: 'In those days, he always struck me as being different from other people, but I little realised what a genius he was to become; but looking back one can see he had this in him from boyhood.'

His genius was certainly not shown in his performances at school. His schooling was anyway a somewhat erratic affair. We have seen how, though they belonged to the conventional upper-middle-classes of Edinburgh, Thomas and Margaret Stevenson didn't possess conventional temperaments, and their uncon-ventionality was nowhere more clearly shown than in their attitude to their son's education. They were without doubt inclined to over-anxiety, and their son was an unusual boy of delicate health. To list the changes of school and those tutors who coached him in interim periods would be tedious. There was, too, a Continental tour on which they took him, lasting several months. The two establishments Louis attended longest were Edinburgh Academy, to which he was sent when he was eleven and where he remained for a year and a half, and Mr. Thomson's School in Frederick Street, Edinburgh, where he was educated—with breaks—from 1864 to 1867. Ill-health kept him away from both schools quite frequently.

Perhaps this accounts for his somewhat disengaged attitude towards school. His position in class was usually low. This was mostly because he was unable to work hard at subjects which made no appeal to his imagination; he found such intricacies as rules of grammar boring and therefore not worthy of his attention. This attitude was never wholly to leave him. On the other hand, he shone at literature and history. A school-fellow at the Academy recorded his astonishment at Louis' precocious knowledge of the novels of Scott and the historical issues they dealt with—the class was studying Scott's *Tales of a Grandfather* at the time, and Louis was able to volunteer an impressive amount of information on these matters. A teacher at Mr. Thomson's stated that he found no sort of promise whatever in Louis' essays. One wonders if this was not because he himself set dull essay topics; certainly we know that Louis was deeply interested in writing throughout his boyhood. We shall return to these early creative efforts later.

From his fellow schoolboys Louis was somewhat apart. This apartness seems to have grown as his boyhood progressed. A clergyman who taught Louis for a brief time before he was sent to Edinburgh Academy, stated quite categorically: 'He was without exception the most delightful boy I ever knew; full of fun, full of tender feeling; ready for his lessons, ready for a story, ready for fun.' We know that Louis used sometimes to amuse his comrades by writing comic verses about the masters and the more noteworthy pupils. But the general impression given by people's recollections of him at school is of someone who very much went his own way. He didn't care for games, he had interests that did not coincide with school activities and curricula. 'He was not the typical schoolboy,' wrote someone who was with him at Mr. Thomson's. 'He was quiet, almost aloof, and showed but little interest in either us or his lessons.'

The quietness is not totally consistent with what we know of Louis at other stages of his life, highly excitable and talkative. Did these sides of his personality show themselves at school? It is hard to believe that they did not. James Milne, who later married one of Louis' cousins, had a vivid recollection of him 'one day in the Academy Yards in a towering rage. Some of the other kiddies were ragging him, and the rim of his straw hat was torn down, and hanging in rings round his face and shoulders.' The picture is the easier to credit as we know Louis was, throughout his adolescence and young manhood, subject to fits of near-hysterical rage and distress. But I think he realized early on in his school career that any public demonstration of strong feeling cost him dear, and, to prevent any such suffering, cut himself off from the life around him. Moreover, Scottish boys more than their English counterparts indulge in fighting and respect handiness with the fists. Louis disliked fights, and, even though he got called 'daftie' and 'softie' for his abstinence, avoided them.

It is significant that though he wrote copiously about almost every aspect of his early life—in essays and poems, stories and novels—Stevenson never once dealt with himself at school. Nor does he describe the school experiences of any of his heroes. There is a passing mention only in *Weir of Hermiston* of Archie in his role of schoolboy, and here the author is at pains to stress his detachment from school affairs. A mental blind seems to have come down in Stevenson's mind over this area of his life. But I do not think the reason for this was misery; after all, Stevenson wrote obsessively about his childhood and boyhood miseries. I think it was rather that he was bored by school, profoundly bored.

But once outside school he came to life again, and showed himself as lively and full of enterprise. One of his school-mates remembered his passion for Natural History, and related how he used to love wandering over the Pentland Hills in Louis' company in search of rare wild flowers and birds' eggs. Once, on such an expedition, Louis spotted a kestrel, marked it to its nest, and would not be satisfied until he had acquired some of the bird's eggs. With great patience he scaled a formidable wall of precipitous cliff until he had successfully reached the nest, from which he transferred the eggs to his schoolboy's cap.

This love of nature later bore fruit in the many beautiful and detailed descriptions of the countryside in his novels. He always seems particularly aware of the songs of the various birds; and there is an intense feeling for the changes the individual seasons cause in a landscape. David's wanderings through the Highlands in *Kidnapped* and Archie's exile on the family estate in the Border Country in *Weir of Hermiston* spring to mind immediately as showing Stevenson's power to evoke the world of the country.

Perhaps the happiest times of his boyhood were spent at North Berwick. These indeed were to the years between eleven and sixteen what the days spent at the Manse at Colinton had been to his childhood, and their importance in his development cannot be under-estimated. His parents, together with various Edinburgh families with whom they were friendly, spent the late summer weeks on this lovely part of the eastern Scottish coast.

'The place was created seemingly on purpose for the diversion of young gentlemen', Stevenson wrote later. 'A street or two of houses, mostly red and many of them tiled; a number of fine trees clustered about the manse and the kirkyard, and turning the chief street into a shady alley; . . . a smell of fish, a genial smell of seaweed; whiffs of blowing sand at the street corners; shops with golf-balls and bottled lollipops; another shop with penny pickwicks (that remarkable cigar) and the *London Journal*, dear to me for its startling pictures, and a few novels, dear for their suggestive names: such, as well as memory serves me, were the ingredients of the town. These, you are to conceive posted on a spit between two sandy bays, and sparsely flanked with villas— enough for the boys to lodge in with their subsidiary parents . . . a haven in the rocks in front: in front of that, a file of grey islets: to the left, endless links and sand-wreaths, a wilderness of hiding-holes, alive with popping rabbits and soaring gulls; to the right, a range of seaward crags, one rugged brow beyond another; the ruins of a mighty and ancient fortress on the brink of one; coves between—now charmed into sunshine quiet, now whistling with wind and clamorous with bursting surges: the dens and sheltered hollows redolent of thyme and southernwood, the air at the cliff's edge brisk and clean and pungent of the sea—in front of all, the Bass Rock, tilted seaward like a doubtful bather, the surf ringing it with white, the solan-geese hanging round its summit like a great and glittering smoke.'

There were ten or twelve boys of roughly Louis' own age and once with them, gone was the aloofness that characterized his behaviour at school: Louis was adventurous and full of fun. The other boys realized that he had an unusual cast of mind for someone their age, and they accepted the fact that he wouldn't want to take part in the more conventional pastimes of golf or football. But they treasured his company, his ability to make romantic escapades out of any enterprise they embarked on, his capacity for warm friendship. He must indeed have been a fascinating friend to have had.

'Always,' wrote David Lewis, many years later, 'there was some fresh weirdness in his imaginings of what happened long ago.

The most memorable, however, of my memories of that time is of our secret meetings, at what, for us, was the dead of night, in a small cave or fissure in the rocks at Point Garry. These were entirely Stevenson's idea, and he ruled over them autocratically.'

We remember how he was the organizer of the other children's activities at the Manse; the boy at North Berwick was the logical heir to the child at Colinton. These 'secret meetings' held a very special place in Stevenson's own remembrances; indeed, he describes them very fully and affectionately in one of his best—and best-known—essays: 'The Lantern Bearers'.

'Towards the end of September, when the school-time was drawing near and the nights were already black, we would begin to sally from our respective villas, each equipped with a tin bull's-eye lantern. The thing was so well known that it had worn a rut in the commerce of Great Britain; and the grocers, about the due time, began to garnish their windows with our particular brand of luminary. We wore them buckled to the waist upon a cricket belt, and over them, such was the rigour of the game, a buttoned top-coat. They smelled noisomely of blistered tin; they never burned aright, though they would always burn our fingers; their use was naught; the pleasure of them merely fanciful; and yet a boy with a bull's-eye under his top-coat asked for nothing more. The fishermen used lanterns about their boats, and it was from them, I suppose, that we had got the hint; but theirs was not bull's-eyes, nor did we ever play at being fishermen. The police carried them at their belts, and we plainly copied them in that; yet we did not pretend to be policemen. Burglars, indeed, we may have had some haunting thoughts of; and we had certainly an eye to past ages when lanterns were more common, and to certain story-books in which we had found them to figure very largely. But take it for all in all, the pleasure of the thing was substantive; and to be a boy with a bull's-eye under his top-coat was good enough for us.

'When two of these asses met, there would be an anxious "Have you got your lantern?" and a gratified "Yes!" That was the shibboleth, and very needful too; for, as it was the rule to keep our glory contained, none could recognise a lantern-bearer, unless (like the pole-cat) by the smell. Four or five would sometimes climb into the belly of a ten-man lugger, with nothing but the thwarts above them—for the cabin was usually locked; or choose out some hollow of the links where the wind might whistle overhead. There the coats would be unbuttoned and the bull's-eyes discovered; and in the chequering glimmer, under the huge windy hall of the night, and cheered by a rich steam of toasting tinware, these fortunate young gentlemen would crouch together in the cold sand of the links or on the scaly bilges of the fishing-boat, and delight themselves with inappropriate talk. Woe is me that I may not give some specimens— some of their foresights of life, or deep inquiries into the rudiments of man and nature, these were so fiery and so innocent, they were so richly silly, so romantically young. But the talk, at any rate, was but a condiment; and these gatherings themselves only accidents in the career of the lantern-bearer. The essence of this bliss was to walk by yourself in the black night; the slide shut, the top-coat buttoned; not a ray escaping, whether to conduct your footsteps or to make your glory public; a mere pillar of darkness in the dark; and all the while, deep down in the privacy of your fool's heart, to know you had a bull's-eye at your belt, and to exult and sing over the knowledge.'

What do these nocturnal adventures tell us about the boy Louis? They show, above all, his ability to cast an intense romantic glow over his—and his companions'—doings and situations. In the essay from which I have quoted, he uses the nightly meetings in North Berwick to bring home to the reader a philosophic truth. An outsider, he says, might have come by and seen a group of teenagers huddled over smelly lanterns in a cold, wind-blown spot talking either extravagant nonsense or the usual schoolboy indecencies; the participants, however, saw themselves in the midst of a most thrilling undertaking. Romance springs from within. And looking back over the exploits, Stevenson saw them as representative of the hunger for romantic experience that is at the heart of every man. He also makes the difference between what the casual passer-by might have made of the Lantern-Bearer meetings and what the boys themselves felt about it, a justification for the kind of fiction which he had chosen to write. The normal realistic writer describing such a group of boys could not have done justice to the emotions and excitement that they were feeling; only a romancer could do that. In writing *his* kind of story, Stevenson was describing a deeper kind of reality.

This has taken us away from the boy on the North Berwick beaches, but it is relevant. Stevenson the writer can be found in his behaviour in these late summer months of his boyhood. In the essay he minimizes his own part in the adventures; the reports of others make it clear that they owed their inspiration and their peculiar intense quality to Louis alone. Perhaps without him the other boys wouldn't have felt the mystery with which Louis' enthusiasm and ready mind invested these doings. So in a sense Louis' later career had already begun; here he was appealing to the romantic instincts and love of adventure within his comrades and using his considerable imaginative powers to do so. Was he not to do the same, to a wider public, with *Treasure Island* and *Kidnapped*?

The success of these North Berwick exploits suggest his charm, his ability to fascinate and win over others, and his capacity for enjoyment. These attributes were always to stay with him.

By himself, as in his early childhood, Louis' imaginative life was equally active. The majority of his imaginative adventures were based on the books he read so vividly. It was no doubt his love of these that made him decide to become an author; frequent loneliness intensified his capacity for weaving stories, and from a very early age onwards, he was scribbling ones of his own. The very act of setting down sentences on paper was beloved by him; at no stage of his life was he not writing. This addiction to the process itself is perhaps an author's most valuable single asset.

It is a nice touch of fate that the first author Louis had the good fortune to meet was R. M. Ballantyne, whose *The Coral Island* must come close to Stevenson's own *Treasure Island* (which indeed it must have influenced) as one of the most popular boys' adventure-stories of the nineteenth century. But the meeting was not an unqualified success.

Mr. Ballantyne had decided to write a novel the hero of which was to be based on Louis' grandfather, Robert Stevenson, the greatest pioneer of lighthouse construction. First he went to Bell Rock to examine some of Robert Stevenson's achievements; then he visited Louis' uncle to find out more about his subject. Louis was invited to dinner and was mildly excited at the prospect. R. M. Ballantyne turned out to be a very vigorous and good-looking man, who sang songs to the piano and drew sketches for the entertainment of the company. This consisted among others of Louis' cousins and they, unlike Louis, were not shy of the author. They were able to talk to him and enjoy his company, while Louis, smitten with embarrassment, wasn't able to say a word. And the irony of it was that it was Louis, not they, who *really* cared for the man's work. After he had gone home, Louis would dream of the situation having been reversed, and of himself having charmed Ballantyne. But the experience strengthened rather than otherwise his desire to be a writer.

Ballantyne soon gave way to Dumas, for whose romances Stevenson was always to feel a certain affection. Bunyan's *Pilgrim's Progress* was a continual source of wonder and awe to him; he early on acquired a taste for Defoe, and, perhaps, more unexpectedly, Thackeray. Indeed, he wrote a version of Thackeray's comic work, *The Book of Snobs*, about the townspeople of Peebles, where he'd spent some holidays. But his greatest delight in reading came from the novels of Scott. Scott was a lifelong idol of his, and a profound influence on him. Stevenson thought him the greatest novelist ever to write in English. Of all Scott's books, his favourite was *Rob Roy*, and later on echoes of it can be found in Stevenson's own best works of fiction, *Catriona* and *Weir of Hermiston*. He was always to remember his first reading of it, indeed, he doubted if he would ever enjoy a book as much as he did *Rob Roy* that first time.

Scott, of course, wrote of the history of Scotland and in doing so appealed to Louis' already acute sense of the past of his country, which was more and more coming to be a dominating force in his inner imaginative life.

But there was torment too in his interior life: the hypersensitive strain responsible for so much of his suffering in the child Louis, was very much there in the boy. When Louis passed on from Cummy's influence to his parents', the religious teaching he received was less narrow-minded and bigoted, though none the less rigid and ardent. Margaret Stevenson was shocked by things her son told her about Cummy's views; she didn't at all disapprove of light reading or cards or wine, and was amused by the way in which Cummy, during a foreign tour, distributed Presbyterian tracts in a beautiful Catholic cathedral they'd been visiting. But the sense of guilt and sin was still kept alive in the adolescent Louis had become, and alive too was his fascination for what was considered sinful.

There is a strange poem, 'Stormy Nights', written probably when he was twenty-four, which describes the tortured nights, which in boyhood as in childhood, were an ever-present unpleasant element in his experience:

Do I not know, how, nightly, on my bed
The palpable close darkness shutting round me,
How my small heart went forth to evil things,
How all the possibilities of sin
That were yet present to my innocence
Bound me too narrowly,
And how my spirit beat
The cage of its compulsive purity;
How—my eyes fixed,
My shot lip tremulous between my fingers
I fashioned for myself new modes of crime,
Created for myself with pain and labour
The evil that the cobwebs of society,
The comely secrecies of education,
Had made an itching mystery to meward.

Do I not know again,
When the great winds broke loose and went abroad
At night in the lighted town—
Ah! then it was different—
Then, when I seemed to hear
The storm go by me like a cloak-wrapt horseman
Stooping over the saddle—
Go by, and come again and yet again,
Like some one riding with a pardon,
And ever baffled, ever shut from passage:
Then when the house shook and a horde of noises
Came out and clattered over me all night,
Then, would my heart stand still,
My hair creep fearfully upon my head
And, with my tear-wet face
Buried among the bed-clothes,
Long and bitterly would I pray and wrestle
Till gentle sleep
Threw her great mantle over me,
And my hard breathing gradually ceased.

Even allowing for the self-dramatizing element so often present when Stevenson is writing about himself, this poem is clearly the working-out of guilt about nocturnal boyhood fantasies. What these were we cannot, of course, ever properly know; the most we can do is to hazard some guesses. Louis was such an outwardly good little boy, well-behaved at school, civil and obedient. He even submitted to such curious impositions of his parents as a graded series of fines for every slang-word he used—surely intolerable treatment of a young boy, for why *shouldn't* he use the slang that every other Edinburgh schoolboy used? He must surely have longed to behave in ways that would shock them, and, for that matter, everyone else he knew, to prove his independence by flouting their laws of behaviour, and night-time, when he lay undisturbed in bed, lent itself to protracted indulgence in elaborate plans of how he could achieve this. His interest in people who lived outside the moral law—pirates, vagabonds, thieves, even murderers—from now on became obsessive. While he cannot be blamed for these imaginative explorations, it is only fair to say that they did come to constitute a rather unhealthy neurotic vein in his mental life. They were responsible, it is true, for some valuable insights into human psychology—and without his love of pirates, we shouldn't have had *Treasure Island*, a misfortune indeed! But, on the whole, what is finest in Stevenson's creative work doesn't spring from these interests; the sense of guilt that accompanied or followed them, on the other hand, does indeed add a powerful dimension to his fiction, But, as I will show later, it was the healthier and highly romantic elements in his imagination that were the most productive.

Again, these thoughts that made miserable and guilt-ridden so many nights may have been connected with the advent of sexuality. Given the puritanical atmosphere of his home, it seems unlikely that this vital subject would have been presented to him in a very enlightened or open manner, and the first stirrings of sex would most probably have aroused feelings of bewildered shame.

Louis was both fortunate and unfortunate in that he responded to every experience in an intense and emotional manner. He was easily bubbling over with happiness, easily cast down into despair.

One day, when he was thirteen, a tragic awareness of what

being alive meant suddenly broke over him. The sadness of life seemed all at once too much to bear:

'. . . one melancholy afternoon in the early autumn, and at a place where, it seems to me, looking back, it must always be autumn and generally Sunday, there came suddenly upon the face of all I saw—the long empty road, the lines of the tall houses, the church upon the hill, the woody hillside garden—a look of such a piercing sadness that my heart died; and seating myself on a doorstep, I shed tears of miserable sympathy. A benevolent cat cumbered me the while with consolations—we two were alone in all that was visible of the London Road; two poor waifs who had each tasted sorrow—and she fawned upon the weeper, and gambolled for his entertainment, watching the effect, it seemed, with motherly eyes.

'For the sake of the cat, God bless her! I confessed at home the story of my weakness . . . It was judged, if I had thus brimmed over on the public highway, some change of scene was (in the medical sense) indicated; my father at the time was visiting the harbour lights of Scotland; and it was decided he should take me along with him around a portion of the shores of Fife; my first professional tour, my first journey in the complete character of man, without the help of petticoats.'

This was the first of a number of journeys in which Louis was to accompany his father. For there was no doubt in Thomas Stevenson's mind that his only son would go into his engineering business, just as he himself, the dreamer and school idler, had followed his own father. A visit to the coast of the Kingdom of Fife would serve as an excellent introduction to the life and work that would be Louis' when grown-up. Louis has left us an account of this trip in an essay: 'The Coast of Fife', and a very revealing essay it is, too. It has remarkably little to say about the lighthouses they visited, and the engineering problems that had taken his father to Fife seem hardly to have engaged Louis' mind at all. The personal attributes of the various lighthouse-keepers and their fellows he did, however, note quite acutely—already showing his faculty for perceiving essential traits in other people. Stronger, though, was his response to the natural scenery of the district, and stronger still his awareness of the historical associations of the places he went to. His knowledge of the history of his own country is indeed astounding. 'History', he wrote, 'broods over that part of the world like the easterly *haar*.' (The *haar* is the East of Scotland sea-mist.) In particular, he was interested by a stretch of country outside St. Andrews—Magus Muir.

This had been the scene of an ugly murder in the seventeenth century, ugly but, according to the murderers, justified. In May 1679 a band of Covenanters, those extreme Protestants mentioned earlier, had hacked to pieces James Sharp, the Archbishop of St. Andrews, who had always opposed them and their beliefs.

Stevenson's description of the effect the scene of the crime had on his boyish imagination tells us a good deal about him at that period of his life:

'From St. Andrews, we drove over Magus Muir ... It is a road I have often travelled, and of not one of these journeys do I remember any single trait. The fact has not been suffered to encroach on the truth of the imagination. I still see Magus Muir two hundred years ago; a desert place, quite unenclosed; in the midst, the primate's carriage fleeing at the gallop; the assassins loose-reined in pursuit, Burley Balfour, pistol in hand, among the first. No scene in history has ever written itself so deeply on my mind; not because Balfour, that questionable zealot, was an ancestral cousin of my own; not because of the pleadings of the victim and his daughter; not even because of the live bum-bee that flew out of Sharp's 'bacco-box, thus clearly indicating his complicity with Satan; nor merely because, as it was after all a crime of fine religious flavour, it figured in Sunday books and afforded a grateful relief from *Ministering Children* or the *Memoirs of Mrs. Katherine Winslowe*. The figure that always fixed my attention is that of Hackston of Rathillet, sitting in the saddle with his cloak about his mouth, and through all that long, bungling, vociferous hurly-burly, revolving privately a case of conscience. He would take no hand in the deed, because he had a private spite against the victim, and "that action" must be sullied with no suggestion of a worldly motive; on the other hand, "that action" in itself was highly justified, he had cast in his lot with "the actors", and he must stay there, inactive but publicly sharing the responsibility. "You are a gentleman—you will protect me!" cried the wounded old man, crawling towards him. "I will never lay a hand on you," said Hackston, and put his cloak about his mouth. It is an old temptation with me, to pluck away that cloak and see the face—to open that bosom and to read the heart. With incomplete romances about Hackston, the drawers of my youth were lumbered. I read him up in every printed book that I could lay my hands on. I even dug among the Wodrow manuscripts, sitting shamefaced in the very room where my hero had been tortured two centuries before, and keenly conscious of my youth in the midst of other and (as I fondly thought) more gifted students. All was vain: that he twice displayed (compared with his grotesque companions) some tincture of soldierly resolution and even of military common-sense, and that he figured memorably in the scene of Magus Muir, so much and no more could I make out. But whenever I cast my eyes backward, it is to see him like a landmark on the plains of history, sitting with his cloak about his mouth, in-scrutable. How small a thing creates an immortality! I do not think he can have been a man entirely commonplace: but had he not thrown his cloak about his mouth, or had the witnesses forgot to chronicle the action, he would not thus have haunted the imagination of my boyhood. . . .'

It is not only the detail and depth of Stevenson's knowledge of history that is remarkable here—it is his ability to see the conflicts and confusions in a man of an age remote to his own, his desire to understand and delve below the surface, and his capacity for visualizing—like a gifted film-director—the significant and curious aspects of the scene or event. A normal boy who was imaginative and interested in history might have been fascinated by the episode of the murder of Archbishop Sharp, perhaps only Stevenson himself would have seized on the mysterious figure of Hackston, in his complex moral role of abstaining from participa-tion in the crime and yet emotionally identifying himself with it, or been riveted by the physical detail of his hiding his mouth behind his cloak. The pages that Stevenson covered with research and imaginative writings about Hackston have not survived. But we can see that his absorption in this marginal historical figure foreshadows his other absorptions in characters caught in moral dilemmas—David Balfour, the Lord Prestongrange, Archie Weir.

So while the journey to Fife may not have set Louis thinking about matters concerned with lighthouse construction, it was certainly a turning-point in that from then on he was hard at work planning romances which had as their setting the troubled and convoluted past of Scotland.

As it happened, it was not until he was thirty-one that he actually completed a full-length work of fiction, this being, of course, *Treasure Island* itself. But from his return from Fife onwards, he was always scribbling chapters and scenes for novels. He tells us about this in the introduction to *Treasure Island*:

'Sooner or later, somehow, anyhow, I was bound to write a novel. It seems vain to ask why. Men are born with various manias; from my earliest childhood it was mine to make a plaything of imaginary series of events; and as soon as I was able to write, I became a good friend to the paper-makers. Reams upon reams must have gone to the making of *Rathillet*, the *Pentland Rising*, the *King's Pardon* (otherwise *Park Whitehead*), *Edward Darren*, *A Country Dance*, and *A Vendetta in the West* . . .'

We only know the subjects of two of these works—*Rathillet* deals with Hackston on Magus Muir, *The Pentland Rising* with the tragic last days of the Covenanters. This second was also the subject of Stevenson's first published work—also called *The Pentland Rising*. Louis was only sixteen when it was issued—thanks to his father's money—and it was written to commemorate the two-hundredth anniversary of the battle of Rullion Green. *The Pentland Rising*, published as a 'slim green pamphlet', shows how saturated in the history and ideas of the Covenanters Louis was—his knowledge of historians is astonishing in a boy of his age, especially in one whose academic performances were largely indifferent, but even more astonishing is his penetration of the frame of mind of the Covenanters in their fanatical, hunted last days. It has already been made clear that Louis' familiarity with the Covenanters was brought about by Cummy and her dramatic stories concerning them—however, it is obvious from his work that Louis himself must have given them much thought, and his ability to identify and sympathize with them must mean that they appealed deeply to his imagination.

The time has come then, before discussing this first entry into print, to say something about the Covenanters themselves, because throughout his life Louis was fascinated by them, and mention will be made of them again. It is also important to understand a little of their beliefs and history because they played such a vital part in Scottish cultural history, and are still part of the imaginative heritage of contemporary Scots.

The Covenanters take their name from a document, the National Covenant, drawn up and sworn to in February 1638. By this time Scotland had been united with England—through having a common king, though not a common parliament—for thirty-five years. The cultural climates of the two countries were, as could be expected, very different. Both England and Scotland had undergone the Reformation but in dissimilar forms. The Scottish form of Protestantism took its inspiration and doctrine essentially from Calvin—that is, they believed in the doctrine of salvation and damnation by predestination. The fact that God had decided on your spiritual destiny did not mean, however, that strict moral behaviour was not expected from you, and the practices that we associate with Puritanism (rigid Sunday observance, strong penalties for drunkenness or sexual indulgence, a general insistence on subjecting the senses to severe discipline, plain services with the emphasis on the sermon and on readings from the Bible, rather than on the Sacrament of Communion) were prevalent earlier and to a stronger degree in Scotland than in England. Under the union of the crowns, the Scots came to see their religion as a vital part of their identity, marking them off clearly and decisively from the English, and the first Covenant was made to ensure that it was preserved intact.

The reign of Charles I was a time of enormous tensions within Britain, and in these tensions religion played the central role. Charles I's High Church ways met with a very unfavourable response in Scotland and this was aggravated by the fact that he displayed little knowledge of or sympathy with Scottish affairs. While the Puritan faction in England grew to powerful proportions, the more extreme Protestants in Scotland, antagonized by Charles' attempts to impose his ideas on them, became more and more convinced that their divinely appointed duty lay in seeing the Calvinist kirk dominate and regulate every aspect of life, not only in Scotland, but in the sister-country of England as well. A second Covenant, generally known as the Solemn League and Covenant, was undertaken in September 1643. The Scots placed great hopes in Cromwell and the Parliamentarians, hopes that were to be disappointed. And after the Restoration of Charles II, the majority of the Scots, though still adhering to a different

37

brand of the Protestant faith from their English neighbours, a state of affairs that continues to this day, accepted the situation as an unfortunate one perhaps, but one to which they had to be resigned. There were, however, some, particularly in the South-West of Scotland (the part of the country known as Galloway), who felt that their acceptance of the situation was compromise with the ungodly; they looked on themselves as bound by the Covenant to do all they could against a worldly Government. It is to these last-ditch upholders of the promise that the term Covenanters usually refers. Even inside Scotland they were not particularly popular, but the English saw them as a nuisance which needed putting down.

In their views and in their conception of morality the Covenanters were not either particularly admirable or attractive—fanatical and bigoted, and with an intolerably unforgiving attitude towards human frailties. There is though, it must be admitted, a splendour about their last days—their awareness of the glory and presence of God, their unswerving loyalty to what they believed to be right, and their amazing bravery in the face of unavoidable destruction. Across the span of the years, they appear a noble handful of men hounded by a cruel outnumbering force—their secret prayer-meetings in the hidden valleys of wild hill districts (hence their name of the 'men of Moss Hags') have the stamp of heroism upon them, and their deaths, in what came to be called the 'Killing Time', take on the nature of martyrdom.

As has already been said, the nineteenth century saw a revival within the Scottish Church of extreme Calvinist ideas—this caused the famous 'Disruption' of 1843—and Cummy, and those of like mind to her in matters of faith, glorified the Covenanter heroes, who seemed to them to have stood out for God's will against a corrupt and time-serving world.

Louis, in dealing with the tragic story of the Covenanter uprising that was quelled at Rullion Green, was influenced by the talk of Cummy to such an extent that he dwells on the heroic, noble sides of the men concerned without considering, as he was to do later, the constricting nature of their ideas, ones which had already been responsible for sufferings in his own life and which, had he lived in a society where they were dominant, he would have found quite insufferable. But then what fascinated him most was these men's intense devotion to their beliefs in the face of almost certain death. And he had, of course, a heightened feeling for the romance of their situation.

Here is Louis describing the Covenanter rebels in their encampment by the Rullion Burn, on the evening before their crushing defeat:

'The sun, going down behind the Pentlands, cast golden lights and blue shadows on their snow-clad summits, slanted obliquely into the rich plain before them, bathing with rosy splendour the leafless, snow-sprinkled trees, and fading gradually into shadow in the distance. To the south, too, they beheld a deep-shaded amphitheatre of heather and bracken; the course of the Esk, near Penicuik, winding about at the foot of its gorge; the broad, brown expanse of Maw Moss; and, fading into blue indistinctness in the south, the wild heath-clad Peeblesshire hills. In sooth, that scene was fair, and many a yearning glance was cast over that peaceful evening scene from the spot where the rebels awaited their defeat; and when the fight was over, many a noble fellow lifted his head from the blood-stained heather to strive with darkening eyeballs to behold that landscape, over which, as o'er his life and his cause, the shadows of night and of gloom were falling and thickening.'

Indeed, *The Pentland Rising* is an impressive performance for a boy of sixteen, and his father, with whom he would solemnly and detailedly discuss the work, must have been proud of his clever son. We can see in it the various elements which, properly and maturely developed, were to distinguish Louis' later works— a gift for feeling his way back into a past period, for communicating excitement and a sense of destiny to his readers, for fastening on the really telling and haunting detail, and for bringing to one's attention instances of the complexities of the workings of human nature. Just as he was fascinated by the contradictions of Hackston's attitudes on Magus Muir, so he was struck by the character of one of the leaders of the persecutors—Sir James Turner. Renowned for the savagery of his treatment of the Covenanters, he is written about by Louis as follows:

'And now we must turn to Sir James Turner's memoirs of himself; for, strange to say, this extraordinary man was remarkably fond of literary composition, and wrote . . . a large number of essays and short biographies . . . The following are some of the shorter pieces: *Magick, Friendship, Imprisonment, Anger, Revenge,*

Duells, Cruelty, A Defence of some of the Ceremonies of the English Liturgie, to wit-Bowing at the Name of Jesus, The frequent repetition of the Lord's Prayer and Good Lord deliver us, Of the Doxologie, Of Surplesses, Rotchets, Cannonicall Coats, etc. From what we know of his character we should expect *Anger* and *Cruelty* to be very full and instructive. But what earthly right he had to meddle with ecclesiastical subjects it is hard to see.'

Religion was in the near future to bring acute unhappiness to Louis both in his relationship with his family and in his inner self. But in *The Pentland Rising* we see that in his adolescence Louis had a fervent faith. With what feelings he recalls the last words of the Covenanter martyrs:

' "And now I leave off to speak any more to creatures, and begin my intercourse with God, which shall never be broken off. Farewell father and mother, friends and relations! Farewell the world and all delights! Farewell meat and drink! Farewell sun, moon, and stars! Welcome God and Father! Welcome sweet Jesus Christ, the Mediator of the new covenant! Welcome blessed Spirit of grace, and God of all consolation! Welcome glory! Welcome eternal life! Welcome Death!" '

Chapter 4

Louis was not quite seventeen when he began his studies at Edinburgh University. The spring before he became an undergraduate, his parents took out the lease of Swanston Cottage, where they were to spend the summer months for the next fourteen years. The village of Swanston is set in a little hollow in the Pentland Hills, and when the Stevensons knew it, it appeared to be, though only in fact a few miles from Edinburgh, deep in the countryside. From the first Louis loved it, delighting in long walks over the moor-covered hills, accompanied by his little Skye terrier, Coolin.

Coolin was a dog of unusual intelligence and independence of mind, but at Swanston, his urban breeding showed itself and he got into trouble with the local shepherd for worrying the sheep. Some of the blame fell on Louis himself, of course, but in fact good came out of the stormy interview, for the shepherd, whose name was John Todd, and Louis soon became friendly. Louis would quite often take himself to Swanston for week-ends in the winter, and then 'it was a settled thing for John to "give me a cry" over the garden wall as he set forth upon his evening round, and for me to overtake and bear him company'. Louis found John Todd's tales of his adventures in following the shepherd's calling a source of endless fascination; he liked his stories of clever dogs and of hard tasks performed on wild moorland tops. He took pleasure too in the rich Scottish Lowlands dialect the man would use for the telling. In after-years Stevenson attributed his love of hillsides in all their intimate aspects to John Todd:

'It was through him the simple strategy of massing sheep upon a snowy evening, with its attendant scampering of earnest, shaggy aides-de-camp, was an affair that I never wearied of seeing, and that I never weary of recalling to mind: the shadow of the night darkening on the hills, inscrutable black blots of snow shower moving here and there like night already come, huddles of yellow sheep and dartings of black dogs upon the snow, a bitter air that took you by the throat, unearthly harpings of the wind along the moors; and for centre-piece to all these features and influences, John winding up the brae, keeping his captain's eye on all sides, and breaking, ever and again, into a spasm of bellowing that seemed to make the evening bleaker. It is thus that I still see him in my mind's eye, perched on a hump of the declivity not far from Halkerside, his staff in airy flourish, his great voice taking hold upon the hills and echoing terror to the lowlands; I, meanwhile, standing somewhat back, until the fit should be over, and, with a pinch of snuff, my friend relapse into his easy, even conversation.'

Another friend in Swanston was the old gardener, Robert Young, an elderly religious man with a passion for vegetables (the only flowers he really cared for were foxgloves!), a deep and close knowledge of the Bible (Biblical texts and phrases were always on his lips), and a peace-loving yet stern disposition. Louis saw him as an heir to the Covenanting tradition.

So Swanston really extended Louis' knowledge of people and ways of life. The upper-middle-class Edinburgh boy learnt to know the countryside not just as a beautiful backcloth, but as a place for living and working in all weathers and seasons.

The author of *The Pentland Rising* was quick to respond to the historical association of the village. In the folds of the hills that tower a thousand feet above Swanston, hidden from their enemies, the Covenanters had held their secret nocturnal prayer-meetings, and at intervals during these, the worshippers would slip down to Swanston Farm, where cheese and bannocks, brandy and milk were kindly left waiting for them. From the hills too had come in 1745 (the second Jacobite uprising), the followers of Bonnie Prince Charlie. They had demanded breakfast from the farmer's family; the great-grandfather of the man who owned the farm in Stevenson's day remembered all his life long being awakened as a child by rough Highland soldiers. Perhaps it was hearing such tales that stirred Louis' interests in the Jacobite past of Scotland, which later bore such splendid fruit in *Kidnapped* and *Catriona*.

For all during his youth Louis was working away at works of fiction with settings in the past—usually that of his own country. And it seems likely that, young though he was, he went up to University determined that writing would be his career. Outwardly, however, he made no attempt to resist his parents' plans for his future, which were very different. Thomas Stevenson was in no doubt about what Louis should do in adult life—he must go into the family firm. Louis was after all his only son; had he himself not followed *his* father? So Louis enrolled as an engineering student in the University, and not only were term-times thus taken care of, but vacations as well. It would be sensible for Louis to learn practical as well as theoretical knowledge of engineering problems. The firm was engaged on several light-house projects on the Scottish coast, and to these places Louis must go in his holidays to study matters at first-hand.

Louis, his head full of plans for romantic explorations of history, cannot have found the idea of the studies ahead of him very appetizing. He was, anyway, beginning to resent the roles his parents thrust on him. Though aware of their deep affection and concern for him—had not Swanston itself been principally taken because of himself? and his parents always kept a room ready there, to put up any friend he chose to invite—and though aware of his own affection for them, he certainly felt an exasperation at the 'good boy' part he was always supposed to play. *The Pentland Rising*, in which he championed the narrow Protestant faith of zealots dead for two centuries, marks a turning-point in Louis' story. The adventures and escapades he had longed for in the secret quiet of the nights now did not seem so totally unrealizable after all; he wanted to spurn the tract-child, the

43

religious pattern side of himself, which had persisted to some extent even into his sixteenth year. So not only did he start his University course with a lack of enthusiasm for the actual work that would be demanded of him, he started with an incipient resentment of being diligent and dutiful and doing what he was asked.

What people who met him for the first time during this period of his life noticed above all about him were his burning, intense eyes, set in an emaciated face, which seemed the more emaciated because of the length—Bohemian French, rather than Scottish or English—of his hair. He was thin, fragile-looking even, though, in fact, his health was less troublesome during his student days than at other times of his life. (Even so, it was weak enough!) His mouth suggested both humour and a general readiness with words, and his voice had, so people said, a haunting musical quality. As for his dress, it varied between the dandyish and the tatterdemalion; he became especially addicted to a velvet jacket and a cloak, so much so that in one of the drinking-dives he frequented his nickname was 'Velvet Coat'.

The University of Edinburgh itself is a handsome, silver-stone affair, standing in the heart of the Old Town, that romantic complex of old, tall, grim buildings that climb up to the Castle itself. Near the University there were—and to some extent still are—some of the worst slums of the city. Dark and sordid though they are, these 'wynds', as the alleys and closes are called, have a fascination all of their own; high houses, black with soot and age, hem them in so that they seem like curious canyons, houses often seven or eight storeys high, full of people in somewhat the same way as a warren is full of rabbits. Though not far away in distance, how different it all seems from the elegance of the New Town. And this was the journey—from New Town to Old— that Louis made every day he went to the University. To him, too, the journey cannot have seemed only a physical one! He was leaving behind a genteel ordered society for a richer, more complicated, more stimulating and, at times, more unsavoury one. Louis, as we know, possessed almost a sixth sense for associations with the past. In the New Town one thinks of the intellectuals who made distinguished Edinburgh's Augustan Age. In the Old Town one is reminded of very different people. In the Royal Mile itself, for instance (the street that descends from the Castle

44

to Holyrood Palace), we can find a pub dedicated to the memory of a Deacon Brodie and see the house where John Knox lived. Deacon Brodie, who lived in the last part of the eighteenth century, was by daytime a respected and competent Edinburgh cabinet-maker, and at night, an equally competent and inventive burglar. He intrigued Louis so much that not only did he write about him in his book on Edinburgh, but he later made him the subject of a play written in collaboration with the poet W. E. Henley, and he clearly stands behind that famous study of man's divided nature, *Dr. Jekyll and Mr. Hyde*.

'A great man in his day was the Deacon; well seen in good society, crafty with his hands as a cabinet-maker, and one who could sing a song with taste. Many a citizen was proud to welcome the Deacon to supper, and dismissed him with regret at a timeous hour, who would have been vastly disconcerted had he known how soon, and in what guise, his visitor returned. Many stories are told of this redoubtable Edinburgh burglar, but the one I have in mind most vividly gives the key of all the rest. A friend of Brodie's, nested some way towards heaven in one of these great *lands* [the name for the tall houses that have just been mentioned above] had told him of a projected visit to the country, and afterwards detained by some affairs, put it off and stayed the night in town. The good man had lain some time awake . . . when suddenly there came a creak, a jar, a faint light. Softly he clambered out of bed and up to a false window which looked upon another room, and there, by the glimmer of a thieves' lantern, was his good friend the Deacon in a mask. It is characteristic of the town and the town's manners that this little episode should have been quietly tided over, and quite a good time elapsed before a great robbery, an escape, a Bow Street runner, a cock-fight, an apprehension in a cupboard in Amsterdam, and a last step into the air off his own greatly improved gallows drop, brought the career of Deacon William Brodie to an end.'

Already, perhaps, Stevenson was noting the timidity and hypocrisy which lurked beneath the surface of conventional professional-class society.

No one brought up in the Church of Scotland could be other than mindful of the great figure of John Knox (1505-1572), guiding spirit of the Scottish Reformation, inspired, passionately godly, and later the subject of a sympathetic and imaginative short study by Stevenson himself. This part of Edinburgh is also haunted by the memory of the sinister Burke and Hare and the Resurrection men, who first rifled newly dug graves but then went on to murder people, in order to supply medical men with bodies for research. This macabre chapter of Scottish history was also to receive treatment by Stevenson, in a spine-chilling story, *The Body-Snatcher*. And there, somewhere in the black jumble of houses, lived the sad Major Weir and his devoted sister, two pious people—he known as Angelical Thomas, she famous for her gifts of prayer—both doomed to horrible deaths at the hands of the superstitious rabble of Old Edinburgh, the Major being burned, the old woman hanged. In the pubs of the Old Town, the poets Fergusson and Burns had drunk and talked away hours. The University and the Law-Courts had known Louis' hero, Scott, whose books he continued to read with intense fascination and attention. All the while then that he wandered round the Old Town in his student-days, Louis' imagination was at work, receiving as it were the spirit of the place, formed by those who had once lived there, and perhaps even at that time, he was busy considering how it could best be given imaginative fictional treatment. No one could have been a greater explorer and brooder about the Old Town than Louis. He loved to retreat to the Greyfriars Kirkyard, last resting-place of the persecuted Covenanters, and contemplate their lives and deaths; he loved to penetrate the dark wynds and feel in contact with people and ways and conditions of living utterly different from those he had always known himself, and which were curiously enough endemic to his own native city.

'In one house, perhaps, two score families herd together; and, perhaps, not one of them is wholly out of reach of want . . . In the first room there is a birth, in another a death, in a third a sordid drinking-bout, and the detective and the Bible-reader cross upon the stairs. High words are audible from dwelling to dwelling, and children have a strange experience from the first . . . Social inequality is nowhere more ostentatious than at Edinburgh . . . to the stroller along Princes Street, the High Street callously exhibits its back garrets. It is true that there is a garden between. And although nothing could be more glaring by way of contrast, sometimes the opposition is more immediate; sometimes the thing lies in a nutshell, and there is not so much as a blade of grass between the rich and poor. To look over the South Bridge and see the Cowgate below full of crying hawkers, is to view one rank of society from another in the twinkling of an eye.

'One night I went along the Cowgate after every one was abed but the policeman, and stopped by hazard before a tall *land*. The moon touched upon its chimneys and shone blankly on the upper windows; there was no light anywhere in the great bulk of building; but as I stood there it seemed to me that I could hear quite a body of quiet sounds from the interior; doubtless there were many clocks ticking, and people snoring on their backs. And thus, I fancied, the dense life within made itself faintly audible in my ears, family after family contributing its quota to the general hum, and the whole pile beating in tune to its time-pieces like a great disordered heart. Perhaps it was little more than a fancy altogether, but it was strangely impressive at the time, and gave me an imaginative measure of the disproportion between the quantity of living flesh and the trifling walls that separated and contained it.

'There was nothing fanciful, at least, but every circumstance of terror and reality, in the fall of the *land* in the High Street. The building had grown rotten to the core; the entry underneath had suddenly closed up so that the scavenger's barrow could not pass; cracks and reverberations sounded through the house at night; the inhabitants of the huge old human bee-hive discussed their peril when they encountered on the stair; some had even left their dwellings in a panic of fear, and returned to them again in a fit of economy or self-respect; when, in the black hours of a Sunday morning, the whole structure ran together with a hideous uproar and tumbled story upon story to the ground. The physical shock was felt far and near; and the moral shock travelled with the morning milkmaid into all the suburbs. The churchbells never sounded more dismally over Edinburgh than that grey forenoon. Death had made a brave harvest; and, like Samson, by pulling down one roof destroyed many a home. None who saw it can have forgotten the aspect of the gable: here it was plastered, there papered, according to the rooms; here the kettle still stood on the hob, high overhead; and there a cheap paper of the Queen was pasted over the chimney. So, by this disaster, you had a glimpse into the life of thirty families, all suddenly cut off from the revolving years. The *land* had fallen; and with the *land* how much! Far in the country, people saw a gap in the city ranks, and the sun looked through between the chimneys in an unwonted place. And all over the world, in London, in Canada, in New Zealand, fancy what a multitude of people could exclaim with truth: "The house that I was born in fell last night!" '

Up to his student days, Louis had led a singularly sheltered and protected life. He must have often resented this at the time; as he came to realize the extent to which this had been the case, his resentment grew. The lives of those born at the other end of the social ladder from himself came to have a potent fascination for him; the struggle for economic survival and the roughness of the texture of their existence roused his compassion, as can be seen in the above passage, and made him—for this period of his life— embrace many of the ideas and principles of Socialism. He was to carry his interest in the outcast and the socially deprived even further as time went on, seeking out the company of seamen, of petty criminals, of prostitutes. There is no doubt that it wasn't only social conscience or even sociological curiosity that drove him to these groups of people, but an increasingly hostile feeling towards his own class and the careful standards of his own parents, and a longing for liberation and escape.

So during the first years of his student life, Louis' mind was receiving many stimulations, but it will already have been clear that these did not come from his official studies at Edinburgh University. Perhaps the excitement of these other impressions, these fresh areas of knowledge, was such that it prevented him from giving his mind to other matters. Perhaps his increasing awareness that he must become a writer prevented him from concentrating on the subject which others had decreed should be his life's work. Or was it simply that theoretical knowledge of engineering bored him? Certainly the truth is that he soon gave up any attempt to work at his courses. He boycotted the greater part of his lectures, and throughout those he condescended to attend he yawned ostentatiously and daydreamed. His abstracted behaviour obviously aroused the attention of his fellow-students. Periodically, however, they noticed him jotting down something in a notebook. They discovered—not wholly to their surprise— that he was in fact writing down observations of his own, polishing up phrases that had suddenly come to him, scribbling away at subjects which had nothing to do with what was being talked about there and then in the lecture-hall.

How much, during the earlier part of Louis' studenthood, his father realized Louis' total unconcern with his studies is not certain; he must have been conscious of his disengagement from engineering matters. He also was increasingly aware of, and increasingly alarmed at, his son's Bohemian tendencies. But, to begin with, at any rate, he still clung on to the idea that Louis might one day make a successful engineer. He was backed up in this rather obstinate and ultimately groundless belief by two things. First it was clear that when he actually did put his mind to the subject, Louis was not without a certain scientific ability. He did in fact win a prize for an excellent paper on lighthouse illumination. This pleased and encouraged his father greatly. Secondly, Thomas Stevenson must have remembered that he himself had been an idler and a dreamer before he entered the business, and had he not turned out the most distinguished of all the Stevenson family in his work for lighthouse construction?

One result of the misgivings Thomas had concerning his son's conduct and attitude towards life was that he kept him ludicrously short of money. Though he came from a richer family than most, and had, assuming he wished it, a comfortable family business to step into when his studies were completed, Louis' spending-money was considerably less than that of the average fellow-student of his class. Perhaps Louis' parents were wise not to give their son the opportunities for extravagance he undoubtedly would have taken, but it surely is an intolerable way to treat a young man getting on for twenty. His parents imposed other restrictions as well. Thomas Stevenson scarcely allowed Louis to express himself on matters political or religious. No student exists who does not wish to think out his own position with regard to these subjects; Thomas Stevenson, fervent, hot-headed and rigid—a very difficult combination to deal with!—held strongly Conservative views in the political sphere, and in the religious was a staunch member of the established Church of Scotland, one moreover who wrote books defending its teachings. He was having no departure from these ideas in *his* house! Of course, both Louis' father and mother were loving parents; they were pleased to give their son dinner-parties (at which Thomas Stevenson did a very good deal of the talking) and certainly they could not be accused of lack of interest in his welfare. But Louis found himself more and more bored and impatient with conventional Edinburgh society, and the dances and soirées he was forced to go to he would attend with an expression of mildly disdainful lack of interest on his face. He found the impositions on his mental and emotional freedom increasingly hard to bear.

Nor did he, in his first years there, find much solace and enjoyment from the social aspects of the University, in many respects merely an extension of middle-class Edinburgh. Institution life never had any appeal for him anyway, and he soon had open—and, it must be admitted, rather unattractive—contempt for many of his fellow-students. He despised those who only thought of working hard for their degrees, of obtaining eventual good places in some firm, government office, or legal concern. Were they not ignoring the deeper, more instinctive aspects of existence? Were they not turning blank eyes to joy and pain, and the whole serious business of being alive? Anyway, they had ambitions which, even if at times he pretended to share them, meant little to him. All his life Louis was never really able to appreciate the worth of much bourgeois life. Members of these student circles didn't much care for Louis either. Questioned later on as to why they hadn't known the future eminent writer better, many of them replied that they didn't want to; they hadn't cared for the company he kept. One contemporary added tartly that much of Stevenson's contempt for conventional activities was anyway both hypocritical and easy. Unlike many of the hard-working students he affected to look down on, he knew that he had a family concern and fortune to fall back on. They were also annoyed by his general appearance and behaviour. Why had he, they asked themselves irritatedly, to dress so zanily? On fine days (the only days he came to work) he would stroll into lectures wearing over long hair a strange, battered straw hat which had been wisely cast aside by his grandfather. With the hat would be worn duck trousers, a black shirt, loose in the collar, and a tie that could have been a strip torn from a threadbare carpet. And when he sat down in the lecture-hall, he had a sneer on his face, or so they thought. One can't be very surprised that he didn't make himself popular with the more orthodox students.

On the other hand, Stevenson didn't care for the society of the young bucks of the University either. He liked neither the would-be smart set, of whom he wrote that 'flirtation is to them a great social duty, a painful obligation, which they perform on every occasion in the same chill, official manner, and with the same commonplace advances', nor the profligate groups whose main communications with each other seemed to him to consist principally of 'mutual bulletins of depravity'. So, for the earlier part of his University career, Louis was lonely. He was, however, also shut off from his fellows, his work and his family by a profound and secret melancholy. It was inevitable that sooner or later Louis, impetuous and romantic, would fall in love. But before he was twenty, Louis had been seriously involved—emotionally and physically—with a girl, and the affair had ended tragically —in separation.

Tantalizingly little is known about it; we are ignorant even of when exactly it took place, and much energy has been spent in trying to establish an identity for the girl. Biographers often refer to her as 'Claire' after the eponymous heroine of a novel Louis later wrote and at his wife's instigation destroyed. This dealt with a love-affair between a young man and a girl of humble station and poor reputation.

'Claire' is perhaps most commonly believed to have been the daughter of the Swanston village blacksmith, whom Louis got to know during one of his solitary visits to the cottage. Compton Mackenzie in his short study of Stevenson (1968) gives the affair a rural context but tells how he himself heard from the owner of a farmhouse (Buckstane, near Swanston) that as a young man Stevenson had been a frequent visitor there and had fallen in love with the youngest daughter of the family, Christina. This story accords the most closely of all the ones available with the love affair at the centre of Stevenson's last and most personal work, *Weir of Hermiston*. The hero in this novel falls in love with a girl whose full name is Christina, and their trysting-place is a Weaver's Stone, which is also to be found in the vicinity of Buckstane.

Other stories relate, however, how Louis encountered Claire in one of his low haunts in Edinburgh. J. A. Steuart in his life of Stevenson (1924) claims like Compton Mackenzie to have heard from private sources (to which he does not give names) the real identity of Claire, a more lurid one than the Christina of Buckstane. She was a girl from the Highlands called Kate Drummond. Steuart attributes Stevenson's later and undoubted fascination for the Scottish Highlanders to this girl with her soft voice and Gaelic phrases. Steuart gathered from people who had seen her, that when Louis knew her she was very young and pretty with jet-black hair, a slim figure and a fresh complexion, though when he himself saw her she was coarsened and exhausted-looking. For she was a prostitute, though one superior to the occupation she had been virtually forced to practise. That Stevenson did visit prostitutes or associate with girls who were more or less of that calling seems almost beyond doubt—but the scantiness of the evidence makes one reluctant to ascribe such an identity to 'Claire'. The Highland ancestry of the loved girl fits in very well with the tender and beautiful descriptions of Catriona in the novel of the same name, and the surname Catriona uses (her real one being forbidden) is significantly Drummond.

We must, it seems, await further research still before we can have any satisfactory picture of who 'Claire' was and how and where the affair took place. What we do know, however, is that Louis was very strongly attracted to and bound up with a girl from a lower social level, and class differences being much more strongly respected and believed in in those days, Louis' parents thought a permanent alliance with such a girl out of the question for their son. For Louis, and it is surely a tribute to his chivalry and honour, wanted to marry 'Claire'. His parents retorted that Louis was not ready for marriage, and one has to admit that they were probably quite right. And if one takes a commonsensical attitude towards the affair, one has to say that Louis, too, was right in giving in as he did to his parents' ban on the relationship. But this wasn't how he felt himself. He felt he had betrayed the one he loved. And he felt emotionally bereft.

For what the affair with 'Claire' had given Louis was a sense of rapture—necessary to the youth kept so long an emotional prisoner—a sense too of being valued, perhaps adored, for his own sake alone, not for the sake of any excellence he might attain. Now he was left with the feeling that the glories of such a sexual union were inevitably destined to come to a wretched end and this accounts for much of his behaviour during the ensuing ten years.

It is not surprising then that so many of his earliest poems—and we possess few written before the age of twenty-one—are obsessed with the theme of a tragic love-affair in the recent past.

In some of the poems he speaks as if the loved one were dead, but this is most probably a device signifying that she is dead as far as he is concerned. But all the verses on the subject emphasize the poet's present solitary condition:

> The relic taken, what avails the shrine?
> The locket, pictureless? O heart of mine,
>   Art thou not less than that,
> Still warm, a vacant nest where love once sat.
>
> Her image nestled closer at my heart
> Than cherished memories, healed every smart,
>   And warmed it more than wine
> Or the full summer sun in noon-day shine.
>
> This was the little weather-gleam that lit
> The cloudy promontories. The real charm was it
>   That gilded hills and woods
> And walked beside me through the solitudes.
>
> That sun is set. My heart is widowed now
> Of that companion-thought. Alone I plough
>   The seas of life, and trace
> A separate furrow far from her and grace.

And even more poignant are four lines written when Stevenson was twenty-five:

> Love—what is love? A great and aching heart
> Wrung hands; and silence; and a long despair.
> Life—what is life? Upon a moorland bare
> To see love coming and see love depart.

The most considerable testimony to the 'Claire' affair, how-ever, is *Weir of Hermiston* with its account of the love between Archie Weir and Kirstie Elliot. This is written with a burning intensity. Archie, who up to his sojourn in the country has been a student at Edinburgh University, falls in love with a girl who, though in fact she comes from an old Border family, has the manners, the speech and the sexual boldness that would have been lacking in a girl of his own—or Louis' own—class. The growing stages of their love are termed a 'moorland courtship'. Kirstie appears a wild, tender, beautiful creature, almost like some animal denizen of the hills. Behind Archie at the time when he meets Kirstie stand years of an exceedingly strained relationship with his father. He is first struck by Kirstie's beauty when he sees her in church—the minister of which has the same name as the minister at Swanston in the Stevensons' time—and later that day walks out on the hills to find her. He comes across her seated in a little hollow. She seems a:

'. . . womanly figure in the grey dress and the pink kerchief sitting little, and low, and lost, and acutely solitary, in these desolate surroundings . . . By an after-thought that was a stroke of art, she had turned up over her head the back of her kerchief; so that it now framed becomingly her vivacious yet pensive face. Her feet were gathered under her on the one side, and she leaned on her bare arm, which showed out strong and round, tapered to a slim wrist, and shimmered in the fading light.

'Young Hermiston was struck with a certain chill. He was reminded that he now dealt in serious matters of life and death. This was a grown woman he was approaching, endowed with her mysterious potencies and attractions, the treasury of the continued race, and he was neither better nor worse than the average of his sex and age. He had a certain delicacy which had preserved him hitherto unspotted, and which (had either of them guessed it) made him a more dangerous companion when his heart should be really stirred.'

This must surely have been true of Louis himself, whatever 'Claire's' likeness to Kirstie. His intense temperament, which had had for so long to be content with daydreams, the writing of romances and nocturnal fantasies, made it very likely that when he encountered a girl who appealed to him he would respond to the situation with unleashed and violent passion. Like Archie, his earlier life, so extremely restricted, meant not that he would suffer inhibitions in love, but that he would fall complete victim to his feelings and desires. And Kirstie seems at times, as 'Claire' must have done, to use the very last words of the novel, 'a wilful convulsion of brute nature . . .'

Archie forces a parting with Kirstie because of the adverse gossip their relationship has aroused. It would seem Louis with part of himself felt that it was right for him to give into the conventions as represented and upheld by his parents. Stevenson in his moving account of the quarrel between Archie and Kirstie cannot have been doing other than going over in a fictionalized form a painful scene from his own past:

'She could have wept, but pride withheld her. She sat down on the stone, from which she had arisen, part with the instinct of obedience, part as though she had been thrust there. What was this? Why was she rejected? Had she ceased to please? She stood here offering her wares, and he would take none of them! And yet they were all his! His to take and keep; not his to refuse, though! In her quick petulant nature, a moment ago on fire with hope, thwarted love and wounded vanity wrought. The schoolmaster that there is in all men, to the despair of all girls and most women, was now completely in possession of Archie. He had passed a night of sermons; a day of reflection; he had come wound up to do his duty; and the set mouth, which in him only betrayed the effort of his will, to her seemed the expression of an averted heart. It was the same with his constrained voice and embarrassed utterance; and if so—if it was all over—the pang of the thought took away from her the power of thinking.'

There is here the unmistakable accents of guilt. Louis perhaps never altogether laid the ghost of 'Claire'. He may have given into the 'schoolmaster' side of himself, for one did exist, but he must have done so with considerable ambiguity of attitude. So not only did he have to contend with the always painful sorrow of having to be parted from someone with whom there has been emotional involvement, but he had also to live with the disturbing voices of self-reproach. The affair with 'Claire' naturally worsened his relationships with his parents; he must have resented their interference, and they must have produced a further element of guilt in him—for it is unlikely that their views on sexual expression, implanted in him at an early age, would not have caused him acute moral discomfort, even though he may intellectually have disagreed with them. For their part, they must have become doubly anxious as to his spiritual health and ultimate well-being. If we add to this the dissatisfaction Louis felt with his studies and his growing dislike of the career decided upon for him, we can see that he must at this period of his life have been extremely unhappy.

Beautiful city though it is, Edinburgh can seem at times a gloomy place; harassed by mists and swirling rain, its blackness and its harshness of climate can oppress one. Louis came at times to see it as a prison; he used to gaze obsessively at the trains leaving Edinburgh, passing under the splendid North Bridge, and long to be travelling southward on them. He would pace the Canongate Kirkyard—where his favourite poet, Robert Fergusson, lay buried—and long for death. Unhappy in his studies, unhappy with his family, unhappy in love, unhappy in the absence of friends, how was this youth going to bear going ahead with life?

Perhaps it was the thought of Fergusson, who sought relief from the oppressiveness of conventional Edinburgh society in low life, that led Louis in the earlier years of his time at the University to explore the seamier sides of the city. The truth about what exactly this involved is again not easily discernible. Like the 'Claire' episode it has attracted much literary gossip, and many of the more sensational stories can be readily discredited. But it is pretty certain that he patronized disreputable pubs in the Old Town, and several squalid dives in the Leith and Lothian Streets, still not the most salubrious parts of Edinburgh. He became familiar with criminal hangers-about of these establishments, many of which were not at all in good favour with the police, principally for selling liquor at illegal hours. Louis became —or so he says—quite a warmly regarded figure in one such place. Here he could be found, sitting in the corner of the crowded, sanded-floored, none-too-clean saloon, dressed in the velvet coat that earned him his nickname, notebook on his lap, ready to scribble down observations on the whole dingy sordid scene and to make drafts of sonnets inspired by it. Louis later attributed his visits to such places as a result of the small amount of money he was allowed by his parents. These pubs were the only places where one could enjoy oneself—if one needed that sort of pleasure—with such a short supply of cash. But I suspect the real attraction of the establishments was that nothing could have been further from the well-ordered, cultured life of his parents' circle:

'Looking back upon it, I am surprised at the courage with which I first ventured along into the societies in which I moved; I was the companion of seamen, chimney-sweeps, and thieves; my circle was being continually changed by the action of the police-magistrates. . . . I do not believe that these days were among the least happy I have spent.'

It is my opinion that Stevenson is telling less than the truth here. Allowing for exaggeration as to both the extent and the nature of these visits—which may well be considerable—it still does not suggest a very attractive or admirable side of his personality. Minor criminals in slummy Scottish equivalents of speakeasies can't have been very pleasant or inspiring companions, if one tries to consider them in an at all realistic light. In the pages of fiction—as translated into terms of the crooked associates of Long John Silver, for instance—they have a sinister glamour about them. In actual life they were most probably foul-mouthed individuals, their lives a tangle of deceptions, petty larcenies, underhand dealings and minor cruelties. Louis most likely did not, at the time when he knew them, see them or choose to see them 'straight'. The very tone of even this short passage suggests that these 'companions', to whom probably he talked little, were to him like picturesque figures from one of his Toy Theatre productions. But of course he was much too perceptive and sensitive not to know what they were really like. Again we have the evidence in his stories. His first published story, *A Lodging for the Night*, deals with the French medieval poet, Villon. The author of many lyrical poems, François Villon (1431-1464?) led a wild life, during the course of which he committed theft and murder. One might have expected the young Stevenson to have treated him with a certain measure of respect and romance; in fact, he reveals him as a damned soul, whose poetry does not atone for his moral ugliness or the worthlessness of the company with which he chooses to surround himself. *The Ebb-Tide* and *The Wrecker* both present us with a gallery of despicable rogues. The criminal Duncan Jopp and his mistress in *Weir of Hermiston* —both from the depths of Edinburgh—are shabby, mean specimens of humanity. These visits to low haunts clearly troubled Louis more than he cared to admit, which is why he refers to them in so emphatically jaunty a fashion.

Many subsequent writers have been so intrigued by the wilder aspects of Louis' student days that they have neglected many important sides of his life at that time. He may have gone to brothels in Lothian Street but this is based on rumour, and I doubt that he made a habit of it; on the other hand, he did make

E

a habit of going to the house of his Professor, Fleeming Jenkin, whose life he later wrote. This kind, amusing man, full of theories about almost everything, led a delightful social life centring on his own home and family; in particular, he was fond of arranging amateur theatricals. Louis was a constant visitor to their house, was deeply attached to both the Professor and his wife, and responded to the warmth of the atmosphere of the house whole-heartedly. This is true even of the time when Louis was most intensely depressed and lonely. It is important to remember this fact since so much of Stevenson's adult life was spent, not in loose company or in affairs, but in a loving family context. Had the dissipated side of him been the stronger, this surely would not have been the case.

It also should be emphasized what Louis was doing in the low dives was scribbling in a notebook. We have noticed that he did this during lectures on Engineering and Philosophy. For though Louis was generally held, at this time of his life, to be the very model of an idler, a young wastrel, he was in fact, all the time, training himself for what was to be the real business of his life: writing. Always he carried with him two books—an exercise-book in which to record his latest ideas, and a pocket edition of some famous work of prose or poetry. He read intently and widely during his student-days: the Elizabethan dramatists, the essays of Montaigne, Lamb and Hazlitt, the novels of Scott and Dumas, the poetry of such different minds as Ronsard (Renaissance French), Burns (eighteenth-century Scottish) and Whitman (nineteenth-century American). And after a reading which he had particularly enjoyed, he felt a necessity, a compulsion, to write in the manner of the author who had given him pleasure. Later he referred to this as playing the 'sedulous ape', and this has often been quoted against him—as if there is something disgraceful about imitating famous writers. The best defence of the practice was made by Stevenson himself; a young writer needs the discipline of a model; it is, as a rule, not what to say but how to say it that bothers the would-be creative artist. It is by no means destructive to seek to understand how an admired writer achieves the communication of his vision. Furthermore, being a writer means, to a certain extent, being in love with literature, delighting in constructing plots, in making words serve one's will, in weaving together sentence after sentence, paragraph after paragraph. If the thoughts or ideas were all-important, then there would be no reason for specifically wishing to be an author—the platform or the practical carrying-out would be enough. Therefore, Stevenson was, even in these years of lounging about and shunning tasks that were his to do, apprenticing himself to the craft of writing, in much the same fashion as the youth who serves a builder or is articled to an architect learns his trade. Louis, then, is to be praised rather than criticized for his learning through imitation; and the final justification of his approach to writing is the body of mature novels and stories he has left us, completely original and unlike anyone else's.

The writings we have from this period of Louis' life are inevitably apprentice work, though some of his contributions to a College Magazine he and his contemporaries founded have a commendable freshness and individuality about them. One essay, written when he was on holiday with his parents at Dunoon, is of particular interest—it is the first of Louis' many attempts to survey his past life, something few people do when not quite twenty. Yet Louis at this age was proclaiming:

'The future is nothing; but the past is myself, my own history, the seed of my present thoughts, the mould of my present disposition. It is not in vain that I return to the nothings of my childhood; for every one of them has left some stamp upon me or put some fetter on my boasted free will. In the past is my present fate; and in the past also is my real life.'

It is fortunate for us that Louis so naturally inclined towards retrospection. For one thing, it meant that continually throughout his life he was recapturing and assessing events and emotions of earlier years, with the result that we have a pretty complete record of his life at its various stages from his own pen. For another, that his fiction was continually watered from the deep wells of memory. Even stories set in societies very different from his own (*Treasure Island* and *Prince Otto*, for instance) are made the more intense from their indirect drawing upon the author's personal past experiences. Louis acknowledges in this early essay that this tendency to look back and brood over what has happened in previous years was perhaps a sign of self-preoccupation; it is also of course a sign of present unhappiness. How curious it is, in the light of what we know (principally from his own writings) of Louis' childhood to hear him at nineteen years old testifying to its idyllic qualities:

'All my childhood is a golden age to me. I have no recollection of bad weather. Except one or two storms where grandeur had impressed itself on my mind, the whole time seems steeped in sunshine. *"Et ego in Arcadia vixi"* ["And I myself have lived in Paradise!"] would be no empty boast upon my grave.'

The truth was the future—to be dedicated to the family engineering business, to be spent in a society whose beliefs and morality he found intensely constricting to his nature, and to be endured in isolation from the girl he loved—appalled him, and he could find no appetite in himself for it. We can see this in his attitude to the odd little episode that prompted him to write the essay in question. Into the public bar of the Dunoon hotel where they were staying, there came an old, mad Highland woman, dressed in sordid bedraggled clothes, with straggly hair and an uncontrolled manner which ranged through many different moods. 'Her talk was a wild, somewhat weird farrago of utterly meaningless balderdash, mere inarticulate gabble, snatches of old Jacobite ballads and exaggerated phrases from the drama, to which she suited equally exaggerated action.' She insisted on reading Louis' palm, and telling him of his future; and readers of *Catriona* will be reminded of the incident in which the old crazed woman tells David Balfour's destiny by the same means. Louis can hardly be blamed for not knowing that this strange aged hag spoke words of an uncanny truth:

'All that I could gather may be thus summed up shortly: that I was to visit America, that I was to be very happy, and that I was to be much upon the sea, predictions which, in consideration of an uneasy stomach, I can scarcely think agreeable with one another.'

But how wrong he was! Louis' American visits were to be crucial episodes in his life's story, his adult, married life was to be remarkably happy and successful, and he was to undertake adventurous and extensive voyages among the South Seas. The unhappy Edinburgh student greeted these prophecies with unbelief, yet it 'set my mind at work upon the future; but I could find little interest in the study. Even the predictions of sibyl failed to allure me, nor could life's prospect charm and detain my attention like its retrospect.'

The future could not begin to take on a hopeful aspect until he had broken with his father's plans, and to do this must have seemed at times well-nigh impossible. Thomas Stevenson was so sure that both morality and sense were on his side, and in some respects, thanks to his upbringing, Louis must have thought so too. What his father knew about his private life and social habits—and we do not even know the extent of his knowledge—must anyway have made the relationship between the two a tense one, for Thomas Stevenson was inflexible in his views of what constituted right and wrong conduct, and made little allowance for age or temperament. These differences between himself and his father must have caused Louis to doubt the wisdom and humanity of his father's creed on personal grounds. But he was in fact beginning, almost involuntarily, with an independence of mind and spirit wholly admirable, to question the faith in which he had been brought up. And the essential loneliness of most of his life had given him much practice in protracted hard thinking. In his late teens he embarked on a rigorous private examination of the whole basic premises and teachings of Christianity. His conclusions and how he felt about having come to them will be dealt with later in its appropriate place when the issue became the major bone of contention between father and son. What needs to be said now is that this underground dissention from his father's beliefs must have made Louis afraid of bringing fully into the open other matters on which he disagreed—even the vital one of his own career.

It will be remembered that part of his father's plan for Louis's student years was that he spent some weeks of each vacation at various places on the coast of Scotland where lighthouse construction was in progress. So accordingly Louis was sent to Anstruther (on the coast of Fife), to Wick up in the desolate county of Caithness (the northernmost in Scotland) to the Shetlands, to Dunoon, and to the little island of Earraid off Mull. As a matter of fact, he derived much intense pleasure from these visits, but, as was the case with that boyhood trip to Fife, it was the aesthetic aspects of them that pleased him—the thrill of wild coastal scenery, small lonely fishing-villages, lighthouses standing sentinel on rocky promontories, and turbulent seas—he was not truly occupied with the various engineering problems that were on hand. A later essay, 'The Education of an Engineer', expresses—with perhaps almost unconscious insight into his own personality—the merits and demerits of the engineering profession as far as he was concerned:

'It takes a man into the open air; it keeps him hanging about harbour-sides, which is the richest form of idling; it carries him to wild islands; it gives him a taste of the genial dangers of the sea; it supplies him with dexterities to exercise; it makes demands upon his ingenuity; it will go far to cure him of any taste (if ever he had one) for the miserable life of cities. And when it has done so it carries him back and shuts him in an office! From the roaring skerry and the wet thwart of the tossing boat, he passes to the stool and desk; and with a memory full of ships, and seas, and perilous headlands, and the shining pharos, he must apply his long-sighted eyes to the petty niceties of drawing, or measure his inaccurate mind with several pages of consecutive figures. He is a wise youth, to be sure, who can balance one part of genuine life against two parts of drudgery between four walls, and for the sake of the one, manfully accept the other.'

Doesn't this make it clear that Louis would never have been able to deal with the minutiae of office life? But while respecting his self-knowledge and honesty in realizing that a career in engineering was incompatible with his temperament, one must also recognize that these lines reveal some very real deficiencies in Louis' make-up and in his vision of things, ones which must have troubled and infuriated his father. For he *does* speak as if the only function of a career, indeed the only function of life itself, is to provide one with memorable and in the main aesthetic experiences. The idea of helping society through work—for wild coasts *need* lighthouses, otherwise lives will be lost—and that doing this must inevitably involve unpicturesque labour, doesn't appear to have occurred to him. An engineer is, after all, sent on necessary commissions to the Scottish coasts, not on pleasure excursions, and there he meets problems which, however dramatic the original appearances, demand hours of patient and probably tedious paper-work. Irrelevant then for him to bewail the fact that he is not riding the seas on a tossing boat! But of course to someone whose heart was in the matter, the hours of poring over diagrams and figures at a desk would have a fascination of their own.

The weeks spent on the Scottish coast were, though, formative ones in Stevenson's career. They catered for his taste for the adventurous and active, which hitherto—owing to his ill-health—had been frustrated. Louis enjoyed descending into the cold waters of Wick Harbour in a diving-suit, he liked signalling from some water-stairs at Lerwick Harbour in the Shetlands for a boat to come ashore for him, he was proud when someone on the harbour-side pointed to him and said, 'That's the man that's in charge.' And seascapes fill his later work.

Perhaps Stevenson's most vivid evocations of the Scottish coast are to be found in two works: a longish short story, *The Merry Men*, and *Kidnapped*. In both instances Louis drew on the weeks he spent on the islet of Earraid. In *The Merry Men* he made it the home of the Lowlands hero's haunted uncle; in *Kidnapped* it is where David Balfour is cast ashore, alone, hungry, feverish and troubled. (It may perhaps have played a part in the invention of *Treasure Island* itself.) Certainly Earraid was present always in Stevenson's mind as an exemplar of wild beauty. He wrote a delightful essay, 'Memoirs of an Islet', on this subject.

'The little isle of Earraid lies close in to the south-west corner of the Ross of Mull: the sound of Iona on one side, across which you may see the isle and church of Columba; the open sea to the other, where you shall be able to mark, on a clear, surfy day, the breakers running white on many sunken rocks. I first saw it . . . framed in the round bull's-eye of a cabin port, the sea lying smooth along its shores like the waters of a lake, the colourless, clear light of the early morning making plain its heathery and rocky hummocks . . . it was no accident that had brought the lighthouse steamer to anchor in the Bay of Earraid. Fifteen miles away to seaward, a certain black rock stood environed by the Atlantic rollers, the outpost of the Torran reefs. Here was a tower to be built, and a star lighted, for the conduct of the seamen . . . The lighthouse settlement scarce encroached beyond its fences; over the top of the first brae the ground was all virgin, the world all shut out, the face of things unchanged by any of man's doings. Here was no living presence, save for the limpets on the rocks, for some old, gray, rain-beaten ram that I might rouse out of a ferny den betwixt two boulders, or for the haunting and the piping of the gulls. It was older than man; it was found so by incoming Celts and seafaring Norsemen, and Columba's priests.

The earthy savour of the bog plants, the rude disorder of the boulders, the inimitable seaside brightness of the air, the brine and the iodine, the lap of the billows among the weedy reefs, the sudden springing up of a great run of dashing surf along the sea-front of the isle, all that I saw and felt my predecessors must have seen and felt with scarce a difference. I steeped myself in open air and in past ages . . .

'And all the while I was aware that this life of sea-bathing and sun-burning was for me but a holiday. In that year cannon were roaring for days together on French battlefields; and I would sit in my isle . . . and think upon the war . . . And I would think too of that other war which is as old as mankind, and is indeed the life of man: the unsparing war, the grinding slavery of competition; the toll of seventy years, dear-bought bread, precarious honour, the perils and pitfalls, and the poor rewards. It was a long look forward; the future summoned me as with trumpet calls, it warned me back as with a voice of weeping and beseeching; and I thrilled and trembled on the brink of life, like a childish bather on the beach.

'There was another young man on Earraid in these days, and we were much together, bathing, clambering on the boulders, trying to sail a boat and spinning round instead in the oily whirlpools of the roost. But the most part of the time we spoke of the great uncharted desert of our futures; wondering together what should there befall us; hearing with surprise the sound of our own voices in the empty vestibule of youth. As far, and as hard, as it seemed then to look forward to the grave, so far it seems now to look backward upon these emotions; so hard to recall justly that loath submission, as of the sacrificial bull, with which we stooped our necks under the yoke of destiny.'

We can see from this essay that Louis was from his youth onwards capable of what the French call 'participation mystique' with nature, when he felt one with his surroundings, became as it were part of a mysterious whole to which the rocks and the trees, the hills and the water around him also belonged. And it is also clear from what he has to say that he felt the professional reasons for his visit to the island comparatively uninteresting and unimportant. He and the boy who became his friend for those few magical summer weeks both felt that the future was placing an imposition on them; they felt it to be a yoke.

64

Certainly Louis could not begin to find happiness until he had of his own accord removed this burden which impeded any hope or joy in what lay ahead. Daily it became clearer to him that he had to tell his father that he wished to devote his future not to engineering but to literature, for which his temperament had so completely designed him.

Chapter 5

And at last he brought himself to do it. On 8 April 1871 Thomas and Louis Stevenson went on a walk to Cramond, on the Firth of Forth. Later on in his life, Louis planned to write a story called *The Devil on Cramond Sands*, and whatever the tale was about, one cannot help wondering if the associations of Cramond with the Devil did not derive from Louis' difficult experience of the place that day. He was afterwards to speak of the walk as 'dreadful'. During its course he finally broke the two-fold news to his father; that he could not go on with his engineering studies, and that he wished to make writing his career.

Thomas Stevenson was certainly dismayed, though he cannot surely have been altogether surprised. It had been not long before the walk that Louis had written the successful paper on lighthouse illumination which Thomas had chosen to see as a portent of things to come. He was undoubtedly upset, upset among other things that the Stevenson father-son continuity was to be broken. However, considering his volatile disposition and capacity for strong righteous indignation, he was reasonably accepting of what Louis had to tell him. He made no bones about putting little trust in a future dependent on Louis' writings; he thought of them as scribblings merely for private amusement rather than for public consumption and payment. But he did appreciate the unusual temperament and turn of mind of his son, and perhaps inwardly he conceded that Louis had the makings of a writer. Outwardly his behaviour showed a combination of sympathy to his son and strong adherence to his own values. Louis could indeed make writing his career later, but under one condition: he must be trained for a profession, if only to be able to fall back on it. Engineering, Thomas admitted reluctantly, had failed; he now proposed as an alternative, the Law. Legal studies would suit Louis' voracious interest in people and their affairs; their discipline would stand him in excellent stead when it came to serious writing. Furthermore, the Law was a highly respected and socially invaluable calling, above all in Scotland. Scotland, which has a legal system different from England's, has for some centuries valued lawyers extremely highly; indeed, its most characteristic eighteenth-century culture, that of the New Town of Edinburgh, was partly shaped by its plethora of eminent legal figures.

And Louis agreed to his father's proposition. Perhaps his principal reason for doing so was: 'Anything rather than become an engineer!' but he probably realized the sense of his father's plan and saw that his putting it forward showed a certain understanding of his nature and predicament. This was borne out by later events; he found his legal studies far more interesting and involving than his previous engineering ones, and they did culminate in the desired success in the final examinations; he could, if he had chosen, have had a career at the Scottish Bar. The connections between the Law and Literature are, as Thomas Stevenson had pointed out, strong, and the fact that other writers—most notably Scott himself—had trained as lawyers may have endeared this new course of study to Louis; it must surely have appealed too to his already developed propensity for careful examination of the past. In studying Scottish Law he was learning about a very important and individual aspect of his own country's history. And Stevenson's legal studies did leave their mark on his writing. His ability to see round a case, to present evidence fairly, must have been considerably developed by them. Many of his major characters are lawyers—for example, David Balfour of *Kidnapped* and *Catriona* becomes one at the end of the second book, Lord Prestongrange in *Catriona* and Adam Weir in

Weir of Hermiston both hold the post of Lord Advocate, Archie Weir is a law student at Edinburgh University. *Dr. Jekyll and Mr. Hyde* and *The Master of Ballantrae* are both presented somewhat in the manner of legal case-histories, while *Weir of Hermiston* is distinguished by a remarkable manner of narration, in which characters and events are considered, weighed in the balance, and judged, with great compassion, great knowledge, and, as far as possible, emotional objectivity: all qualities expected from a distinguished lawyer.

So Thomas did not make a bad choice for his son, and the walk of 8 April 1871 was by no means the black event it must have seemed at the time. The change of course, together with the feeling that he had unburdened an oppressive secret and that his greatest desire, that of being a writer, was now acknowledged as a fact, must have made Louis feel as if an abscess had been lanced. This explains why the next years of his life were so much happier than those just described. And, as far as it lay within his capacity to do so, Louis took his law studies seriously, sometimes indeed producing work of a high standard, and his brief experience of a lawyer's office (part of his course) did not dishearten him as that of an engineer's had done. Not that the strained relationship with his parents diminished—indeed tension, especially with his father, mounted. But in other respects things were a lot better.

Up to now Louis' story has been a record of solitude. Most of his joys—imagining, reading, writing, responding to beautiful effects of Nature, thinking about the insoluble question of life's meaning, even exploring the underworld of a large city and tasting the sullied pleasures of the flesh—had been experienced alone—and almost *all* his miseries had been unshared. Indeed the pain would not have been so great had there been some sympathetic and young friend at hand, a brother or sister to confide in. Louis—perhaps because of habits formed in his unusual and parent-dominated early life—had never really had a proper confidant, nor indeed a companion constantly available simply to do things with. Only in his earliest years had there perhaps been such a one, his cousin Bob, inventor and monarch of Nosingtonia, with whom breakfast-times had been so tremendously enjoyable and exciting. And now in 1871, after an absence of many years, Bob came back into his life.

'The mere return of Bob changed at once and for ever the

68

course of my life; I can give you an idea of my relief only by saying that I was at last able to breathe. The miserable isolation in which I had languished was no more in season, and I began to be happy. To have no one to whom you can speak your thoughts is but a slight trial, for a month or two at a time, I can support it almost without regret; but to be young, to be daily making fresh discoveries and fabricating new theories of life, to be full of flimsy, whimsical, overpowering humours, that seem to leave you no alternative but to confide them or to die, and not only not to have, but never to have had a confidant, is an astounding misery. I now understand it best by recognising my delight when that period was ended. I thought I minded for nothing when I had found my Faithful; my heart was like a bird's; I was done with the sullens for good; there was an end of green-sickness for my life as soon as I had got a friend to laugh with. Laughter was at that time our principal affair—'

The lively and imaginative small boy had grown up into an equally lively and imaginative young man, brimful of fun and ideas and curious plans. Stevenson later described Bob as 'the man likest and most unlike to me that I have ever met. Our likeness was one of tastes and passions, and, for many years, at least, it amounted in these particulars to an identity.' Bob had a restlessly active mind and many talents; he painted, read widely, and had acquired an extraordinary knowledge of many and often curious subjects. He loved talking, and Louis and he would—as friends of the same sex at this stage of life often will—consume hour after hour in enthralling conversation, exploring any alleyway of a topic, any avenue of life that mutually intrigued them. Bob possessed Louis' own love of fantastic imaginative pursuits; in this respect he had retained much of his childhood self, just as Louis himself had. He still liked to talk about made-up countries and would apparently devote a week's leisure time to 'regulating the expenses of an imaginary navy'. Like Louis, too, he had intense likes and dislikes, yet was without resentment, or any mean desire for revenge. He loved jollity and jokes and called forth Louis' own—hitherto somewhat untapped—love of them too.

Practically every morning now Louis would call for Bob; they were inseparable—they shared a whole world of humour, adventure, ideas and enterprises. It would seem that Louis admired his cousin as he had never admired anyone before. In his essay on conversation, 'Talks and Talkers', Louis pays Bob the compliment of calling him, under the title Spring-Heel'd Jack, 'the very best talker' he had ever known.

'I say so, because I never knew any one who mingled so largely the possible ingredients of converse. In the Spanish proverb, the fourth man necessary to compound a salad, is a madman to mix it: Jack is that madman. I know not which is more remarkable; the insane lucidity of his conclusions, the humorous eloquence of his language, or his power of method, bringing the whole of life into the focus of the subject treated, mixing the conversational salad like a drunken god. He doubles like the serpent, changes and flashes like the shaken kaleidoscope, transmigrates bodily into the views of others, and so, in the twinkling of an eye and with a heady rapture, turns questions inside out and flings them empty before you on the ground, like a triumphant conjurer.'

How well one can understand Louis wishing to spend as much time as he could with such a person!

It must have been very salutary for Louis to laugh and enjoy himself so whole-heartedly. Activities which seem hilarious at the time in the company of an intimate friend seldom sound other than silly when set down in cold print. Louis and Bob, for instance, had a whale of a time as a result of making up a person called John Libbel, but what they did doesn't sound particularly funny now. They would pawn goods in his name, they would issue visiting-cards on his behalf, some of which had eccentric indecencies scribbled at the bottom. They would call at various guest-houses asking anxiously if Mr. Libbel had turned up. One shop at which they were inquiring for this fictitious individual was the scene, however, of a rebuff which at the same time caused the two young men inordinate delight. The assistant suddenly lost his temper and said: 'I know who you are, you're the two Stevensons!' Fame at last! To their surprise the man proceeded to invite them to tea, but they never went.

It is not so astonishing that Thomas Stevenson looked on this friendship between his son and his nephew with a certain suspicion. Their behaviour must have smacked to him of both the frivolous and the irreverent. It was through him, of course, that the two young men were related, and one cannot help wondering if Thomas did not realize that the histrionic, excitable qualities which both possessed belonged to the Stevenson family itself for all the worthiness and piety of many of its members, and that he himself had—in different guises admittedly—his full share of them.

But Louis' pleasures were not all idle. Even before Bob came back to Edinburgh to transform his existence, his social life at the University had become fuller and steadier, and he had begun to form good relations with some of his contemporaries. Now in this new period of comparative happiness these were able to blossom forth into friendships. He had also become involved with two University institutions, one old, long-established, the other partly of his own founding. The first was the University's debating club, the Speculative Society. Louis was proud to be elected to this exclusive society of only thirty members. To start with, he was perhaps drawn to the society because of its past associations and traditions and by the romantic dignity of its meetings; it had behind it a long history of being the rhetorical nursery of many of Scotland's most eminent laywers and political figures; and Scott himself had been a member of it. How potent was the atmosphere of the Spec.'s rooms, situated in the University buildings themselves, on the winter evenings when most of the debates were held! A Turkey-carpeted hall would be lit up by fire and candles, and the portraits of the distinguished past 'alumni' would look down on the present generation of intently arguing students. Beyond the hall was the library, happy hunting-ground for Louis. The motions that Louis proposed as a student-member testify to his being no mere idler. We hear, for instance, of him trying to organize a discussion on the iniquity of capital punishment, to be proposed under highly dramatic circumstances in the same society by his hero Archie Weir in his last book. On 12 November 1872 he read before the Spec. a paper on 'Two Questions on the Relations between Christ's Teaching and Modern Christianity'. Other papers he contributed included significantly 'The Influence of the Covenanting Persecution on the Scottish Mind', 'Notes on the Nineteenth Century', 'Notes on *Paradise Lost*' and 'Law and Free Will'. This shows the bent of much of Louis' thoughts. He was— even at this period of his most lunatic enterprises, snowballing, dancing about, skipping and roaring with laughter down

Leith Street—profoundly concerned with working out his own attitude towards orthodox Christianity, with finding out how much of it he really could believe in, what moral system he really could accept, and what meaning could be discerned in the bewildering contradictory complexities of life. But his father would have shuddered at the very idea of the debating society's motion.

Before going on any further, it is perhaps important to say that the years when Louis was a young man—the 1860's and 70's—were years when many thinking young people felt that the Christianity their parents accepted and practised rested on uncomfortably shaky foundations, and that the whole problem of what to believe, of what aspects of religion could be considered scientifically and rationally valid, had to be thrashed out anew for themselves. Two revolutionary intellectual events—both taking place in the late 1850's—had brought about this state of affairs. First, the publication of Darwin's theory of Evolution. Perhaps no new idea has ever caused such mental upheaval as this. For how could Evolution be reconciled with the idea of God having created man as the centre of the universe? That humankind was only the logical development over millions of years of a species of animal seemed to refute utterly the whole Christian teaching of the immortal soul. Now Christians find that Darwin's discoveries and the centuries-old dogmas of their own faith are not mutually exclusive; but new ideas dazzle, and the shock of Darwinism led to panic on both sides of the fence, traditionalists maintaining either that it was unsound or else diabolically inspired, modernists feeling that it heralded in an age during which religion must die. The second event in the world of ideas had taken place largely in Germany. This was the serious historical examination of Biblical texts. Put through a rigid scrutiny, the Scriptures could no longer be looked at as inspired error-free transcriptions of the workings of God. Both Darwinism and the New Criticism of the Bible dealt Christianity shattering blows. Now we live in an age when disbelief and atheism are taken for granted. To understand the anguish that many people such as Louis went through, we must realize how cataclysmic for this generation was the idea that central doctrines of their faith might be scientifically untenable. For if Christianity were not true, what pattern *was* there in life and death, what reasons *were* there for behaving well, for justifying morality, and what indeed *was* a human being? In a way, of course, we still haven't come to terms with these problems now. But they have not the stunning newness about them to fill us with the excitement and fear that they had then, nor do we today feel in considering them the lurking guilt that most young men in Louis' generation did.

So Louis' mind was engaged on problems of the utmost seriousness, and the Spec. was an excellent channel for his pre-occupations. And the second institution appealed equally to his thoughtful side. One day as he sat reading in the loved library of the Spec., it was put to him by James Walter Ferrier, a new friend, that a College Magazine was needed and should be founded, and that he should be contributor and part-editor. Louis responded with all the ardour of his youth. The magazine did not exactly have a long life; in point of fact, it ran for four months only:

'The first number was edited by all four of us, with prodigious bustle; the second fell principally into the hands of Ferrier and me; the third I edited alone; and it has long been a solemn question who it was that edited the fourth.'

But if the magazine died an early death, it was not because of any lack of hard work on Stevenson's part; the essays he contributed were fresh and characteristic; and one of them, that on the shepherd of Swanston, has been quoted earlier in this book. Moreover, as the majority of his early pieces made their first appearance in magazines, working on this one stood him in excellent stead.

Ferrier, mentioned above, was one of a circle of friends which now came into being and existed on terms of equality of friendship—Louis was not more dominating than the others. These friendships intensified rather than otherwise after the arrival of Bob Stevenson on the scene. It is as if Louis was liberated from the prison of over-self-preoccupation by his cousin's companionship, and consequently was able to give himself to others as never before.

Of these new friendships perhaps the most durable was that with Charles Baxter. Louis remained on terms of the greatest and tenderest intimacy with him till the day of his death. Charles, who later became an eminent lawyer, seems indeed to have been a remarkably sympathetic person; himself a man of many moods and facets, he was perhaps the best able of all Louis' comrades to enter into his varying states of mind and emotional problems, and certainly Louis seems to have confided in him to a greater extent than in any of the others. In point of fact, in his letters to Charles he told him things he never spoke so frankly about to anyone else. Not that their conversation always partook of the confessional. He had jokes with Charles just as he had with Bob. Charles and Louis delighted in observing and parodying Scottish mannerisms and attitudes and wrote humorous letters to each other, partly in mock-dialect, in which they pretended to be two old Scotsmen called Thomson and Johnson. Louis often included verses in his letters to Charles, again often employing the Scots tongue:

> Noo lyart leaves blaw ower the green,
> Reid are the bonny woods o' Dean,
> An' here we're back in Embro, frien', (Edinburgh)
>   To pass the winter.
> Whilk noo, wi' frosts afore, draws in,
>   An' snaws ahint her.

Sir Walter Simpson was another friend. With him, Louis' conversation was more consistently serious. They had many interests and tastes in common but Walter's temperament was slower, less mercurial and fiery than those of the other members of the circle. Louis and he went on several walking tours together, both delighting keenly in the countryside. *An Inland Voyage*, one of Louis' most praised early works, describes a holiday spent with Sir Walter.

James Walter Ferrier is, Bob apart, perhaps the most intriguing personality of the group of friends. The son of a distinguished professor of moral philosophy and political economy at St. Andrews University, he was a young man of great gifts, capable too of considerable kindness of deed and thought. He was also self-indulgent and dissipated, frequently guilty of selfish and debauched conduct. Consequently he never made the most of his talents or merits. Like Louis he was tubercular, and the combination of persistent ill-health and loose-living killed him prematurely; he was, sadly, to die in his early thirties. Louis was

74

devastated by his death, and could not for a time bear to have it so much as mentioned.

Later, Louis declared that Ferrier was under a kind of curse which prevented him from fully doing justice to his own moral and intellectual merits, and the tragic story of his friend, one which had uncomfortable parallels with certain aspects of his own, he told, without mentioning Ferrier's name—in one of his most moving and feelingly expressed essays: 'Old Mortality'.

'In his youth he was most beautiful in person, most serene and genial by disposition; full of racy words and quaint thoughts. Laughter attended on his coming. He had the air of a great gentleman, jovial and royal with his equals, and to the poorest student gentle and attentive. Power seemed to reside in him exhaustless; we saw him stoop to play with us, but held him marked for higher destinies; we loved his notice; and I have rarely had my pride more gratified than when he sat at my father's table, my acknowledged friend. So he walked among us, both hands full of gifts, carrying with nonchalance the seeds of a most influential life.

'The powers and the ground of friendship is a mystery; but, looking back, I can discern that, in part, we loved the thing he was, for some shadow of what he was to be. For with all his beauty, power, breeding, urbanity, and mirth, there was in those days something soulless in our friend. He would astonish us by sallies, witty, innocent, and inhumane; and . . . demolish honest sentiment. I can still see and hear him, as he went his way along the lamplit streets, *La ci darem la mano* on his lips, a noble figure of a youth, but following vanity and incredulous of good; and sure enough, somewhere on the high seas of life, with his health, his hopes, his patrimony and his self-respect, miserably went down.

'From this disaster, like a spent swimmer, he came desperately ashore, bankrupt of money and consideration; creeping to the family he had deserted; with broken wing, never more to rise. But in his face there was a light of knowledge that was new to it. Of the wounds of his body he was never healed; died of them gradually, with clear-eyed resignation; of his wounded pride, we knew only from his silence. He returned to that city where he had lorded it in his ambitious youth; lived there alone, seeing few;

striving to retrieve the irretrievable; at times still grappling with that mortal frailty that had brought him down; still joying in his friend's successes; his laugh still ready but with kindlier music; and over all his thoughts the shadow of that unalterable law which he had disavowed and which had brought him low. Lastly, when his bodily evils had quite disabled him, he lay a great while dying, still without complaint, still finding interests; to his last step gentle, urbane and with the will to smile.

'The tale of this great failure is, to those who remained true to him, the tale of a success. In his youth he took thought for no one but himself; when he came ashore again, his whole armada lost, he seemed to think of none but others. Such was his tenderness for others, such his instinct of fine courtesy and pride, that of that impure passion of remorse he never breathed a syllable; even regret was rare with him, and pointed with jest. You would not have dreamed, if you had known him then, that this was that great failure, that beacon to young men, over whose fall a whole society had hissed and pointed fingers. Often have we gone to him, red-hot with our own hopeful sorrows, railing on the rose-leaves in our princely bed of life, and he would patiently give ear and wisely counsel; and it was only upon some return of our own thoughts that we were reminded what manner of man this was to whom we disembosomed: a man, by his own fault, ruined; shut out of the garden of his gifts; his whole city of hope both ploughed and salted; silently awaiting the deliverer. Then something took us by the throat; and to see him there, so gentle, patient, brave and pious, oppressed but not cast down, sorrow was so swallowed up in admiration that we could not dare to pity him.'

The narrative of Ferrier's distressing but moving last days has taken us in time beyond the years we have been dealing with, but I have quoted it now because it shows the strength and depth of Louis' feelings for his friends. He accused himself, and others were to accuse him—and with reason—of egotism, but never did this mean that he was unable to respond to those he loved or that he was incapable of taking the very keenest interest in all they did or felt. The essay just quoted from shows that he was able to see his friends clearly for what they were, that because they were his friends, he loved them even with their faults, and that he had a generosity of vision where they were concerned.

One cannot wish for better qualities in someone with whom one is intimate.

Louis and his friends had, of course, many mutual interests, tastes and pursuits. They all delighted in vigorous, lively conversation, which they liked to hold in pubs, in long country walks, in books and ideas, in flouting many of the stuffier conventions of Edinburgh society, and in hammering out a philosophy of life for themselves. As to this last, they all, but Louis above all, were influenced by the writings of Walt Whitman (1819-1892). Louis circulated his poems among the group. Whitman was a figure who was arousing much admiration and controversy at this time: later, Louis wrote a thoughtful essay on him. A shaggy-looking American who had taken part in the Civil War, about which he had written very feelingly, Whitman wrote poems to defy the orthodox notion of what poetry should be like. Whitman's is a highly individual form of free verse; there is something of the psalm about a poem of his; his work is incantatory in manner and full of bold and often rousing use of repetition. Passionately democratic, he asserted the rights and brotherhood of all men, the sheer beauty of being alive, and the wonderful exhilaration that could come from feeling oneself part of the whole world of nature. Conventional religion and morality he despised as much as he did the conventional rules of poetry. There is a splendour and nobility of mind in Whitman's work, and Louis and his friends, fed up to the teeth with the narrowness and the sin-and-guilt obsessions of Scottish Presbyterianism, found his optimism invigorating indeed. Whitman seems now above all a poet for youth. His proclamations that he cannot find one fault or flaw in the universe can, it must be admitted, ring hollow when the initial response to the singing freedom of his work is over, but Louis found his poetry and philosophy at this time of his life inspiring antidotes to the teachings he had been subjected to hitherto. Whitman's direct influence can be found in Louis' own essays, and we can hear echoes of him in certain lyrical passages in almost all his books. Louis' later infatuation with the forests of France, the mountains of California and the islands of the Pacific may even have been partly the result of his falling so much under Whitman's spell at a formative stage of his intellectual development; in various lists of what had shaped him as a complete literary personality he always rated Whitman very high. But, as I hope this book has shown, the sufferings that Louis had undergone in his early years had penetrated too deep into his personality to be banished by optimism such as Whitman's. Moreover, the years when he 'found' Whitman were also the years of excessive psychological strain, so that even when he was most under the American poet's influence, he was never so much as he hoped—being always, in spite of himself, aware of darker, more troubled aspects of life.

The friends delighted in one particular pub in the 'Advocates' Close in the Old Town of Edinburgh for their meetings; a dark old place, it had been frequented by Burns himself. Here they organized themselves into a club, the L.J.R. as they called it. For a long time biographers of Stevenson were at a loss to know what these initials meant; now it is believed that they stood for Liberty, Justice, Reverence. It is thought that there were six members of it—we know that Louis and Bob, Charles Baxter and James Walter Ferrier were its moving spirits. The club believed in emancipating themselves from conventional prejudices and constrictions; and devising blueprints for a new enlightened society. They even drew up a constitution for it, which had a memorable opening sentence: 'Disregard everything our parents taught us.'

An exciting if rather adolescent maxim! Perhaps it shouldn't be taken too seriously. Unfortunately, though, the document got into the hands of one particular and easily aroused parent— Thomas Stevenson himself—and his anger and sorrow were dramatic and extreme. Of course his worries about Louis were increasing almost daily. He found himself caring for Bob less and less and thought him a bad influence; he saw Louis applying himself to his legal studies with not so greatly more diligence than he had shown for the engineering course. He saw him absorbed in writing literature to what he thought an alarming extent, and his life with his comrades—which seemed to be characterized by a general fecklessness—he found highly suspect. Now, worst of all, it would seem that Louis, not content with frivolity and licence, was actually professing disregard of all that he himself held dear and sacred. For some time he prepared himself for a frontal attack on Louis concerning his spiritual position, and for the same length of time Louis must have inwardly braced himself for it. Then on 31 January 1873 the attack came. The following

Sunday Louis wrote a letter to Charles Baxter telling him all about it:

'The thunderbolt has fallen with a vengeance now. You know the aspect of a house in which somebody is still waiting burial: the quiet step, the hushed voices and rare conversation, the religious literature that holds a temporary monopoly, the grim, wretched faces; all this is here reproduced in this family circle in honour of my (what is it?) atheism or blasphemy. On Friday night after leaving you, in the course of conversation, my father put me one or two questions as to beliefs, which I candidly answered. I really hate all lying so much now—a new-found honesty that has somehow come out of my late illness—that I could not so much as hesitate at the time; but if I had foreseen the real hell of everything since, I think I should have lied, as I have done so often before. I so far thought of my father, but I had forgotten my mother. And now! they are both ill, both silent, both as down in the mouth as if—I can find no simile. You may fancy how happy it is for me. If it were not too late, I think I could almost find it in my heart to retract, but it is too late; and again, am I to live my whole life as one falsehood? Of course, it is rougher than hell upon my father, but can I help it? They don't see either that my game is not the light-hearted scoffer; that I am not (as they call me) a careless infidel. I believe as much as they do, only generally in the inverse ratio; I am, I think, as honest as they can be in what I hold. I have not come hastily to my views. I reserve (as I told them) many points until I acquire fuller information, and do not think I am thus justly to be called "horrible atheist"; and I confess I cannot exactly swallow my father's purpose of praying down continuous afflictions on my head.

'Now, what is to take place? What a damned curse I am to my parents! As my father said, "You have rendered my whole life a failure!" As my mother said, "This is the heaviest affliction that has ever befallen me." And, O Lord, what a pleasant thing it is to have just *damned* the happiness of (probably) the only two people who care a damn about you in the world.'

What were they all to do in the face of this new disaster?

Chapter 6

The situation seemed well-nigh insoluble. Louis' intellectual honesty could not allow him to recant, Thomas' stern creed forbade him to see his son's loss of faith as anything but culpable heresy. Eventually, though neither could have then known it, time would heal the breach; both parties would come to realize that the love each entertained for the other was far more important than specific religious convictions. Before this took place, however, six whole years were to be devoured by differences, tensions, and quarrels, all of which took a very heavy toll indeed of Louis—in fact, the physical and psychological strain they imparted changed the course of his life. In the years following the declaration of his departure from his father's faith, Louis was never either well or happy in Edinburgh, and was obliged to live away from Scotland as much as possible. Often this restored him to slightly better health, though during these prolonged absences, he would frequently be extremely homesick. And the struggle between himself and his father had the greatest possible bearing on the fiction that Louis later produced—he explores the rift again and again in his books with obsessive interest and

80

emotional concern, and his last and best novel, *Weir of Hermiston*, has the conflict for its central theme.

The house in Heriot Row must have at times seemed a hellish prison. Thomas Stevenson flung his abundant emotional and nervous energy into any quarrel he had with his son; his tears and tempests seemed too often impossible to cope with. Louis, already guilt-strung as a result of his upbringing, was made to feel that he was a living sorrow to his parents, that he was a bringer of misery and destruction. Such opinions of himself were not comfortable to live with, especially as, for all his wildness and silliness, he was an affectionate son, quick to forgive and to respond with love, and, beneath all his posturing, serious-minded. No truly frivolous being would have bothered, as Louis did, to stand up for his own beliefs when attacked in such terms as Thomas Stevenson employed—he would have lazily acquiesced. Louis himself appreciated this aspect of the situation—indeed, in one of his letters he compares himself to Luther, father of Protestantism, who had the courage to speak out for what he believed against the authority of the church. 'Hier stehe ich!' he had said. ('Here I stand!') 'Ich kann nicht anders!' ('I cannot do otherwise!') Thomas Stevenson didn't see this at all—determined to view Louis as an ungrateful 'scoffer', he threatened to disinherit him unless he had guarantee of a return to the faith. No heir of his should be a rebel against the Christian religion.

Thomas Stevenson behaved both unwisely and unsympathetically, giving his son little or no credit for any good motives in taking up the position he did. But it would be wrong to condemn him for this. For one thing, he was just as much the victim of *his* temperament as was his son—and it was a temperament that had many points in common with Louis': over-emotional, histrionic, unreasonable. For another, Louis had so often in the past tried his patience, he had not been the dutiful student it had been hoped he would be, and he had shown himself many times as irresponsible and extravagant. And there must have been numerous scrapes and instances of dissipation that Thomas Stevenson knew about that have not been passed down to posterity—sordid episodes taking place in the shady haunts of Lothian Street or with girls of dubious reputation up among the shadowy hummocks on top of the Calton Hill—that had made him despair of his son's essential virtue. And in addition to these factors, one must take into consideration Thomas Stevenson's own religious convictions. He believed that he who has had the opportunity to know Christ and receive His teaching and yet has chosen of his own volition to reject Him has brought himself in danger of eternal punishment. What father could face with equanimity the prospect of his beloved son being eternally damned? Would he not do all he could to rectify the situation? It is Calvinism rather than Thomas Stevenson whose harshness is at fault.

Nevertheless, the fact remains that life at home produced an almost unbearable strain, and in July 1873 a pattern was begun that recurs throughout Stevenson's subsequent life—Louis went south to find solace for his exhausted condition, and had there beneficial experiences that would not have been available to him in Scotland. In this case the trip was only to England, to the Suffolk village of Cockfield. Yet it was far enough in spirit from the New Town of Edinburgh. Louis went to stay with his cousin and her husband—Professor and Mrs. Babington—whose home was the rambling, peaceful Cockfield Rectory. Though he had been to England, indeed to Suffolk before, he had never responded to it as he did this particular time. He delighted in the kindness of the English countryside which bespoke centuries of harmonious living alongside nature, so different from the wildness and intractability of the Scottish. And—more important still—he found himself among a set of people who, though every bit as responsible and morally upright as his parents, held different views about what constituted salvation. Better still, they were prepared to look on him not as a rebel against righteousness who should be taken to task, but as a lovable and interesting person in his own right, whose attitude to religion was his own affair.

He certainly made an enormous and almost immediate impact on the Cockfield household, and one which was to have lifelong repercussions. In the rectory there was staying a young woman, Mrs. Sitwell, and her small son. Long afterwards she was to treasure her recollection of Louis' arrival at the house. It was a scorchingly hot day and Mrs. Babington had told her that she was expecting her young cousin from Scotland. Looking up from where she was lying on a sofa placed by an open window, Mrs. Sitwell saw, making his way up the dusty avenue, 'a slim youth in a black velvet jacket and straw hat, with a knapsack on his back'. Mrs.

Babington opened the French windows to let in the youth, who appeared very shy and spoke diffidently about his long walk from Bury St. Edmunds made in the glaring heat. This rather faltering account was broken into by Mrs. Sitwell's small boy, who had been staring at Louis intently: 'If you will come with me, I'll show you the moat; we fish there sometimes,' he said. Louis seized the opportunity eagerly, and, a few minutes later, left the room, the small boy's hand in his, looking, so Mrs. Sitwell thought, almost the latter's age. When Louis returned, however, his shyness had evaporated, and he started to talk—in his lively, intimate and individual manner. Before he had been in the rectory twenty-four hours, Mrs. Sitwell felt she had made a life-long friend—which indeed she had—and come into contact with someone of the rarest gifts—which was also the case.

'. . . the hours,' she wrote later, 'began to fly by as they had never flown before in that dear, quiet old Rectory. Laughter, and tears too, followed hard upon each other till late into the night, and his talk was like nothing I had ever heard before, though I knew some of our best talkers and writers. Before three days were over, I wrote to Sidney Colvin, who was then Slade Professor and living at Cambridge, and begged him (with Mrs. Babington's leave) not to delay his promised visit to Cockfield if he wanted to meet a brilliant and to my mind unmistakable young genius Robert Louis Stevenson.'

Sidney Colvin, whom Mrs. Sitwell later married, came as bidden, and he was in no way disappointed. He himself was an up-and-coming art historian and man of letters, he had friends in some of the most distinguished artistic circles in London, and yet he too was utterly captivated by Louis. Not only that—he saw that he had great creative potential. Many a young man babbles of his ambition to become a writer, but Colvin realized from his very first acquaintance with Louis that in this case fulfilment of such dreams was not only likely but inevitable. For Colvin too the meeting at Cockfield was a prelude to a friendship that ended only with Louis' death.

Battered by the experiences of home-life, Louis found the quiet routine of Cockfield Rectory balm to his tired spirit. There were picnics, there were walks in the, to him, unbelievably lush and gentle English countryside, there was a school feast, there were games of croquet. But above all, there was the company of cultured and unprejudiced people who shared his own belief in the seriousness and value of the arts. Refined though Stevenson's parents and their friends were, and fond as they were of books and music, they cannot be described as exactly artistic, indeed the ascetic nature of some of their views on life made it almost impossible for them to be so. This had always been cramping to Louis. Louis' social experience, it must be realized, was, as Colvin later pronounced, a limited one—he knew the Edinburgh *haute bourgeoisie* with whom he did not fit in, he knew rebellious students of his own ways of thinking and behaving, who constituted a somewhat closed society, and he knew the riff-raff who patronized the same low haunts as himself. In particular, he knew very few young women with whom he could really feel himself; the middle-class girls of Edinburgh were too bound to tiresome conventions for his liking, and with the more disreputable girls he realized that conversation on many important topics would have been an impossibility. This fact, in addition to her own charm and kindly disposition, made Mrs. Sitwell seem a heaven-sent confidante; Louis took to her almost at once and poured out all his troubles and aspirations to her. Long afterwards the thought of the shade of the large tree in the Rectory garden underneath which the two of them had such intimate conversations was to comfort him. A world which could contain such repose and proffer someone capable of such sympathy couldn't be all bad.

The visit to Cockfield helped Louis to put the difficulties of home into a certain perspective. He realized what, for all his knowledge of the cultural history of his own country, he had never before adequately appreciated, that his was a specifically Scottish predicament. One always takes the society in which one grows up for granted and assumes that its ideas and practices are either those of the world at large or else the only sensible ones possible; and this seems to be the case even if one finds oneself in rebellion against them. Louis came to see that his parents' theological views, though consistent with the prevalent Calvinist religion of Scotland, were thought strange in England, where the Protestant faith had for several centuries developed along very different lines. Stevenson therefore came to understand that ideas which had been presented to him as universal, eternal truths were in fact part of a specifically Scottish culture; realizing this must have eased his burden considerably—the lone fighter in his own land turned out to have multitudes of like-minded allies in another. Nevertheless, he could not help feeling that England was the *odder* country of the two:

'I cannot get over my astonishment,' he wrote to his mother shortly after his arrival, '. . . at the hopeless gulf that there is between England and Scotland, and English and Scotch. Nothing is the same; and I feel as strange and outlandish here as I do in France or Germany. Everything by the wayside, in the houses, or about the people, strikes me with an unexpected unfamiliarity: I walk among surprises, for just when you think you have them, something wrong turns up.'

His awareness of his own Scottishness, which increased with each extended stay he made outside his native country, was a tremendously important factor in his growth as a creative person. While his early essays take Scottish themes for treatment, they took some time to emerge in his fiction. Perhaps a writer always needs to get away from his own environment, at least for a time, to be able to view it with the necessary objectivity. Stevenson certainly became the more appreciative of Scotland the more he could stand back from it. For the comparisons did not always by any means work against his own country. Scottish people were readier to talk about personal matters and serious subjects, he noted, than their English counterparts. If he found it a relief to get away from burning discussions about life and death, he also found—particularly on later visits to England—the social chit-chat, the lightness and well-turned pleasantries and pieces of gossip of English life hard to stomach. He thought the Suffolk country people sluggish and mentally lazy compared to the Bible-quoting, articulate villagers of Swanston, steeped in local history and ancient lore. There was in fact an intensity about Scottish life which English life could never, and never did, provide him with.

However, he was very sorry to leave England after that summer visit in 1873 and he crossed the Tweed into his own land with feelings of acute misgivings. Mrs. Sitwell and Sidney Colvin had given him confidence in his own resolution to be a writer— Colvin would give him introductions to many important figures in the English literary scene. But they had been adamant that he must finish his law studies. In counselling thus they were probably not thinking so much of his having a profession to fall back on, but of the psychological effect any further dissension from his parents would have. Generally they had advised him to try to heal the breach between himself and his father.

But when he returned to Edinburgh, the situation was as fraught as ever. Louis had expected Bob to be at the station to greet him, but he wasn't. And though he saw him the next day, he was soon to realize that something had happened while he was away that was to have unpleasant consequences for both Louis and Bob. Thomas Stevenson, in thinking over his son's fall from grace, had come to the conclusion that Bob, whose mercurial personality had for some time past grated on him, was partly responsible for Louis' lapses—indeed, might have been their prime cause. Thomas Stevenson had by no means forgotten the constitution of the L.J.R.

However, Louis felt he had one bastion against all the turmoils and troubles of home, Mrs. Sitwell, and to her he wrote almost every day. He was to continue to pour himself out to her with amazing frequency for the next three years. The tensions of the months that followed Louis' return from Cockfield are indeed best told through quotations from these letters, which are remarkable documents, vibrant with emotion and sensibility. Egocentric though they are, they must have been fascinating to receive. Throughout the time in which the following were written Louis was not only coping with the strained home situation, he was also working with success for his law examinations (so much so that the Lord Advocate recommended that he read for the English Bar and present himself to one of the Inns of Court) and getting on with writing various essays of his own. He was also suffering from bouts of severe illness.

(September 1873)

'. . . I am still rather tired, but well. I cannot pretend that I am glad to be back in Edinburgh. I find that I hate the place now to the backbone and only keep myself quiet by telling myself that it is not for ever.

'They [his parents] were glad to see me and in a kind of way so was I; but that is a horrid subject.'

(Saturday, 6 September 1873)

'I have been to-day a very long walk with my father through some of the most beautiful ways hereabouts; the day was cold with an iron, windy sky, and only glorified now and then with

86

autumn sunlight. For it is fully autumn with us, with a blight already over the greens, and a keen wind in the morning that makes one rather timid of one's tub when it finds its way indoors.

'I was out this evening to call on a friend, and, coming back through the wet, crowded, lamp-lit streets, was singing after my own fashion, *"Du hast Diamanten und Perlen,"* when I heard a poor cripple man in the gutter wailing over a pitiful Scotch air, his club-foot supported on the other knee, and his whole woe-begone body propped sideways against a crutch. The nearest lamp threw a strong light on his worn, sordid face and the three boxes of lucifer matches that he held for sale. My own false notes stuck in my chest. How well off I am! is the burthen of my songs all day long—*"Drum ist so wohl mir in der Welt!"* and the ugly reality of the cripple man was an intrusion of the beautiful world in which I was walking. He could no more sing than I could; and his voice was cracked and rusty, and altogether perished. To think that that wreck may have walked the streets some night years ago, as glad at heart as I was, and promising himself a future as golden and honourable.

'*Sunday*, 11.20 A.M.—I wonder what you are doing now?—in church most likely, at the *Te Deum*. Everything here is utterly silent. I can hear men's footfalls streets away; the whole life of Edinburgh has been sucked into sundry pious edifices; the gardens below my windows are steeped in a diffused sunlight, and every tree seems standing on tiptoes, strained and silent, as though to get its head above its neighbour's and *listen*. You know what I mean, don't you? How trees do seem silently to assert themselves on an occasion. . . .

'I wish I could make you feel the hush that is over everything, only made the more perfect by rare interruptions; and the rich, placid light, and the still, autumnal foliage. Houses, you know, stand all about our gardens: solid, steady blocks of houses; all look empty and asleep.

'*Monday night*.—

'. . . You would require to know, what only I can ever know, many grim and many maudlin passages out of my past life to feel how great a change has been made for me by this past summer. Let me be ever so poor and thread-paper a soul, I am going to try for the best . . .'

'I was sitting up here working away at John Knox, when the door opened and Bob came in with his hands over his face and sank down on a chair and began to sob. He was scarcely able to speak at first, but he found voice at last, and I then found that he had come to see me, had met my father in the way and had just brought to an end an interview with him. There is now, at least, one person in the world who knows what I have had to face, and what a tempest of emotions my father can raise when he is really excited. I am so tired at heart and tired in body that I cannot tell you the result to-night. They shook hands; my father said that he wished him all happiness, but prayed him, as the one favour that could be done him, that he should never see him between the eyes again. And so parted my father and my friend. To-morrow I shall give more details.

'*Wednesday*.—The object of the interview is not very easy to make out; it had no practical issue except the ludicrous one that Bob has promised never to talk Religion to me any more. It was awfully rough on him, you know; he had no idea that there was that sort of thing in the world, although I had told him often enough—my father on his knees and that kind of thing. O dear, dear, I just hold on to your hand very tight and shut my eyes. If it had not been for the thoughts of you, I should have been twice as cut up; somehow it all seems to simplify when I think of you; tell me again that I am not such cold poison to everybody as I am to some.

'3 p.m.—I hope you are well. To continue the story, I have seen Bob again, and he has had a private letter from my father, apologizing for anything he may have said, but adhering to the substance of the interview. If I had not a very light heart and a great faculty of interest in what is under hand, I really think I should go mad under this wretched state of matters. Even the calm of our daily life is all glossing, there is a sort of tremor through it all and a whole world of repressed bitterness . . .

'I take it kind in Nature, having a day of broad sunshine and a great west wind among the garden trees, at this time of all others; the sound of wind and leaves comes in to me through the window, and if I shut my eyes I might fancy myself some hundred miles away under a certain tree.'

(Friday, 12 September 1873)

'. . . *Saturday*.—. . . After lunch, my father and I went down to the coast and walked a little way along the shore between Granton and Cramond. This has always been with me a favourite walk. The Firth closes gradually together before you, the coast runs in a series of the most beautifully moulded bays, hill after hill, wooded and softly outlined, trends away in front till the two shores join together. When the tide is out there are great, gleaming flats of wet sand, over which the gulls go flying and crying; and every cape runs down into them with its little spit of wall and trees. We lay together a long time on the beach; the sea just babbled among the stones; and at one time we heard the hollow, sturdy beat of the paddles of an unseen steamer somewhere round the cape. I am glad to say that the peace of the day and scenery was not marred by any unpleasantness between us two. . . .'

(Tuesday, 16 September 1873)

'. . . I have been up at the Spec. and looked out a reference I wanted. The whole town is drowned in white, wet vapour off the sea. Everything drips and soaks. The very statues seem wet to the skin. I cannot pretend to be very cheerful; I did not see one contented face in the streets; and the poor did look so helplessly chill and dripping, without a stitch to change, or so much as a fire to dry themselves at, or perhaps money to buy a meal, or perhaps even a bed. My heart shivers for them.

'*Dumfries . . . Sunday*.

. . . Do you know, I find these rows harder on me than ever. I get a funny swimming in the head when they come on that I had not before—and the like when I think of them.'

(Monday, 22 September 1873)

'I have just had another disagreeable to-night [*sic*]. It is difficult indeed to steer steady among the breakers: I am always touching ground; generally it is my own blame, for I cannot help getting friendly with my father (whom I *do* love), and so speaking foolishly with my mouth. I have yet to learn in ordinary conversation that reserve and silence that I must try to unlearn in the matter of the feelings.

'. . . *Much Later*.—I can scarcely see to write just now; so please excuse. We have had an awful scene. All that my father had to

G

say has been put forth—not that it was anything new; only it is the devil to hear. I don't know what to do—the world goes hopelessly round about me; there is no more possibility of doing, living, being anything but a beast, and there's the end of it.

'It is eleven, I think, for a clock struck. O Lord, there has been a deal of time through our hands since I went down to supper! All this has come from my own folly; I somehow could not think the gulf so impassable, and I read him some notes on the Duke of Argyll [i.e. on his book, *The Reign of Law*]—I thought he would agree so far, and that we might have some rational discussion on the rest. And now—after some hours—he has told me that he is a weak man, and that I am driving him too far, and that I know not what I am doing. O dear God, this is bad work!

'I have lit a pipe and feel calmer. I say, my dear friend, I am killing my father—he told me to-night (by the way) that I alienated utterly my mother—and this is the result of my attempt to start fair and fresh and to do my best for all of them.

'I must wait till to-morrow ere I finish. I am to-night too excited. . .'

(Wednesday, 24 September 1873)

'. . . *Friday*.—I was wakened this morning by a long flourish of bugles and a roll upon the drums—the *réveil* at the Castle. I went to the window, it was a grey, quiet dawn, a few people passed already up the street between the gardens . . . I heard the noise of an early cab somewhere in the distance, most of the lamps had been extinguished but not all, and there were two or three lit windows in the opposite façade that showed where sick people and watchers had been awake all night and knew not yet of the new, cool day. This appealed to me with a special sadness: how often in the old times, my nurse and I had looked across at these, and sympathised.'

Such protracted strain was bound to have evil effects. Not only did he frequently feel tired and weak, he suffered from giddiness and from pains in the head and behind the eyes. At the suggestion of his father's friend, the Lord Advocate, Louis made a journey down to London to present himself for admission at one of the Inns of Court. He was to be given an examination there. However, it was clear both to himself and to his friends, notably Sidney Colvin, that an examination of another kind was called for. Consequently Louis consulted a Sir Andrew Clark, a well-known physician, who found him suffering from acute nervous exhaustion. Much more worry, and he undoubtedly would have suffered a complete breakdown. Sir Andrew ordered immediate rest, to be taken somewhere where there was plenty of sunshine, and to be taken alone.

Louis' parents, when they were informed of the doctor's pronouncements, were not only concerned about their son's health, they feared that living by himself abroad might be bad for his character (if it were possible for that damaged entity to suffer any further deterioration). However, they could not go against medical opinion. It was decided that Louis should stay at Mentone on the French Riviera, which he had once visited as a child with his mother. The prospect thrilled him: 'I do look forward to the sun and I go with a great store of contentment—bah! what a mean word—of living happiness that I can scarce keep bottled down, in my weatherbeaten body.'

Chapter 7

'By a curious irony of fate,' Stevenson wrote in a later essay, 'the places to which we are sent when health deserts us are often singularly beautiful.' He certainly found the Riviera so, though there were times when its exotic charms seemed too alien for comfort. But despite bouts of loneliness and melancholy, Louis was glad to be away from Edinburgh. Mentone did not have quite the compatible company to offer that Cockfield had had, but he became a member of a small circle of expatriates, living *en pension* in various hotels in the town. All were, like himself, in search of health, tranquillity and sunshine. Principal among them were two Russian sisters, both about fifteen years Louis' senior. They were women of volatile temperaments and quick-changing moods, and one of them, Madame Garschine, seems to have tried to start up a little flirtation with him. Judging by Louis' letters to Mrs. Sitwell, this caused him some embarrassment at first, though he may have ended up by lightly responding. The sisters were accompanied by their children; one of them, a little girl, Nelitchka, earned herself a very firm place in Louis' affections. When he got back to Scotland, he would talk for hours about this enchanting creature—to such an extent that some visitors to Heriot Row privately admitted to themselves that Louis was a bore on the subject. But his friendship with this little girl shows once more his almost uncanny ability to get on well with children, to talk to them and share their interests as if there were no dividing gulf of years between them.

Apart from this small company, Louis was a great deal alone. He read as much as his now limited supply of energy would allow him to, particularly exploring French literature. During the years that immediately followed, Louis was a fervent admirer of the great French novelist, Balzac (1799-1850). Balzac's insights into the workings of society and of human psychology found expression in a vast series of loosely related novels to which he gave the general name 'Comédie Humaine'. Louis' work certainly shows the influence of Balzac; Edinburgh and the Scottish landscape play a role in his work comparable to Paris and the Tourraine in Balzac's; Stevenson follows Balzac's practice of mentioning characters in one story who have appeared in another, and of including real people from history in his fictions. (The character of Alan Breck Stewart in *Kidnapped* is a case in point.) And one of his very greatest works, *The Master of Ballantrae*, seems to me to have a plot with a marked resemblance to one of Balzac's masterpieces, *La Rabouilleuse* (called *The Black Sheep* in the English translation), with its theme of the conflict between two brothers.

Louis was, of course, writing as well as reading. He was at work on various essays which were intended for publication, and he poured himself out in letter after copious letter to Mrs. Sitwell. Sometimes—with the feverish anxiety of the sick person —the fact that he wasn't getting down his impressions exactly as he would have liked obsessed him, perhaps because this was so much what he wanted to do in his life's work of writing.

'Do you notice how for some time back you have had no descriptions of anything? The reason is that I can't describe anything. No words come to me when I see a thing. I want awfully to tell you to-day about a little *piece* of green sea, and gulls, and clouded sky with the usual golden mountain-breaks to the southward. It was wonderful, the sea near at hand was living emerald; the white breasts and wings of the gulls as they circled above—high above even—were dyed bright green by the reflection. And if you could only have seen or if any right word would only come to my pen to tell you how wonderfully these illuminated birds floated hither and thither under the grey purples of the sky!'

For all his worries he does not seem to have done so very badly in bringing the scene before the reader.

But much of the time he felt ill and very, very exhausted. Once he felt so low that he decided to take a far stonger dose of opium than he had ever before done, opium being recommended then by doctors to patients. The drug produced the oddest effects on him. First sensations of near-delight rippled through his body; then, as day gave way to night, he was beset by terrifying tremblings. He may later have drawn on this experience when he wrote the memorable passage describing Dr. Jekyll's taking the drug which turns him into Mr. Hyde.

The outside world was brought to him by letters from Mrs. Sitwell, his mother, Charles Baxter, Sidney Colvin and his cousin, Bob. Sidney Colvin, in fact, came out to stay a few weeks with him. At Mentone, too, Stevenson met Andrew Lang, already a name in literary circles, later to become one of the most influential critics and men of letters of his day. He was also to play an extremely important part in establishing Louis' literary reputation; his reception of *Treasure Island* was to be rapturously enthusiastic and to arouse the enthusiasm of others. Almost from the first meeting, Lang recognized that Louis possessed true, unmistakable talents, though he was also somewhat irritated by him. He didn't care for Louis' affected cloak or his, to his mind, over-long hair. Louis for his part found something lady-like, prim and languid in Lang, even though he was, like himself, Scottish (he had grown up in beautiful country of the Tweed in Southern Scotland) and shared his own interests in romance and the legends of the past. (Lang's serious interest in folk-tales and ability to present them in literary form were responsible for the marvellous series of 'coloured' Fairy Books—the Red, the Yellow, the Blue, etc., which for almost a century have been valued members of English children's bookshelves.) The relationship with Lang was to be maintained until Louis' death, but there was always to be something that held Louis back from full friendship with him; Louis was a wilder, tougher individual, he was also warmer, more spontaneous, and more tender, and he was never entirely able to join the kind of London literary life that Andrew Lang so thrived in.

The long, intimate letters Louis received show how, for all his egotism, Louis had won a firm place in the hearts of several people, a rare and precious achievement. Of nobody was this more true than his cousin, Bob, now studying art in Paris. These next years were to be ones of trial to Bob as well as to Louis. Plunged into the thick of artistic life in France, he led a life full of pleasure, yet hazardous and erratic; often he ran out of money, often he had little to eat, often his lodgings left much to be desired. For all his belief in a carefree existence, Louis often found himself worrying about Bob, and indeed begged him to have enough food. But—more painful—Bob was also having gradually to come to terms with an uncomfortable truth, that of the absence in himself of any real creative drive or talent in his painting. For someone to have to abandon long-cherished dreams is a sad and nerve-wracking task. Bob was, however, not to lose his interest in art, even after his self-discovery; he later became well-known as an art-historian, writing a much respected book on the great Spanish painter Velasquez, and for a short time he held a Professorship at Liverpool University.

Bob was at this time making another disturbing discovery; he felt strangely lost without Louis' company. One day he brought himself to write a letter to his cousin, telling him this. The letter disconcerted Louis—though, of course, it moved him too; he told Mrs. Sitwell about it.

'. . . He cannot get on without me at all, he writes; he finds that I have been the whole world for him; that he only talked to other people in order that he might tell me afterwards about the conversation. Should I—I really don't know what to feel; I am so much astonished, and almost more astonished that he should have expressed it than that he should feel it; he never should have said it, I know. I feel a strange sense of weight and responsibility.'

But Louis himself had been aware that, in the company of Bob, he himself felt such a sense of empathy between them that it was as if the two of them possessed a single identity.

On his way back home from Mentone, Louis went to stay with him in Paris, where Bob was pleased to introduce him to the society of various Bohemian artists and students. For his part,

Louis was delighted with his new acquaintances; the concept of Bohemianism was very much in the air at that time, and for none did it have a more potent appeal than himself. This way of life had been given name, romance, and popularity by a novel, one which was in its day a best-seller, though in our century the author is virtually unknown: *Scènes de la Vie de Bohème* by Henri Murger. It is the story of a group of impoverished but talented Parisians for whom love and art were of infinitely greater importance than material goods, security or respectability. The book had long been a great favourite with Louis, who, in common with other young men of his time, saw Paris drenched in the light of Murger's romantic story. Later in his own writings Louis was to make two of his heroes experience Bohemian life in Paris: Dick in *The Story of a Lie*, and Loudon Dodd in *The Wrecker*. Both visit Paris significantly at a time when relationships with their fathers are exceedingly strained.

'Every man,' says Loudon Dodd, 'has his own romance, mine clustered exclusively about the practice of the arts, the life of the Latin Quarter students, and the world of Paris as depicted by that grimy wizard, the author of the "Comédie Humaine". I was not disappointed—I could not have been; for I did not see the facts, I brought them with me ready-made . . . At this time we were all a little Murger-mad in the Latin Quarter. The play of the *Vie de Bohème* . . . had run for an unconscionable long time . . . the same business, you may say, or there and thereabout, was being privately enacted in consequence in every garret of the neighbourhood, and a good third of the students were consciously impersonating [the characters] to their own incommunicable satisfaction. Some of us went far, and some farther. I always looked with awful envy (for instance) on a certain countryman of my own, who had a studio in the Rue Monsieur le Prince, wore boots, and long hair in a net, and could be seen tramping off, in this guise, to the worst eating-place of the quarter, followed by a Corsican model, his mistress, in the conspicuous costume of her race and calling. It takes some greatness of soul to carry even folly to such heights as these; and for my own part, I had to content myself . . . by wearing a smoking-cap on the streets, and by pursuing, through a series of misadventures, that extinct mammal, the grisette.'

Louis found French culture and ways of life infinitely more

sympathetic to him than those of his own country, and for that matter, to those of England. He spoke French almost perfectly, and, as we have seen, read it easily and voraciously. He admired in the French what is often called their *douceur de vivre*, their art of making life pleasant and aesthetically satisfying. What a welcome contrast this seemed to the cultivated austerity of Scotland! The French laid far greater emphasis on the importance of the arts than did the British, and even today the artist there occupies a very different position in society from his counterpart in our country. He found the French far more willing to discuss ideas than the English, and far more flexible in the way they did so than the Scots. And he admired their sexual freedom and tolerance; in this respect he thought them the most sensible and enlightened race in the world. French culture, he claimed, could never die or do other than dominate once it had taken root in a country. And, in some respects indeed, his own art shows itself as stamped with a French mark; the passionate belief in the perfection of literary craftsmanship is something more commonly found in the French writers of his time than in the English; it is associated with Flaubert and de Maupassant, not with Hardy or George Eliot. People who met Louis in his twenties claimed that he could have been mistaken for a Frenchman, whereas no one would have ever thought him English. And for their part, French people could mistake him for one too. Once in Nice, tired after a long walk, he sat down in a scruffy café to have a drink. At the next table to him two 'villainous-looking fellows' stopped talking and paid him the closest attention. They looked him up and down, they strained their ears while he gave his order; satisfied, they then resumed their conversation, the subject of which was their utter hatred of the English people and their intention of drugging and robbing the first Englishman who entered that particular café.

So this first really extended stay in France was a turning-point in Stevenson's life since it revealed to him the culture which he felt had most to give him and which could both refresh and stimulate him.

Back in Edinburgh, things were a little better. True to the promise he had made Mrs. Sitwell, Louis worked hard at law. But there was pleasure too amid the stresses of work. The household of Professor Fleeming Jenkin was, even more than ever, a source of delight to him, and he played increasingly big parts in their famous 'home theatricals'. There is a touching story of Louis at this time of his life, one which shows well his instinctive compassion. In the middle of the night, Louis came across a small child, only three years old, crying in the street. He had lost his parents. Louis picked the boy up, wrapped him in his greatcoat, and carried him all round Edinburgh in search of them—an unsuccessful search!

As for his law studies, he eventually passed his examinations with credit. How pleased he was, though he had not the slightest intention of practising his newly proved skills! But perhaps he was principally pleased because he had done something at last which he knew would gladden his parents. A young cousin of his was staying with the Stevensons at the time when the good news came through, and later she remembered the great rejoicing there had been:

'Well can I remember the afternoon in which we drove into town from Swanston to hear the result of the examination. The excitement and joy were tremendous when we heard that he had *passed*, and was a full-blown advocate. We were driving in the big open barouche, and nothing would satisfy Louis but that he would sit on the top of the carriage, that was thrown back open, with his feet on the seat, between his father and mother, when they were sitting; and he kept waving his hat calling out to people he passed, whether known or unknown, just like a man gone quite mad.'

And so the following winter he was able to put up a brass plate on the door of Heriot Row announcing himself as a qualified lawyer. He bought himself the traditional wig and gown of the profession, and had a share, along with four other young men, of a law clerk. His legal career was, of his own choice, short and scarcely dazzling. His earnings came to a glorious total of four guineas, and the only two times he had to present a brief in court he was so overcome with nerves that someone else had to speak on his behalf. And all he had to say was three words: 'Intimation and Service?' It would seem that the Bar did not lose a very enterprising or dedicated practitioner in Louis.

But he was occupied with other things. The next four years were unsettled ones, during which he divided his time between three countries (Scotland, England and France). It is perhaps helpful to give a brief chronological summary of his whereabouts in this complex and crucial period.

The spring of 1875 was Louis' first extended French holiday; then it was that he was taken by Bob to the artists' colonies in the Forest of Fontainebleau. In the summer of the same year he sat the examinations mentioned above, the date of his triumph being 14 July 1875. On 25 July, however, he was off to France again, back to his haunts in Fontainebleau, but he spent the following autumn and winter in Scotland. In the summer of 1876, after a holiday with his parents in the West Highlands, he returned to France, spending once more most of his time in the Fontainebleau forest and in various artists' quarters of Paris. In 1878 also he spent several months in France; it was in this year that he made a celebrated journey with a donkey in the Cevennes hills. 1879 was likewise spent in Scotland, in London and in France, though by the close of the year Stevenson was in America.

It will be clear that these were exceedingly restless years during which Louis felt himself to be tugged in many directions, and yet, at the same time, rootless, perhaps doomed to be a wanderer upon the face of the earth. But they were years of profound emotional experience and of creative achievement. It is important to remember that, however disorganized his life, Louis never ceased from working hard at his writings. These four years saw him build up for himself a very considerable reputation as a young author of promise. Essays and articles began to appear in various periodicals, notably *The Cornhill*, edited by the distinguished critic and man of letters, Leslie Stephen, and he was also engaged on fiction. Right from the start, Louis' writings seem to have made a strong impression on the reading-public. The kind of essays he was principally producing at this time is of a species generally known as 'belles-lettres'. It is rather out of fashion at the moment, and seems unlikely ever to return. Each essay partakes of the nature of a seemingly rambling series of observations and speculations prompted by contemplation of an object, an incident, a view, a book. Much rather vacuous stuff was turned out by writers using this form—elaborately turned nothings which derived from literature rather than from life. But Stevenson's essays, even his very early ones, which were really more trials of the pen than anything else, are not like that, though they may at first seem to have some of the faults of the genre. Stevenson's voice is always a personal one; he shows, even in his most immature work, a fascinating gift for selecting the really interesting or haunting episode and instance for mention; his language is always alive and vigorous, despite the affectations of style he could fall into, and he always chose to write on matters that appealed to the most creative elements within him. Most of the essays are personal in subject, and provide a treasure-trove for the reader interested in knowing Stevenson more intimately in all his various moods. And when one thinks of how young Louis was when most of these were written, they seem astonishing performances indeed. Of his fictional work, I shall speak later.

His other preoccupation was with life in the artists' colonies of the Forest of Fontainebleau. As can be seen from the number of times he stayed there, he was almost a resident of them—indeed, he once said that for three years at least, his true address was 'care of the Forest of Fontainebleau'.

It was Bob who, having introduced him to various artistic circles in Paris, persuaded Louis to accompany himself and his friends to the beautiful area of wooded countryside which lies to the south of Paris and is bordered by the limpid waters of the river Loing. This landscape was a magnet for whole flocks of artists, particularly in the summer, who would come out from Paris and settle in one of several little villages, the favourites being Barbizon and Grez-sur-Loing. They derived inspiration from their surroundings and from the uninterrupted company of each other, worked at their paintings and consumed hours in talk.

The magic of the forest worked on Louis from the first, and the closer became his acquaintance with it, the more he loved it. He felt it healed him in body and spirit.

'. . . it is not so much for its beauty that the forest makes a claim upon men's hearts, as for that subtle something, that quality of the air, that emanation from the old trees, that so wonderfully changes and renews a weary spirit. . . . It is the best place in the world to bring an old sorrow that has been a long while your friend and enemy; . . . With every hour you change. The air penetrates through your clothes, and nestles to your living body. You love exercise and slumber, long fasting and full meals. You forget all your scruples and live a while in peace and freedom, and for the moment only. For here, all is absent that can stimulate to moral feeling . . . For the forest takes away from you all excuse to die. There is nothing here to cabin or thwart your free desires. Here all impudence of the brawling world reach you no more. You may count your hours, like Endymion, by the strokes of the lone wood-cutter, or by the progression of the lights and shadows and the sun wheeling his wide circuit through the naked heavens. Here shall you see no enemies but winter and rough weather.'

It is clear that Louis found the forest balm for his neuroses; air and light seemed to heal the wounds caused by the tense relationship with his parents, by years of grappling with subjects that did not correspond with his real interests, by giving into and feeling guilt over his sexual promptings, by recriminations of his undoubted dissipation of his time. But he also liked the forest for itself and delighted in its particular as well as its general aspects. He was tireless in exploring it and familiarizing himself with its glades, its rises, its charming villages—Franchard, Barbizon, Melun, Grez—its arcane houses, its meadows and little pools and above all perhaps the bends of the jewelled Loing itself. He was responsive to the legends and stories from the past associated with it, for once it had been a great hunting ground of the French Kings. It was also intimately bound up with modern movements in art. There is a school of painters known as the Barbizon painters. Principal among them was Jean François Millet (1814-1875), whose painting combines a scrupulous realism with a feeling for light and colour. He believed—as did his followers—in getting away from academy conventions and popular notions of serious subjects and concentrating on depicting everyday life, yet endowing it with significance and beauty. Perhaps his most famous picture is that idyllic evocation of the nobility of labour in the countryside, 'The Gleaners'. By a coincidence, the blinds were drawn in the village inn because of Millet's death the day Stevenson first arrived in Barbizon.

Millet was perhaps the presiding deity of the many artists who came to Fontainebleau. Individualistic though they were, mixed though they were in nationality (English, American, French, Swedish), they had certain views on both life and arts in common with each other. Their belief in the supreme importance of works of art, in the necessity for having the time not only to execute them but to discuss and analyse them with kindred spirits, struck a sympathetic note in Louis, though he, of course, was not much concerned with painting as such. And the general way of life could scarcely have suited Louis—or Bob for that matter—more, for it was as Bohemian and 'free and easy' as they could have wished.

Inn-keepers took for granted that food and drink would be on 'tick'; the importance of friendship and the delights of conversation were articles of faith; there was a prevailing *bonhomie*. If you were the right sort of person, you were accepted, easily and without any awkward, inquisitive questions; on the other hand, the wrong sort of person, the person who could perhaps destroy the prevailing harmony, was soon made to feel out of place and before very long, he left. There was a general freedom of attitude towards the relationship between the sexes. Girls accompanied the artists down from Paris. At the same time there was a generally accepted code of honour and chivalry. All the artists enjoyed not only talking about life and art but also such simpler pleasures as performing feats of gymnastics and conjuring, singing, boating on the river and general congenial foolery.

Some of the artists who made up the colony were colourful and extravagant enough characters to suit Louis' tastes very well. One in particular is intriguing, and Louis' friendship with him is revealing of his own temperament.

This man's name was Salis, and he arrived in Fontainebleau announcing to the colonists that he was an escaped convict who dared not return to Paris or indeed to any sizeable French community for fear of being caught again, and sent back off to New Caledonia. His crime was his anarchic philosophy held in the 1870's, time of the rebirth of French revolutionary fervour; he had been what is called a 'communard'. Louis took to him at once, and when a law was passed, granting forgiveness to all 'communards' he made it his concern to find a suitable job for Salis to return to in Paris. He summoned a special meeting of the colony to debate about 'Question Salis' and in his opening address declared his own solution. Salis must run a café in Paris, and a special and joyous café at that! Members of the colony would cover its walls with paintings, others would during the evenings recite verse or play music to clients in return for free wine. The other colonists were enthusiastic and one in fact suggested a name for the café—'The Black Cat'. Salis agreed to this. On his last evening in the colony at Grez before departing for Paris, Salis took a boat out on the river, rowed up to the house of an old miller, who was generally believed to have murdered his mother, and shouted at him to come out. The miller did and Salis recited to him with bloodthirsty gestures a melodramatic poem by Victor Hugo called 'The Assassin'. Wild escapade after Stevenson's own heart! The strange thing was that Salis' café became a great success and indeed made him very rich, so much so that he eventually became a member of the Senate.

The story is interesting because it shows Louis' taste in men; he liked those who had defied bourgeois conventions, who had had the courage to stick their necks out, and had had adventures. Yet at the same time he admired what can best be termed 'romantic worldliness'; those he got on with best while certainly unconventional and bold nevertheless had too much energy and force of personality to want to hide altogether from society— something indeed drove them to prove themselves before other men. And Louis was like that himself!

Louis and Bob were tremendously popular in the colony, becoming indeed pivots of the community, admired for their invention, talent, and fun. Though Louis' high spirits and charm were valued he was thought to be something of an idler. How could men think otherwise when while they were working hard at their canvases, they saw him lounging around, reclining by a tree, his straw hat pushed over his face, or rambling through the woodland? They weren't to know that, all this time, ideas were turning in his head. A strolling player and his somewhat pathetic Bulgarian wife were later written about in a story, *Providence and the Guitar*; glades and woodland dells were to be celebrated in such collections of essays as the *Forest Notes*. Scenes suggested incidents to Louis, and throughout his life inspiration for fiction was to come from places he saw. For example, noticing a loft above the stables of an inn, he imagined a doctor being summoned to the death-bed of an old quack who was forced to use the room as his last on earth. In a dark corner of the shadowy room skulked a boy. 'He had a great arched skull, the forehead and the hands of a musician, and a pair of haunting eyes. It was not merely that these eyes were large, or steady, or the softest ruddy brown. There was a look in them, besides, which thrilled the Doctor, and made him half uneasy.' The childless doctor would be, Louis felt, so moved by this boy that he would adopt him and take him to live in his own comfortable home—a house in another village called Bourron which Louis had noticed, with a long garden which terminated in a wharf by the river. Louis pictured the doctor musing on the mysteries of health by the river's bright waters. And then the doctor would become involved in a search for treasure, a search in which the adopted boy would play a significant part. And the treasure would be sought at Franchard, for the tales of the treasure-chests hidden by hermits in the hill-side of the rocky gorge so that they would not fall into the hands of the English conquerors in the Hundred Years War, had called forth an excited response in Louis when he listened to them from local inhabitants. Later on, he knew, he would weave all these elements into a single story. And he did, and *The Treasure of Franchard* is one of the best of Louis' earlier tales, evoking charmingly the peaceful, secret countryside of this part of France.

But among the colonists of Fontainebleau it was Bob not Louis Stevenson who was thought to be the genius, and no one seemed to have had this view of him more than Louis himself. People were much moved by the obvious deep affection and ease of relationship between the two young men. Bob's talk was of a brilliance and inventiveness that held the company spellbound. Louis would throw in a remark, an idea, a question, that would unleash all the imaginative energy and exuberance in his cousin. In fact, Bob's conversation stimulated his own fancy and intelligence. A fellow-colonist remembered Bob one evening planning a curious scheme for romantic-minded men who were tired of life. Once a month at midnight a train was to leave Charing Cross Station, and was to carry as its passengers any people who during that month had come to the conclusion that life had no further meaning or enjoyment for them. The train was to be luxury incarnate. There would be a dancing-car, and a dining-car where the most gastronomically exquisite dishes would be served; wine and liqueurs would be provided. There was one real peculiarity about the train, how-ever: there were to be no engine-driver and train crew. The train was to run of its own accord along the line until it went over the cliffs of Dover at a point in time and space unknown to the passengers. It is not hard to see in this extravagant piece of nonsense the genesis for the story *The Suicide Club* in the *New Arabian Nights*.

It will have become apparent that the Fontainebleau colonies were on the whole male affairs; girls were there as accompaniments to the men, rather than in their own right. The particular blend of work and talk, the particular amusements indulged in, were masculine ones. News came to Louis when he was in Britain that an American woman had joined the colony in an independent capacity, and the news, though it may have intrigued him, did not please him. What kind of woman could she be?

One September day in 1876, Bob and Walter Simpson having gone on before him, Louis journeyed by himself to Grez-sur-Loing. If you want to recreate for yourself the probable atmosphere of the occasion, listen to the music of Delius, the great English composer who came in the 1920's to live in Grez—his enchanted tone-poems, 'Summer Night by the River' and 'Song of Summer' conjure up the dreamy fragrance of the Loing landscape. It was dusk when Louis moored his little boat, and he walked across the lawn to the long, low hotel where a whole host of his artist friends were seated at supper. The lamps were lit, the evening smelt sweet, there was food and wine to be had, and everyone was delighted to see him and greeted him enthusiastically. But there were among the company the woman he had been hearing about and her seventeen-year-old daughter. They were presently introduced to him as Fanny Van de Grift Osbourne and Isobel.

Louis' meeting with Mrs. Osbourne was perhaps the most important single event of his life.

Chapter 8

The arrival of Louis was excitedly witnessed by a small boy, the only child among the eighteen people seated at the dinner-table. This was Lloyd, Mrs. Osbourne's eight-year-old son, commonly known as 'Pettifish' by the artists. He and his mother and sister had been in Grez some time, finding it greatly to their liking; they had been informed, however, that their presence in so predominantly male a society might well be objected to by the Stevensons and had come to dread their advent.

Then, one day, when Lloyd had been standing beside his mother at their bedroom window, looking down at the inn-yard, he had seen his sister talking to a swarthy, slim, handsome young man, colourfully but roughly dressed, wearing trousers spattered with paint; this stranger turned out to be the feared Bob Stevenson. Bob and the Osbournes had taken immediately to each other, and won over by his charm and interesting talk, the American family realized that Louis himself might be agreeable, might not come as an enemy after all. Lloyd's mind had begun indeed to play on the idea of Louis, who now assumed heroic proportions:

'Louis, it seemed, was everybody's hero; Louis was the most wonderful and inspiring of men; his wit, his sayings, his whole piquant attitude towards life were unending subjects of conversation. Everybody said: "Wait till Louis gets here", with an eager and expectant air.

'All my previous fear of him had disappeared, and in its place was a sort of worshipping awe. He had become my hero, too, this wonderful Louis Stevenson, who was so picturesquely gliding towards Grez in a little sailing canoe, and who camped out every night in a tent . . .'

And Lloyd was not disappointed. From that very first dinner-time, he fell under Louis' spell. After dinner was over and Louis had been well and truly fêted by the company, they all went down to the river to inspect the two canoes, the *Cigarette* and the *Arethusa*, both celebrated by Stevenson in the pages of *An Inland Voyage*. Louis displayed his usual kindness to children by setting up the diminutive masts and sails for Lloyd's benefit, and allow-ing him to sit in the boat.

'While the others talked,' Lloyd wrote later, 'I appraised him silently. He was tall and slight, with light brown hair, a small golden moustache, and a beautiful ruddy complexion; and was so gay and buoyant that he kept everyone in fits of laughter. He wore a funny-looking little round cap such as schoolboys used to have in England; a white flannel shirt, dark trousers, and very neat shoes.' Looking back over his mother's friendship with Louis, Lloyd said later: 'Young as I was, I could not help noticing that R.L.S. and my mother were greatly attracted to each other; or rather how they would sit and talk interminably on either side of the dining-room stove while everybody else was out and busy, under vast white umbrellas, in the fields and woods. I grew to associate them as always together, and in a queer, childish way I think it made me very happy.'

It was as well that Lloyd took to Louis; for Louis and Mrs. Osbourne, were, within a very short space of time, to fall in love. Mrs. Osbourne was almost eleven years Louis' senior. At this time of her life, she was apparently very pretty, though her portraits do not exactly suggest this, making her look in fact somewhat forbidding and strong-willed. Louis, whose emotional and sexual career had been complex and chequered, found qualities in her that he had not ever encountered in a woman before. It seems likely that he thought of marrying her within only a few weeks of his having first made her acquaintance. Within a month or so he was certainly writing to Charles Baxter, now a fully fledged lawyer, to find out the legal aspects of marriage to a woman who would soon be an American divorcée.

For such was Mrs. Osbourne's position. Her history was certainly a stormy and colourful one, as much as any heroine of the romantic novels Louis was addicted to, and, it must be admitted, she comes out of it rather well.

She had grown up, a wild, forward child, in the Indiana backwoods. When she was only seventeen, she married her sweetheart, a young man of twenty-one, Samuel Osbourne, who even at that age had all the makings of a regular adventurer. Theirs was a highly unstable and restless married life, in which they wandered all over the United States. Samuel Osbourne first took his wife and family to a rough little mining-camp in Nevada, where there were only six other women in the vicinity. They lived there for seven years. Next, the Osbournes moved to Virginia City, wilder and more lawless still, and after that to San Francisco. Here Samuel left Fanny for such a long time that she presumed he was dead, and bought herself widow's clothes. No such luck, however, and he returned to make life just as difficult as he always had done. For not only was he a rolling stone, he was also an inveterate gambler and womanizer, and, at last, sick to death of his infidelities and extravagance, Mrs. Osbourne secured a separation from him. For a time she and her daughter studied art in San Francisco, then, wishing to develop her talent further, she took her family to Paris. As well as a girl, she had two sons, Lloyd and Hervey. In Paris, however, tragedy struck. Hervey, by all accounts a beautiful and sweet-natured little boy, fell ill of diphtheria and died, and so hard up was his mother that he had to have a pauper's burial in a depressing, neglected graveyard in a poor region of Paris. The sad event distressed Lloyd greatly, and it was partly for his sake, as well, of course, for her own, that Mrs. Osbourne made the move to the Forest of Fontainebleau. Like Louis, she needed the peace, beauty and solace of the wooded landscape; she needed too to devote herself to her painting as a palliative for her sorrow. Fellow-artists at the Grez colony spoke of the serious interest she had in her work and also said that she did not in any way participate in some of the less morally admirable amorous goings-on.

Her past must indeed have tested her and developed the already abundant strength of character she possessed. It was this feeling of her essential steadfastness under all kinds of hardship that won her Louis' admiration.

It can easily be imagined, however, that Fanny was not the wife that Thomas and Margaret Stevenson had pictured for their son. A woman on the brink of divorce, no matter how wronged she had been by her husband, was still in those days hardly socially acceptable. And her unconventional American ancestry and her presence at so unorthodox an establishment as an artists' colony in France hardly improved her position in their eyes. Moreover, Mr. and Mrs. Stevenson had had good reason for not having a particularly rosy picture of their son's amorous tastes, and, despite Louis' protestations, could not believe well of Mrs. Osbourne. The truth must be confessed that Louis' sexual irregularities continued all the time he was in Edinburgh—and with girls of fairly low repute. These entanglements may not have meant much to him or to the girls, though Louis was always emotional and impulsive. But it resulted in his parents greeting the idea of Louis' marriage to an American divorcée with horror!

Louis, whose time during these years was spent more in France than in England, and more in England than in Scotland, relieved the burden of these new worries by his usual process of pouring his heart out in letters, especially, of course, to Mrs. Sitwell. His parents, however, were never far from his mind, and absence from them certainly revealed to Louis his love and admiration for them—he even respected their views, though he still found himself unable to share them. And from time to time he wrote his mother and father letters which reveal not only his deep concern for them but his similarity in so many important respects to them—they were wrong in their gloomiest moments when they declared themselves to have failed with him. One February day in 1878, Louis, seated in a café in Paris, wrote to his father thus: 'My dear Father,

A thought has come into my head which I think would interest you. Christianity is among other things, a very wise, noble and strange doctrine of life. Nothing is so difficult to specify as the position it occupies with regard to asceticism. It is not ascetic. Christ was of all doctors (if you will let me use the word) one of the least ascetic. And yet there is a theory of living in the Gospels which is curiously indefinable, and leans towards asceticism on one side, although it leans away from it on the other. In fact, asceticism is used therein as a means, not as an end. The wisdom of this world consists in making oneself very little in order to avoid many knocks; in preferring others, in order that, even when we lose, we shall find some pleasure in the event; in putting our desires outside of ourselves, in another ship, so to speak, so that, when the worst happens, there will be something left. You see, I speak of it as a doctrine of life, and as a wisdom for this world. People must be themselves, I suppose. I feel every day as if religion had a greater interest for me; but that interest is still centred on the little rough-and-tumble world in which our fortunes are cast for the moment. I cannot transfer my interests, not even my religious interests, to any different sphere. . . . I have had some sharp lessons and some very acute sufferings in these last seven-and-twenty years—more even than you would guess. I begin to grow an old man; a little sharp, I fear, and a little close and unfriendly; but still I have a good heart, and believe in myself and my fellow-men and the God who made us all. . . . There are not many sadder people in this world, perhaps, than I. . . .

'There is a fine text in the Bible, I don't know where, to the effect that all things work together for good to those who love the Lord. Strange as it may seem to you, everything has been, in one way or the other, bringing me a little nearer to what I think you would like me to be. 'Tis a strange world indeed, but there is a manifest God for those who care to look for him.

'This is a very solemn letter for my surroundings in this busy café; but I had it on my heart to write it; and, indeed, I was out of the humour for anything lighter.—Ever your affectionate son.

ROBERT LOUIS STEVENSON

'*P.S.*—while I am writing gravely, let me say one word more. I have taken a step towards more intimate relations with you, but don't expect too much of me. Try to take me as I am. This is a rare moment, and I have profited by it; but take it as a rare moment. Usually I hate to speak of what I really feel, to the extent that when I find myself *cornered*, I have a tendency to say the reverse.'

Surely no father could fail to be moved and impressed by such a letter, and it is unlikely that Thomas Stevenson did not respond to it with the generosity of heart which he did indeed possess. There are sentences that bespeak the writer's egotism and youth, but what comes over most of all is his deep concern with working out for himself a philosophy of life, his belief (for all his frequent failures to practise it) in living in consideration for others, and his anxiety that cordial relations should be restored between himself and his father. And in that postscript Louis does say something of the profoundest truth with regard to all relationships—one must take the other person as he or she is, one cannot impose one's own ideology or morality on them. To do so is to deny the other person individuality. Louis was prepared to accept his father for all the latter's bigotry and intolerance because he loved him as a man. Surely Thomas could do the same. And, as a matter of fact, he was to be able to accomplish this, and ironically through the very person—at the time when the above-quoted letter was written—he most feared. For not the least strange feature of Louis' life-story is the fact that Thomas was to feel for Mrs. Osbourne, once she had married Louis, a devotion and an admiration he had felt for few other people in his life. But as Louis sat writing that heart-wrung letter in a Paris street-café, that event was still a long way off—in both time and spirit.

Despite, or because of, the problems and conflicts of these years, they were creatively productive. Not only did Louis write the essays that earned him a growing reputation, he also expressed himself imaginatively. Like many writers, Louis was some years before truly finding his creative self. Almost every-thing he wrote is characterized by an individual style and approach, but only after his marriage and his reconciliation with his parents was Stevenson able to face up to Scottish themes and predica-ments, and it was these that provided him with the imagination for his most vital creative achievements.

None-the-less the works he produced in his twenties are by no means unremarkable, especially when one thinks of the emotional situations in which they were written. There are the two stories about the medieval French poet François Villon whose vagabond life and criminal career among the flotsam and jetsam of society had long intrigued him. There are several stories based on encounters in France. And in January 1878 there appeared in the distinguished periodical *The Cornhill*, one of his loveliest performances, *Will o' the Mill*, an allegorical short story. Will as a young man has always dreamt of going down to the plains which he can see from his mountain home. How fair and tempting they look, how he longs to take the initiative and see them for himself. But instead he marries—a pleasant enough girl, Marjory—and has a steady job at the mill. A stranger, a fat young man, comes to the local inn and tells Will that the plains aren't really all that much after all, certainly not worth fretting over, and Will is really only too ready to take him at his word. And so life slips by, and he never ventures beyond the narrow confines of his daily life. And then old age overtakes him, a quiet, unadventurous old age:

'One night, in his seventy-second year, he awoke in bed, in such uneasiness of body and mind that he arose and dressed himself and went out to meditate in the arbour. It was pitch dark, without a star; the river was swollen, and the wet woods and meadows loaded the air with perfume. It had thundered during the day, and it promised more thunder for the morrow. A murky, stifling night for a man of seventy-two! Whether it was the weather or the wakefulness, or some little touch of fever in his old limbs, Will's mind was besieged by tumultuous and crying memories. His boyhood, the night with the fat young man, the death of his adopted parents, the summer days with Marjory and many of those small circumstances, which seem nothing to another, and are yet the very gist of a man's own life to himself—things seen, words heard, books misconstrued—arose from their forgotten corners and usurped his attention. The dead themselves were with him, not merely taking part in this thin show of memory that defiled before his brain, but revisiting his bodily senses as they do in profound and vivid dreams. The fat young man leaned his elbows on the table opposite; Marjory came and went with an apronful of flowers between the garden and the arbour; he could hear the old parson knocking out his pipe or blowing his resonant nose. The tide of his consciousness ebbed and flowed; he was sometimes half asleep and drowned in his recollections of the past; and sometimes he was broad awake, wondering at himself. But about the middle of the night he was startled by the voice of the dead miller calling to him out of the house as he used to do on the arrival of custom. The hallucination was so perfect that Will sprang from his seat and stood listening for the summons to be repeated, and as he listened he became conscious of another noise besides the brawling of the river and the ringing in his feverish ears. It was like the stir of the horses and the creaking of harness, as though a carriage with an impatient team had been brought up upon the road before the courtyard gate.'

The disturbance is caused by the arrival of a stranger whose identity one assumes is death itself.

' "A time comes for all men, Master Will," ' he says, ' "when the helm is taken out of their hands. For you, because you were prudent and quiet, it has been long of coming, and you have had long to discipline yourself for its reception. You have seen what is to be seen about your mill; you have sat close all your days like a hare in its form; but now that is at an end; and . . . you must arise and come with me." '

The meaning of the story is clear and has considerable bearing on Louis' feelings and predicament at the time. No man can escape knowledge of the mysterious forces of life, no matter how hard he tries to protect himself. Will has led an existence as sheltered from harshness and searing joys as any middle-class burgher of evangelical persuasion. Yet he himself had known what it was to long for the seemingly unattainable, had wanted to go out and see the shimmering plains for himself. And in the end life and death caught him up; all his caution could not prevail. Louis must himself have been thinking that at least he had made an attempt to explore the heights and depths of life as, secretly, every human being must feel inclined to do. And the story reflects Louis' own awareness of the passing of time, of the brevity of life, something his perpetual ill-health must have made him more aware of than is the normal person.

Almost all Stevenson's early literary efforts are short-length affairs, triumphs, one might have supposed then, of a miniaturist rather than a larger-scale literary artist. Repeatedly during his twenties, Stevenson found himself frustrated in his attempts on bigger works—and indeed throughout his life Stevenson was to begin stories that he not only could not complete but could not even get on with. In September 1878, he decided to gather material for a longer work. It sounded when he proposed it an eccentric enough plan, but in fact it showed excellent judgement of what he could at that stage of his life handle successfully and interestingly—for out of the plan came one of his, even today, best-known and most-read books. He took himself to a remote area of rural France, the part of the Auvergne known as the

Haute Loire and here he hired a donkey. Modestine, as his donkey was called, turned out as stubborn and self-willed a beast as could be imagined, adept at stopping on steep hillsides and refusing to be budged, adept too at briskly trotting down roads poor Louis had no desire to travel down. But Stevenson's feeling and affection for animals was only just less than that he possessed for children, and this, combined with his heightened response to the world of the countryside, combine to make the book of these experiences, the *Travels with a Donkey in the Cevennes* (published 1879), a delightful one. Some of the actual adventures may have at the time been more trying than delightful, but Stevenson's curiosity always carried him through what befell him. The strange society of the Trappist Monks (those bound to an order of silence) up at the monastery of Our Lady of the Snows he observed with a kindly blend of interest and gentle imaginative respect, even while realizing that such a way of life was neither for him nor consistent with the general philosophy of life he believed himself to possess:

'At night . . . I took my place in the gallery to hear compline and *Salve Regina*, with which the Cistercians bring every day to a conclusion . . . A stern simplicity, heightened by the romance of the surroundings, spoke directly to the heart. I recall the whitewashed chapel, the hooded figures in the choir, the lights alternately occluded and revealed, the strong manly singing, the silence that ensued, the sight of cowled heads bowed in prayer, and then the clear trenchant beating of the bell, breaking in to show that the last office was over and the hour of sleep had come; and when I remember, I am not surprised that I made my escape into the court with somewhat whirling fancies, and stood like a man bewildered in the windy starry night.

'But I was weary; and . . . the cold and the raving of the wind among the pines (for my room was on that side of the monastery which adjoins the woods) disposed me readily to slumber. I was wakened at black midnight, as it seemed, though it was really two in the morning, by the first stroke upon the bell. All the brothers were then hurrying to the chapel; the dead in life, at this untimely hour, were already beginning the uncomforted labours of their day. The dead in life—there was a chill reflection. And the words of the French song came back into my memory, telling of the best of our mixed existence:

> *"Que t'as de belles filles,*
> *Giroflé!*
> *Girofla!*
> *Que t'as de belles filles,*
> *L'Amour les comptera!"*

And I blessed God that I was free to wander, free to hope, and free to love.'

But for all his rejoicing over the quaint specimens of humanity he encountered, and the lovely joyous effects of Nature he witnessed, Stevenson's views on life, indeed his interests, were not quite as triumphantly cheerful as he would have us believe. Readers and commentators of the book have tended to overlook the quite extraordinary interest Stevenson takes in the old French Protestants of the mountains, their history, their fanaticism, their bravery and staunchness, and in their noble-minded, courageous but curious leader, Jean Cavalier, on the subject of whom Stevenson was also to write several poems. Who are we reminded of when we read about these late seventeenth-century Frenchmen?

'In that undecipherable labyrinth of hills, a war of bandits, a war of wild beasts, raged for two years between the Grand Monarch with all his troops and marshals on the one hand, and a few thousand Protestant mountaineers on the other. A hundred and eighty years ago, the Camisards held a station even on the Lozère, where I stood; they had an organisation, arsenals, a military and religious hierarchy; . . . their leaders prophesied and murdered; with colours and drums, and the singing of old French psalms, their bands sometimes affronted daylight, marched before walled cities, and dispersed the generals of the king; and sometimes at night, or in masquerade, possessed themselves of strong castles, and avenged treachery upon their allies and cruelty upon their foes . . . And there, to follow these and other leaders, was the rank and file of prophets and disciples, bold, patient, indefatigable, hardy to run upon the mountains, cheering their rough life with psalms, eager to fight, eager to pray, listening devoutly to the oracles of brain-sick children, and mystically putting a grain of wheat among the pewter balls with which they charged their muskets.'

It is, of course, of the Covenanters that we think, and, as we think this, we notice how the pace of writing quickens. The thought of the Camisards kindles the liveliest creative spirit in the young author, and we realize that the spirit that thrilled to stories of the Covenanters, and was responsible for that strange, ardent little work *The Pentland Rising*, was by no means dead. Indeed, with benefit of hindsight, we can see that Stevenson could only possibly have attained creative fulfilment when he had released the Scottish side of his imagination and interests, when, if you like, he had brought to the surface the buried Calvinist. For, as the very outward events of these years are enough to suggest, he was not, gay though he could be, a mere pleasure-seeker.

He was also much in love, and the *Travels with a Donkey* contains many deliberate references to his feelings for Fanny Osbourne —remarks addressed to her rather than the reader. (Stevenson is here describing a night spent out of doors.)

'And yet even while I was exulting in my solitude I became aware of a strange lack. I wished a companion to lie near me in the starlight, silent and not moving, but ever within touch. For there is a fellowship more quiet even than solitude, and which, rightly understood, is solitude made perfect. And to live out of doors with the woman a man loves is of all lives the most complete and free.'

Stevenson's early writings did, in fact, earn him a growing circle of admirers, while bringing him in virtually no money. Readers of Leslie Stephen's *The Cornhill* delighted in noting the now famous initials R.L.S. at the bottom of an article. He was making friends in the literary world too. He visited and later stayed with George Meredith (1828-1909), one of the most considerable and remarkable novelists of his day. His optimistic philosophy, his generous treatment of love, his sympathy for movements which brought freedom to stifled societies, his verbal brilliance, and complex plots mirroring the complexities of life and of human urges—all fascinated Stevenson, though only *Prince Otto* (and possibly the story mentioned above, *Will o' the Mill*) show his influence at all strongly. Two other literary friends play a far more important part in Stevenson's story: the poet and critic, W. E. Henley (1849-1903) and the man of letters Edmund Gosse (1849-1928).

Stevenson first met Henley in Edinburgh in the winter of 1875. Leslie Stephen, the editor spoken of above, came to

Edinburgh to lecture, called on his young author and took him to see another of his contributors, who was confined to the Edinburgh Infirmary. Like Stevenson himself, Henley's whole life had been and was to be dogged by ill health; he suffered from a tubercular disease of the feet. He had had one foot amputated and had come to Edinburgh to have the other foot saved by the great surgeon, Lister. There is a story, probably apocryphal, that Lister asked Henley why he had consulted him and Henley replied: 'Because others have failed. I was told *you* were no good, so I thought you might be able to do something for me.' Henley was a courageous, romantic-hearted individual, who delighted in the literature of a life of action, from which he himself was debarred, and who had a taste for low life and literary camaraderie. All this was excellent qualification for a real friendship with Stevenson, and the two men indeed took to one another at once. The Infirmary was a grim, unhomely place, and the English Henley—who though born in Gloucester was very much a Londoner—must have felt something of an exile in winter-bound Edinburgh. He has left us a poignant account of his experiences in a poem-sequence, 'The Hospital', and from it, we can build up a picture of the circumstances in which this crucial friendship was formed.

> The gaunt brown walls
> Look infinite in their decent meanness.
> There is nothing of home in the noisy kettle,
> The fulsome fire.
>
> The atmosphere
> Suggests the trail of a ghostly druggist.
> Dressing and lint on the long, lean table—
> Whom are they for?
>
> The patients yawn,
> Or lie as in training for shroud and coffin.
> A nurse in the corridor scolds and wrangles.
> It's grim and strange.
>
> Far footfalls clank.
> The bad burn waits with his head unbandaged.
> My neighbour chokes in the clutch of chloral
> O, a gruesome world.

But this gruesome world, in addition to being peopled by aloof surgeons, motherly elderly nurses, pretty yet coldly efficient young ones, crippled children, failed suicides and desperately ill countrymen, all of whom received poetic treatment from Henley, was to be enlivened by repeated visits from Louis. How kind, how cheerful he seemed! One Sunday, when Edinburgh was imprisoned in its depressing Sabbath-day gloom, Louis arrived laden with bright yellow-bound copies of Balzac which he dumped by the drab bedside. He introduced Henley to his great friend Charles Baxter, and the three of them had such good times together that Henley compared them to the Three Musketeers. Henley read Stevenson's writings and could detect an element of whimsicality and self-indulgence in his literary approach, and he also pointed out the dangers of too much reliance on other people's writings. At the same time—like Andrew Lang before him—he discerned the deep originality of Louis' creative temperament. When he was at length released from hospital and took rooms for a time in Edinburgh, the two men could spend even longer in one another's company. Indeed when his amorous activities or when more than usually heightened tension between himself and his parents kept Louis away from home, Louis would stay with his new friend. In 'The Hospital' sequence there is a poem called 'Apparition', a sonnet to celebrate and analyse Louis at this time of his life:

> Thin-legged, thin-chested, slight unspeakably,
> Neat-footed and weak-fingered: in his face—
> Lean, large-boned, curved of beak, and touched with race,
> Bold-lipped, rich-tinted, mutable as the sea,
> The brown eyes radiant with vivacity—
> There shines a brilliant and romantic grace,
> A spirit intense and rare, with trace on trace
> Of passion and impudence and energy.
> Valiant in velvet, light in ragged luck,
> Most vain, most generous, sternly critical,
> Buffoon and poet, lover and sensualist:
> A deal of Ariel, just a streak of Puck,
> Much Anthony, of Hamlet most of all,
> And something of the Shorter-Catechist.

These are perceptive words, as well as somewhat fulsomely flattering ones. The last three lines suggest Louis' impulsiveness and mercurial make-up, they also suggest the stern morality, derived in part from parents and upbringing but also inherent in his personality, that lay far below the Bohemian surface. For the 'Shorter-Catechism' referred to, is the summary of the belief of the Scotch Calvinists. It is interesting that Henley understood this quality in Louis so early in his career.

The friendship with Henley was to be important and difficult. Certainly, after Louis had married Fanny Osbourne, the relationship was to become extremely strained; Henley was a somewhat neurotic man, for all his belief in good cheer and masculine sense; in reality the champion of romantic patriotism and sportsmanship was a complicated personality, quick to take offence. But during Louis' twenties, he and Henley, as can be testified by the numerous and lengthy letters they wrote to one another, enjoyed an affectionate relationship. And Henley is of great significance to Stevenson's development because, as we shall see, he provided the inspiration for the character of Long John Silver. All the same, I think it is fair to say that Henley's influence on Stevenson was not wholly good, and that it was not altogether a bad thing when the friendship cooled. (Undoubtedly the plays that the two collaborated on are rubbishy works, not worth the energy of either man.)

It always seems to me that there is a somewhat tasteless heartiness in Stevenson's letters to Henley that we do not see to nearly such a degree elsewhere. Both men were invalids, both needed perhaps to escape from invalidism by cultivating the jaunty, the roguish—all that was not associated with the gentle home-life most beneficial to a sick man. But it is not true bravery to live too much in a dream-world of blood-bespattered heroics, and both Stevenson and Henley were guilty of this. Also with it—in Henley's case to a far greater extent than Stevenson's—goes a self-conscious Philistinism—better the games-field or the battleground, on neither of which tubercular patients could play any real part, than the exploration of psychological or spiritual conditions of which they could have had far greater knowledge. As we shall see, as we follow his all-too-short literary career, Stevenson wasted a great deal of time on second-hand, second-rate projects, simply because there was a streak in him which cared for the bogus-hearty and the escapist. The world of letters of the time, as can be seen by the fact that Lang and Henley played important roles in it, tended anyway to favour the falsely adventurous rather than the truly so—the spinning of rattling good yarns rather than the tackling of serious themes and the exploration of the soul. Henley, I think it fair to say, did have a certain corrupting influence on Louis.

Edmund Gosse, on the other hand, did not. He was a serious-minded and deeply literate man of letters, critic, essayist, poet; he also possessed a lively vein of humour. His interest in the world of ideas and in the imaginative and intellectual challenge presented by literature had a very beneficial effect on Stevenson —Gosse was to introduce him to many distinguished writers of the day, and after his death wrote a moving and percipient tribute to him. The contrast with Henley can best be seen by examining the letters Louis wrote to both. The letters to Gosse are warm and full of fanciful invention, but they are also abounding in serious discussion of his work and literary projects.

Gosse was well-equipped to understand Louis, anyway. His own upbringing, though far more extraordinary than Louis', had parallels with his, and can be best read about in the author's book *Father and Son*, one of the most absorbing and moving autobiographical works of English literature. Gosse's father, made early a widower, had been a member of a curious extreme Protestant group, the Plymouth Brethren, and lived in exile in Devon; his career as an eminent naturalist had been broken by his religious objections to Darwinism. Gosse had therefore led a life every bit as secluded and religion-dominated as Louis, and like Louis, religious authority had been embodied in the figure of his father. Like Louis, too, he had emancipated himself from his background through his intense belief in the life of the imagination.

So his late twenties saw Louis establishing a name for himself in the literary world and expanding his circle of friends. He took to the world of the London club, liking the atmosphere of conviviality and good talk. Gosse has in fact left us with a charming account of Louis in London. He remembered him, a laughter-loving young man, 'often . . . excessively and delight-fully silly—silly with the silliness of an inspired schoolboy'; often roaming the streets, often chatting in the Savile Club and wearing the oddest clothes: 'a suit of blue sea-cloth, a black shirt, and a wisp of yellow carpet that did duty for a necktie'.

It was his ability to communicate happiness that most impressed everyone, which went so oddly with his noticeably poor health.

'A pathos was given to his gaiety by the fragility of his health. He was never well, all the years I knew him; and we looked upon his life as hanging by the frailest tenure. As he never complained or maundered, this, no doubt—though we were not aware of it—added to the charm of his presence. He was so bright and keen and witty, and any week he might die. No one, certainly, conceived it possible that he could reach his forty-fifth year. In 1879, his health visibly began to run lower, and he used to bury himself in lonely Scotch and French places, "tinkering himself with solitude" as he used to say.'

Of course it was not only ill-health which came to isolate Stevenson in 1879. He was extremely worried. News came from the States that Fanny Osbourne was in the process of going through with her divorce, and then that she had fallen ill. Stevenson always took the illness of others very seriously (when his cousin, Bob, had fallen seriously ill some time back, Stevenson had been able to think about little else). He realized now how deeply and truly he loved Fanny, and resolved to make her his wife. J. A. Steuart, in his book on Stevenson, says that in fact even while Stevenson was supposedly in love with Fanny, he had been pursuing other girls; indeed, one affair with an Edinburgh girl at this stage of his life involved him in a fight with her father. But this news of Fanny caused him to reappreciate his emotions.

None of the friends whose opinions he consulted, however, thought his idea of going over to America and marrying Mrs. Osbourne, practical, sensible or advisable. Whether they objected to the plan simply because it seemed so wild a one, containing so little thought for building up a solidly sustained future for himself, or whether, as does indeed seem to have been the case, they disapproved of Fanny as a wife, is still not quite certain—both elements presumably were present. Stevenson was depressed but yet not dissuaded. He did realize, however, that, if friends, who held pretty similar views on life to his own, failed to understand or sympathize with him, his parents were unlikely to do so. Really there would be very little point in trying to persuade them over an issue on which their minds were indubitably made up.

Louis was in poor health physically and psychologically.

Doctors had prescribed a return to the Mediterranean, and would obviously have in no way condoned a rough journey first across the Atlantic, then across the States, in conditions of which we shall speak in the next chapter. His parents cut off supplies of money when they heard about this projected scheme, friends were adamant against it. Nevertheless, Louis revealed once more his strength of mind; he set sail for America in the August of 1879.

The account of his last day in London is vividly described by Gosse:

'The day before he started he spent with my wife and me—a day of stormy agitation, . . . for it was not in Louis to remain long in any mood. I seem to see him now, pacing the room, a cigarette spinning in his wasted fingers. To the last we were trying to dissuade him from what seemed to us the maddest of enterprises. He was so ill that I did not like to leave him, and at night—it was midsummer weather—we walked down into town together. We were by this time, I suppose, in a pretty hysterical state of mind, and as we went through Berkeley Square, in mournful discussion of the future, Louis suddenly proposed that we should visit the so-called "Haunted House", which then occupied the newspapers. The square was quiet in the decency of a Sunday evening. We found the house, and one of us boldly knocked at the door. There was no answer and no sound, and we jeered upon the door-step; but suddenly we were both aware of a pale face—a phantasm in the dusk—gazing down upon us from a surprising height. It was the caretaker, I suppose, mounted upon a flight of steps: but terror gripped us at the heart and we fled with footsteps as precipitate as those of schoolboys caught in an orchard. I think that ghostly face in Berkeley Square must have been Louis's latest European impression for many months.'

Chapter 9

Travelling in a hot, crowded train across America, an exhausting journey which consumed some eleven days and nights, Stevenson wrote lines, which, placed together, can be seen as representative of the terrible battle raging in mind and body which took place not only during one crossing of sea and land, but during the whole dark, tragic year in the States. First there is this, from a letter he wrote to Sidney Colvin:

'I had no idea how easy it was to commit suicide. There seems nothing left of me; I died a while ago; I do not know who it is that is travelling.

> Of where or how, I nothing know;
>   And why, I do not care;
>   Enough if, even so,
> My travelling eyes, my travelling mind can go
> By flood and field and hill, by wood and meadow fair,
> Beside the Susquehanna and along the Delaware.
>
> I think, I hope, I dream no more
>   The dreams of otherwhere,
>   The cherished thoughts of yore;
> I have been changed from what I was before;
> And drunk too deep perchance the lotus of the air
> Beside the Susquehanna and along the Delaware.

Unweary God me yet shall bring
  To lands of brighter air,
  Where I, now half a king,
Shall with enfranchised spirit loudlier sing,
And wear a bolder front than that which now I wear
Beside the Susquehanna and along the Delaware.'

On the same journey, he made an attempt to compose a requiem for himself. (The lines have some similarity to the famous requiem lines that were later carved on his grave.)

Now when the number of my years
  Is all fulfilled, and I
  From sedentary life
  Shall rouse me up to die,
    Bury me low and let me lie
    Under the wide and starry sky,
    Joying to live, I joyed to die.
    Bury me low and let me lie.

Clear was my soul, my deeds were free,
  Honour was called my name,
  I fell not back from fear
  Nor followed after fame.
    Bury me low and let me lie
    Under the wide and starry sky, etc.

Bury me low in vallies green
  And where the milder breeze
  Blows fresh along the stream,
  Sings roundly in the trees—
    Bury me low, etc.

There is a curious contrast between the two poems, though, of course, they have a strong resemblance to each other. In the first, Stevenson is expressing, light though his lines are, a frightening feeling of disorientation. Far away from people and places he knew and loved, tortured by anxiety as to the wisdom of what he was doing, as well as of the moral rightness, he felt stripped of his own identity. (And this sensation was to recur repeatedly through his American year, indicating that however much he might make protestations against his homeland, he needed the love and even the presence of the people who had surrounded him from early years.) Nevertheless, as his somewhat Whitmanesque rejoicing in the scenery and in the beautiful and magical sound of American names (surely the most poetic on earth!) shows, he felt he would win through. America *would* bring him the joy he was seeking there.

The second poem takes a very much more cheerful view of his past, and indeed of his present. There is a determined jauntiness in his insistence on the joy of his life. 'Honour was called my name' presumably refers to his feeling that only by fulfilling the vow he had made to Fanny by the river at Grez could he be seen by himself as behaving honourably, and this he was now in the process of doing. And certainly, as he says in the next line, he had not put fame or worldly honour before matters of the heart. But I doubt if he was speaking the truth when he said that his soul was clear, his deeds were free, for all throughout his American year—and indeed, as his fiction shows, afterwards—he was haunted by guilt springing from the nature of his departure from his own country. And perhaps this is why in this seemingly more optimistic poem he consigned himself to death, to a hero's grave, not to a glowing future.

He was right to feel guilt. For the biographer, his treatment of his parents in the matter of his leaving for America is one of the episodes in Stevenson's life most hard to sympathize with or condone. For while realizing that Louis, his mind made up, felt further rows with his parents over the subject of Fanny would be both pointless and distressing, one cannot feel that it was other than cowardly and worse, callous, to leave his parents with only a cursory note and no proper information about his whereabouts, his future plans or even ultimate intentions. And the note itself was a somewhat despicable one; it dwelt almost exclusively on himself and his feelings. It never adequately apologized for, or even seemed to understand, the pain and worry his parents would be bound to go through on his behalf. Life, Louis declared in his egotistical farewell, was at present more like death to him; only by going to the States to marry Fanny could it cease to be so.

All the same, much as Louis is to be censured for his behaviour, had Thomas been a more reasonable, less intransigent parent, this would never have had to happen.

Louis was repeatedly to feel throughout his time in America that the acute nature of his sufferings was due to his sinfulness. For many months he knew himself to be officially cut off from his parents: Thomas (and he had had enough provocation, one must admit) pronounced the sentence of disinheritance. It was not until they heard from Charles Baxter, to whom Louis wrote his usual warm, intimate letters, that he was near death, starving and dwelling in acute poverty, that his parents relented.

'Count on two hundred and fifty pounds annually' said a telegram which arrived in April 1880 from Thomas Stevenson, nine months after his son's departure from Scotland. Stevenson felt the greatest relief and the greatest joy on receiving this bulletin; clearly, important though it was, it wasn't the money that delighted him, but the feeling that his parents—and through them his own country, his own culture, perhaps even his own God—had taken him back. This book has been written to no purpose if it isn't at once obvious that a seemingly final breach with his parents, with whom he had throughout his life enjoyed such an intense if yet strained relationship, would wreak havoc on Louis' soul—the more if he felt the guilt for its existence to rest on his own shoulders.

With this restoration, Louis was able to go ahead with marrying Fanny.

If, as Louis put it, he had for much of the time leading up to this, been living 'in a circle of hell unknown to Dante', there had been ample reason for unhappiness. The whole venture from the outset was dogged by misfortune.

The voyage across the Atlantic itself seemed infernal. Not the least quixotic aspect of Louis' flight to America was that he insisted on travelling 'emigrant class'. The 1870's and 1880's were years of extensive emigration to the United States. There were perhaps three reasons for his choosing to make the journey in these conditions. First—severing himself as he was from his parents—he was short of money and, not himself knowing what lay ahead of him, he had to be very careful how much he spent. Secondly, he was possessed with his frequent anti-bourgeois sentiment which led him in this case to want to feel what travel in these hard conditions—ones which the majority of those bound for the States experienced—was like. And thirdly, he felt that out of what he saw and underwent an interesting book might come, a tougher sort of travel book than the *Travels with a Donkey*. (And indeed one did come: *The Amateur Emigrant*.)

Not only did Stevenson feel strung up with nervous anxiety, not only did he have his usual respiratory trouble, but, the crossing being a rough one, he felt extremely seasick. He managed to secure himself, however, a cabin where there was a table on which he could write. For despite his feeling so ill, he was not inactive on the journey. He read—and how curious an employment in the circumstances—through his father's theological works, by which he was considerably impressed. He also wrote the greater part of a short novel, *The Story of a Lie*. With its mostly English setting, this story cannot be accounted one of Stevenson's successes. The atmosphere of an English squire's household was not one he had much knowledge of. But the hero's Bohemian years in Paris, where he associates with picturesque riff-raff, are clearly based on Louis' own time there with Bob, and the work is further interesting as being Louis' first real attempt to tackle the father/son conflict that had absorbed so much of his own emotional energy. In the story, significantly enough, the father is violently opposed to his son Dick's association with a girl who, because her background is a roughish one, he believes to be unrespectable too. Certain passages parallel the relationship between Louis and his father very closely:

'Old Mr. Nasely had the sturdy, untutored nature of the upper middle class. The universe seemed plain to him. "The thing's right," he would say, or "the thing's wrong"; and there was an end of it. There was a contained, prophetic energy in his utterances, even on the slightest affairs; he *saw* the damned thing; if you did not, it must be from perversity of will, and this sent the blood to his head. . . . He had a hearty respect for Dick as a lad of parts. Dick had a respect for his father as the best of men tempered by the politic revolt of a youth who has to see to his own independence. Whenever the pair argued, they came to an open rupture; and arguments were frequent, for they were both positive, and both loved the work of the intelligence. It was a treat to hear Mr. Naseby defending the Church of England in a volley of oaths, or supporting ascetic morals with an enthusiasm not entirely innocent of port wine. Dick used to wax indignant, and none the less so because, as his father was a skilful disputant, he found himself not seldom in the wrong. On these occasions he would redouble in energy, and declare that black was white, and blue yellow with much conviction and heat of manner; but in the morning such a licence of debate weighted upon him like a crime, . . .'

And all the time Stevenson was writing this somewhat gentle account of his own difficulties in confronting his father, a tossing ship was carrying him farther and farther away from him.

He arrived in America, to be greeted by dense, inhospitable rain. The weather soon changed, however, and for much of the time that he was carried across the continent by the emigrant train, the days were clear, golden and sunny, bespeaking a freshness and unsulliedness fitting for the New World. The virgin beauty of much of the landscape called forth a characteristic delighted response in him. Equally characteristic was his interest in his fellow-passengers, made up of all sorts of nationalities. Quickly he got into conversation with them, and, also true to his nature, performed many little kindnesses for them, particularly for the children. But for much of the time he felt very ill, and utterly weary. He came to San Francisco, at the end of these days, a wreck in mental and physical health. Here, however, he heard the comforting news that Fanny was better, though still very far from well. From San Francisco, Stevenson started to make his way south to Monterey, on the Californian coast, for here Fanny was living with her sister. Little could he have known the difficulties to lie ahead of him.

Stevenson journeyed a hundred and fifty miles to the south of San Francisco, and camped in the Coast Line mountains, some eighteen miles from Monterey. At this point his sorely tested strength gave way; as he put it: 'I was pretty nearly slain; my spirit lay down and kicked for three days'. Lying under a tree in a near stupor, feverish and worn out, he was found by two frontiersmen who took him up to their ranch and took great care of him. One of these men was an old bear-hunter, seventy-two years of age, the other had served in the war in which California was taken by the States. Stevenson was very ill indeed on Angora Ranch, and though the kindness of the two men moved him a lot, he must have been depressed and troubled in spirit, and significantly while he lay in this fever, remote from all he knew, his thoughts turned back to Scotland.

'I am lying,' he wrote to Charles Baxter, 'in an upper chamber nearly naked, with flies crawling all over me and a clinking of goat bells in my ears, which proves to me the goats are come home and it will soon be time to eat. The old bear hunter is doubtless now infusing tea, and Tom the Indian will come in with his gun in a few minutes. How's that for Beadle's American Library? Yet all true. How about J. W. F.? [Ferrier, the dissolute friend described in an earlier chapter] and how for God's sake about my father? Tell me, please, Charles. Since I have gone away I have found out for the first time how much I love that man: he is dearer to me than all except F.'

At last he had recognized the fact, which made the declaration of rejection soon to come the harder to bear.

From the ranch, Stevenson made his way to Monterey. He found it a picturesque town, extremely Mexican in flavour, with adobe houses, an atmosphere of lethargy (except in the saloons where men gambled feverishly over cards all day) and full of horses and men on horseback. Spanish was more frequently heard in the streets than English, and at night serenaders would go about the streets, singing love-songs underneath windows to the accompaniment of guitars. Stevenson found companions who interested him, he found an alien pattern of life that he thrilled to observe. And of course he was also reunited with Fanny who was living with Nelly her sister in a beautiful Spanish colonial house. Behind huge adobe walls was a garden which was a 'riot of flowers'. Here Stevenson would walk up and down and also sit and read out the writings he was engaged on, one of which was one of his most exciting short stories, *The Pavilion on the Links*. Sometimes the three of them, Fanny, Nelly and Louis, would go for walks along the Pacific beach.

'Out of the mist arise memories of walks along the beach—the long beach of clean white sand stretches unbroken for many miles around the great sweeping curve of Monterey Bay, where we watched the tiny sandy-pipers, and the huge Pacific seas . . . Sometimes we walked there at night, when the blood-red harvest-moon sprang suddenly like a great ball of fire . . . above the rim of horizon on the opposite side of the circling bay, sending a glittering track across the water to our feet. To walk with Stevenson on such a night, and watch the "waves come in slowly, vast and green, curve their translucent necks and burst with a surprising uproar"—to walk with him on such a night and listen to his inimitable talk is the sort of memory that cannot fade.'

His sister-in-law's words suggest a more consistent happiness in Monterey than was the case. Despite the joys of Fanny's company, Louis knew great emotional tension. He was at this time expressing to Henley—to whom, as we have seen, he generally liked to put forward his more cheery, optimistic side—such views as these:

'The end of life? Yes, Henley, I can tell you what that is. How old are all truths, and yet how far from commonplace; old, strange, and inexplicable, like the Sphinx. So I learn day by day the value and high doctrinality of suffering. Let me suffer always; not more than I am able to bear, for that makes a man mad; as hunger drives the wolf to sally from the forest; but still to suffer some, and never to sink up to my eyes in comfort and grow dead in virtues and respectability. I am a bad man by nature, I suppose; but I cannot be good without suffering a little. And the end of life, you will ask? The pleasurable death of self: a thing not to be attained, because it is a thing belonging to Heaven.'

It is clear that his very presence in California was a source of great guilt to him, and that this, because it was so intimately linked to his feelings for his parents, revived his childhood sense of sin and of the need for expiation. There is the familiar accent of morbidity in these lines; we know that Louis, rightly, did not really believe himself to be bad by nature, but there were times when, perhaps as a result of having kicked too hard against the pricks, he thought that this was perhaps the case. No man can wholly escape the creed taught him in childhood, can go against the concepts of right and wrong presented by his parents. And certainly Stevenson was only to know peace of mind when he had reconciled himself and his more renegade emotions and desires to his Scottishness and the Scottish religion in which he continued in one part of his being to believe.

Alas! more and deeper suffering was still in store for him.

In December 1879, Stevenson went to San Francisco, where he thought he could get employment as a journalist. In fact, he earned very little money, and the city provided him with one of the grimmest episodes of his life. Here he knew great poverty, near-starvation, bitter loneliness, and torturing ill-health. Needless to say, the romance and adventurous nature of San Francisco were not lost on Louis, and in his descriptions of the city it is of these, not of his own hardships there, that he chooses to speak (*The Old and New Pacific Capitals*):

'There are rough quarters where it is dangerous o' nights; cellars of public entertainment which the wary pleasure-seeker chooses to avoid. Concealed weapons are unlawful; but the law is continually broken. One editor was shot dead while I was there; another walked the streets accompanied by a bravo, his guardian angel. I have been quietly eating a dish of oysters in a restaurant, where, not more than ten minutes after I had left, shots were exchanged and took effect; and one night about ten o' clock, I saw a man standing watchfully at a street-corner with a long Smith-and-Wesson glittering in hand behind his back. Somebody had done something he should not, and was being looked for with a vengeance. It is odd, too, that the seat of the last vigilance committee I know of . . . was none other than the Palace Hotel, the world's greatest caravanserai, served by lifts and lit by electricity; where, in the great glazed court, a band nightly discourses music from a grove of palms. So do extremes meet in this city of contrasts: extremes of wealth and poverty, apathy and excitement, the convenience of civilisation and the red justice of Judge Lynch.'

Stevenson himself came to know far more of the extremes of poverty than those of wealth; and his health received shattering blows as a result of the life he was forced to lead. A contributory factor to the worsening of his condition was an act of great unselfishness; his landlady's little boy fell desperately ill, and Stevenson tended his sick-bed. It was a disastrous thing to do from the point of view of his physical and mental health. He broke down completely, and was nearer to death than ever before.

'I have,' he wrote in a letter to Ferrier, 'truly, been very sick; I fear I am a vain man, for I thought it a pity I should die. I could not help thinking that a good many would be disappointed; but for myself, although I still think life a business full of agreeable features, I was not entirely unwilling to give it up. It is so difficult to behave well; and in that matter, I get more dissatisfied with myself . . . every day.'

This points to a psychological factor in the illness, though its consumptive features were obvious and disagreeable enough—a horrifying catalogue: 'cold sweats, prostrating attacks of cough, sinking fits of cough, sinking fits in which I lost the power of speech, fever, and all the ugliest circumstances of the disease . . .'

The graveness of his descent into illness was not wholly a misfortune; Charles Baxter informed Thomas and Margaret Stevenson. The telegram of forgiveness and financial security was dispatched. On 19 May 1880, Louis, 'a withered bridegroom' as he described himself, was at last able to marry Fanny. The wedding took place in San Francisco, the couple then spent an eccentric honeymoon in a deserted mining-town fifty miles away. The honeymoon was blighted by both Fanny and Lloyd contracting diphtheria. For while Fanny's daughter Isobel had married Joe Strong, an artist, and remained behind in the States (indeed Fanny was now a grandmother!) Lloyd was to live with Louis and Fanny. Plans were now made for the return to Britain.

The year in America irrevocably altered Louis' life. First, it brought him a wife, and for this reason alone it is not to be regretted. The nature of the marriage he embarked on in this fraught year of 1880, is best described by Stevenson himself in a letter to his parents, four years later:

'I cannot think what I have done to deserve so good a gift. This sudden remark came out of my pen; it is not like me; but in case you did not know, I may as well tell you, that my marriage has been the most successful in the world. . . She is everything to me . . .'

And in the atmosphere of love Fanny created, Louis' creative genius could flourish. Secondly, the sufferings he had endured led, as we shall see presently, to a reunion, a recognition of mutual love, between Louis and his parents, scarcely possible perhaps without the calamitous troubles just gone through. This, as we have seen, was deeply necessary to his psyche. Moreover, the proximity of death Louis had twice known had deepened his attitude to life; the poseur, the dilettante, the eschewer of bourgeois domesticity vanish from the scene this year. Again this has beneficial effects on both his character and his writings.

But on the other hand, his bodily condition received such blows as to amount to permanent damage. From this traumatic year onward, Louis' health was such that death or rather the idea of death became as a companion; every illness could be fatal, each new year that presented itself could so very easily be his last. A sick man before he went to the States, he now was irretrievably doomed to a short life, and this he knew and must constantly and sadly been aware of.

Chapter 10

Stevenson's fiction abounds in scenes of significant homecomings. Two in particular spring to mind. From the dead, as it were, the Master of Ballantrae returns one November afternoon to his family home. Behind him are years in which he has experienced defeat, been a pirate and a murderer, roughed it in America, and lived in exile among the Jacobite expatriates of Paris. Wicked though his past career has been, wicked indeed though his very nature is, his old father receives him with forgiveness and love. John in *The Misadventures of John Nicholson* has led a feckless dissipated youth in which he got into scrapes and incurred heavy debts necessitating his leaving Scotland for America. Mr. Nicholson senior has been a stern unbending father, much preoccupied with theological niceties. In the States John has worked his way into a good position in a bank, though even here trouble and bad luck has dogged him, and when after many years he returns to his native Edinburgh there is a cloud over his head. So set against him by now is his father that reconciliation seems at first almost impossible, but it is achieved and that through the auspices of the good woman whom John loves and later marries.

The emotional force of these homecomings derives from Stevenson's own in the August of 1880. It is, of course, particularly noteworthy that in both these scenes of return the figure of the righteous father is dominant. Officially forgiven by Thomas Stevenson, the object of his generosity, and, as we have seen, aware now of the great love he himself had for 'that man', Louis must have had him constantly in mind as he made the voyage across the Atlantic. How would matters really stand between them? Had Thomas truly forgiven Louis for his past malconduct? Above all, how would Thomas react and behave towards Fanny, to whom he had before so violently on principle objected? Could he find it in his intransigent nature to accept her as his son's wife?

In both the fictional cases mentioned above, the central character has been away from his own country many years. So must it have seemed to Louis. He had left Britain unmarried and estranged from his own family, he now left America a married man with a stepson for whom he was to take responsibility, and having known what close proximity to death and poverty was really like; he also left with a deeper knowledge of himself and of his relationships with others. But in fact he had been away only a year—indeed, he left New York for Liverpool on the exact date on which the previous year he had sailed from Clydeside to New York: 7 August. On the voyage, despite his anxieties and excitement, his capacity for making friends was once more exhibited; James Cunningham, with whom he was to keep up a correspondence for some years, remembered long after Stevenson's death the nine or ten days of conversation he had with him on the ship, conversation the like of which he had never known before. Among the topics Louis discoursed on, he recalled, were adventure-stories, particularly those of his boyhood favourite Captain Mayne Reid, of whom he spoke with marked enthusiasm. Was there already present in Louis' mind the idea that he might add significantly to literature for boys? For only a year later the first fifteen chapters of *Treasure Island* were to be written.

Louis' worries about his family's reception of himself and of Fanny were to be swiftly proved ungrounded. Forgiveness was complete. It is a tribute to the remarkable and strong natures of both parents and son that from Louis' arrival in Liverpool onwards, the relationship between them was not only restored to the best of what it had been but developed into something rich and mature and fed by mutual respect. The sufferings both parties underwent during the American year certainly seem to have made each value the other the more highly. And in addition to this, there was the almost immediate liking and regard that the Stevenson parents felt for Fanny, both of which emotions were amply returned, as her memoirs of them show.

There is no doubt that Fanny, mostly out of her deep love for Louis, determined on the conquest of Thomas and Margaret. She must have known of their former disapproval of her previous status, and of the probability of a resentment of her present one. So she must have resolved to use all her charm and diplomacy to make this new relationship a smooth one. It is possible that there were mercenary motives among others. But no amount of deliberate policy and pleasant manners can eradicate real dissimilarities or alien personality traits, and so the only conclusion that can be drawn from the whole-hearted acceptance of Fanny was that her character and her devotion to Louis impressed them greatly and called forth from them the best of their own warm temperaments.

Thomas Stevenson and Fanny, in particular, enjoyed a deep friendship. He was greatly struck by her sense and strength of personality; in fact, he commanded Louis always to show his writings to Fanny before offering them to the world, so sensible would her opinions be. And as has already been said, he was right to advise so, since Fanny was to be Louis' first and shrewdest critic for the rest of his life. Not that Thomas Stevenson failed to recognize the managing side of Fanny's character. But then he thought that Louis needed a wife who possessed such a nature. 'I doot yer a besom,' he said to her, meaning that there was a touch of the shrew about her, but an admirable shrew!

Indeed, perhaps if there had been no Fanny, Louis would never have been truly at one with his parents again. With her pleasant ways—her habit of calling him 'Uncle Tom' or 'Mr. Tommy', for example—Fanny tapped the tender, chivalrous, near-sentimental side of Thomas Stevenson. And this, of course, altered the complexion of his behaviour towards Louis. The dramatic change can be seen by reading through Stevenson's letters. Louis wrote far more frequently to Thomas after his return to this country than ever before. They are letters rich in affection and in interest in each other's ideas and projects, showing in fact an intellectual give-and-take rare in father-son relationships. The father and son who discussed the Pentland Rising together appeared in maturer form. From what we can make out, the tensions and troubles of previous years seem hardly to have been alluded to after the return; certainly, one would not have guessed at what had happened in the past by reading through the correspondence of 1881-1887. Of course in the back of the minds of both men the memories must have persisted; that Louis never forgot the days when each seemed to spell agony to the other is triumphantly present in his books. But we know that love had always existed between them; now circumstances and the emotional journeys both had made united to make love dominant, and with love came friendship and ease of intercourse.

It was, I think, absolutely essential for Louis that this was the case. Psychologically he could not have survived without parental approval and affection. The experiences of his earliest years had made him intensely emotionally bound up with his parents and with his father in particular and while it had been necessary to free himself, to do so in perpetual estrangement would have gone against both his strongest moral feelings and his deepest-seated needs and impulses. If the loving home that Fanny created for him can be thanked for his having had the security in which to produce his series of masterpieces, we owe much of the balance and sanity of viewpoint to the fact that his conscience and his affections were both satisfied in that he had won back through deeds of his own making the admiration and the approval of the parents who meant so much to him.

The years that followed his arrival home also revealed to Louis something which hitherto he had taken for granted or perhaps at times turned his back on: his Scottishness. While, as we have seen, the past of his own country had always been of the greatest interest to him, because of the strained relationship with his father, and indeed with the whole of Edinburgh middle- and upper-class society, he had felt blocks about exploring or coming to terms with his country. He had been a Bohemian, a Frenchman, an emigrant, even a Californian; in both his writings and in his behaviour he had not presented himself to the world as the Scotsman he was. Perhaps he had feared that in doing so he would reveal parallels between himself and his father with whom he was at variance. Now, those fears gone, he could acknowledge

K

his Scottish background and character both to himself and to the outside world.

The most conspicuous instance of this rediscovery was his response to the Highlands after his return to Scotland. Shortly after Louis and Fanny's arrival in Britain, Thomas and Margaret Stevenson took them to Blair Atholl and to Strathpeffer, both of which are in the Eastern Highlands of Scotland. The summer of 1881 was likewise spent in the Scottish mountains—first at Kinnaird Cottage in Pitlochry, then at Braemar, and in the summer of 1882 the Stevensons, after having stayed in the Manse of Stobo in Peeblesshire, went up to Speyside and thence to Kingussie. As a youth Louis had felt a certain distaste of Highland scenery—he had thought it stark and inhospitable, and he had been adamant on how much more attractive to his eyes was lush scenery which seemed to accommodate man, not provide him with obstacles and elemental buffetings. Readers of the *Travels with a Donkey* will remember various unfavourable comparisons the author saw fit to draw between the Highlands and the landscape of the Cevennes. I think part of this standpoint was affectation—Stevenson wanting to appear a cosmopolitan, a French Bohemian, was at pains to conceal from himself and from others a taste for scenery almost deified by his fellow-countrymen. For not only did the Highlands command the fervent admiration of other Scots, and had received numerous celebrations from them, above all, of course, from Scott—in *Waverley* and *Rob Roy*—it was the favourite area of her kingdom of Queen Victoria herself. She adored her seat at Balmoral and had a Highlander ex-gillie, John Brown, as her chosen companion. No wonder the youthful Louis had liked to blaspheme against this beautiful country stamped with the approval of the Scottish and English Establishments. And of course the Highlands can present a very grim aspect, all too reminiscent to Louis no doubt of the grimness of the Scottish religion and ethical system. But it is impossible to believe that Louis did not respond to them when younger, and indeed we have testimonies from those who saw him earlier on holiday in the Highlands that he took an immense delight in the wild Highland scenery. But it is certainly the case that his visits there directly after coming back from the United States almost amounted to a falling in love with the Highlands and to his realizing as he had

138

never done before that they were a part of *his* country. He felt almost guilty that he had never paid them compliments before.

'My dear Colvin,' he wrote, shortly after his arrival in Strathpeffer, 'One or two words. We are here: all goes extremely well with the wife and with the parents. Near here is a valley; birch woods, heather and a stream; I have lain down and died; no country, no place, was ever for a moment so delightful to my soul. And I have been a Scotchman all my life, and denied my native land! Away with your gardens of roses, indeed! Give me the cold breath of Rogie waterfall, henceforth, and for ever, world without end!'

What passion there is in these words! He even went to church in the Highland village they were staying in and wrote to James Cunningham, his friend of the ship:

'Man, I liked the Scotch psalms fine!

And man, of a' 'at I ever saw, I think I ne'er saw the beat o' Tummelside.'

Certainly the Highlands were to find one of their finest celebrants in Robert Louis Stevenson. How magically the world of lowering mountains, fast-flowing burns, of mile upon mile of purple heather, of eagle and deer, pine and rowan, marsh and rock, small kirk and smaller croft is captured in the pages of *Kidnapped*! In his youth Louis had sometimes amused himself by trying to trace—with more imagination than scientific accuracy—a pedigree of his family showing its Celtic roots. From his stay in Strathpeffer onwards, the history and culture of Highland Scotland tugged strongly at both his intellect and his imagination.

Here it seems necessary to say something about what this history and culture consists of.

The Highland experience has been radically different from the Lowland. Geography has inevitably been responsible for this. The intractable terrain of so much of Highland Scotland resulted in its having a poor but agrarian-centred economy, and in its inhabitants preserving an ancient social structure. This is the case with many mountain communities (Montenegro, for example). Hills are an obstacle to external influences. Certainly the Highlanders retained their clan system with all its complicated practices and priorities into the mid-eighteenth century; in the west, Gaelic speech persisted (as in a very limited form it does today), and idiosyncrasies of dress were also preserved.

(The kilt, it should be remembered, is a Highland not a Lowland garment.) Being so obviously different in their way of life from the rest of Britain made the Highlanders feel alien to all others and to be looked on as such too! And this included their fellow-Scots on the other side of the Highland line. Indeed, tension grew up between the two divisions of the Scottish nation, and there were many reasons why this should be the case. A sizeable number of the Highlanders, for instance, were Catholic, and as we have even seen from the behaviour of nineteenth-century Cummy, Catholicism is inimical to the average Puritan. And their sense of values was at variance with that of the other North Britons. One feature of a poor society is that, unable because of its very nature to accumulate riches, it develops a certain nonchalance in matters of husbandry and industry. This aroused the contempt of both the Lowland Scots and the English, who dismissed the Highlanders as rough and feckless. Moreover, their clan system, encouraging a paramount belief in loyalty, was responsible for a certain savagery. Highlanders came to have regard for deeds of violence and to have disregard for the restraints more civilized communities put on revenge, hatred, territorial coveting, etc. This rendered them barbarous in the eyes of outsiders. On the other hand, they preserved a sense of the continuity, indeed the presence, of the past which communities living close to nature tend to possess. They had kept alive a beautiful mythology, a rich store of music and ballads, tales and proverbs, together with a lovely language (the Gaelic), and a passionate approach to existence that challenges the more materialistic and careful ones of differently organized nations.

(No better picture of the differences between Highland and Lowland cultures can be found than *Kidnapped* and *Catriona*.)

The Highlanders for the most part gave their support to the Stuarts in their claim to the British throne. There were two major uprisings against the Hanoverian regime—the '15 (1715) in championship of the Old Pretender, 'James III', and the '45 (1745) in which the rallying figure was the Young Pretender, 'Bonnie Prince Charlie'. After the defeat of the Jacobites at the ill-fated Battle of Culloden, the Highlanders were treated with some severity by authority of the British government. A recalcitrant district of the country was not to be tolerated. Butcher Cumberland subdued the region with a blend of unimaginative callousness and calculated cruelty. Estates of rebels were temporarily confiscated, the Gaelic tongue was forbidden, the Highland customs and dress made illegal. All this incurred much resentment. But in fact the Government also showed foresightedness. They tried to develop the Highlands as an economic region, ensured a wider spread of religion and education, and after the restoration of the estates, removed the ban on the Highland traditions and practices. By the end of the eighteenth century, the two Scotlands had, if you like, become not only reconciled to each other but united. Scott, himself a Lowlander, helped to make his countrymen proud of their Gaelic heritage—instead of being ashamed of their cousins on the other side of the Highland line; the Scots, and the English too for that matter, were taught to rejoice in it, and once the threat implicit in the Jacobite upsurges was no longer a reality, the bravery and the nobility displayed in them were treasured.

But there was more sorrow in store for the people of the Highlands. In order to secure income from this wild country, thousands of crofters were driven from their homes by their landlords to make room for herds of sheep or cattle. 'The Highland Clearances' is one of the saddest stories of British history. Today the Highlands remain a depopulated area—whole communities have vanished and indeed, sad to relate, the process is by no means over yet. The Highlander is still unfeelingly disregarded by governments.

Stevenson's first published book, *The Pentland Rising*, had been, after all, a work of a historical nature. Now he felt a renewal of imaginative concern about the past of Scotland, and this area of it, which for the reasons just gone into he had tended to ignore, now became of burning interest to him. As Louis passed the spot where the Earl of Mar had raised the standard of rebellion in 1715—ostensibly as a deerhunt to which three hundred men came—as he gazed out on to the magnificent purple slopes of Ben Vrackie, so dear to the Gaelic soul, his creative pulse quickened, he felt a new sense of identity with the entirety of his country's culture and past. In addition to this, he felt—now the old harmonious relationship with his parents had been restored—a reversion to the serious-minded person, with a special gift for the understanding and analysis of a past period, that he had once been. Only he was able to approach the past now with a more *objective* understanding; gone was the emotional partisanship that one finds in *The Pentland Rising*. The breadth of mind he had acquired during his Bohemian days and wander-years equipped him admirably to examine the complexities of feelings and attitudes of past people. Sooner or later he would be bound to give these developed insights literary expression.

Scotland may have agreed with him spiritually better than ever before, but climatically it was just as harsh and hostile. Louis' health was still very far from good. America, as we have seen, had been responsible for a serious deterioration of his condition, and his mother's brother, Dr. Balfour, pronounced him unfit to endure the rigours of the Scottish winter. He suggested the Swiss Alps. Somewhat reluctantly Louis agreed, and so he, Fanny and Lloyd spent the winters of 1880-1881 and 1881-1882 in Davos; Scotland was reserved for the summer seasons only.

Though appreciative of the magnificence of the Alps in winter, Stevenson resented his confinement in Davos Platz and both Fanny and he frequently felt ill and low in spirits. Sidney Colvin, as staunch a friend as he had ever been, came out to stay with him, and other close friends—Bob, Gosse, Charles Baxter—regaled him as usual with letters. Also in Davos because of his afflicted lungs was another man of letters, later to acquire a reputation for himself, John Addington Symonds (1840-1893). Whereas for the most part Louis had always been more widely read than those he came into contact with, John Addington Symonds was a man of far-ranging literary and artistic tastes that seemed to Louis to show up his own limitations. Louis liked Symonds' company, though he found something 'sickroom' in his whole approach to life. Lloyd Osbourne, with a child's perception, thought there was something condescending in Symonds' own treatment of Stevenson. Whether this was the case or not, it is undoubtedly true that Louis became increasingly critical of his own dilletante streak.

His writings, it is true, had begun by now to earn him a small reputation, but they amounted to a somewhat unsubstantial achievement. At the age of thirty he had not, for all his attempts and all his ambitions, produced one single full-length book. Nor had he made himself a real expert on any one subject, even on those dear to his heart. He vowed now to remedy this. Less energy must go on ephemeral trifles, more on the exploration of matters that really interested him. This does not mean, of course, that the idea of Romance and of adding creations of his own to its literature was any the less dear to him.

So, in between the resting, the seeing of a limited society of expatriates and invalids, and the great fun of tobogganing, an amusement in which his boyish nature delighted, Louis planned a work which certainly would stretch his intellect to the full. It was to be a history of the Highlands. Eagerly and industriously Stevenson began making notes and ordering books. His letters to his father are full of his project. He intended his book to begin immediately after the '15, and to fall into five parts tracing the history of the Highlands to the years following the tragic clearances and dealing with their writers, their lore, and with the many remarkable and colourful persons they had produced.

His absorption in this task led to one of the most extraordinary episodes in Louis' story. Louis, the lazy, dissolute student who had tended to scoff at those who took their studies seriously, heard that the Chair of History and Constitutional Law was vacant at Edinburgh University, and decided to apply. He wrote round to his various literary and academic friends (Colvin, Gosse and Lang were of their number) asking them to give testimonials concerning his worth to the Faculty of Advocates at Edinburgh. This they did; their words show the high opinion they had of Louis, but few of them can really have thought of him as a likely member of a university staff, let alone as a Professor. Edinburgh must have been amazed; only seven or eight years before, this candidate, competing against hard-working scholars, had been cutting classes and spending his time in dissipation rather than industry. Admittedly Louis had not been a history student, and history—could they have known it—was a true passion with him. But for all the eminence of his sponsors, Louis—not surprisingly —did badly in the election, receiving indeed only three votes on his behalf.

The letter he wrote to Colvin asking him for recommendation is an interesting document to the student of Louis' personality.

'In short, sir, I mean to try for this chair. I do believe I can make something out of it. It will be a pulpit in a sense; for I am nothing if not moral, as you know. My works are unfortunately so light and trifling they may interfere. But if you think, as I think, I am fit to fight it, send me the best kind of testimonial stating all you can in favour of me and, with your best art, turning the difficulty of my never having done anything in history, strictly speaking . . . it would be a good thing for me, out and out good. Help me to live, help me to *work*, for I am better of pressure, and help me to say what I want about God, and life.'

This reveals the dissatisfaction with himself that Louis was feeling at this time. His writings did not really satisfy him— he knew he was capable of far stronger, more searching work than any he had tried so far. His coming back to Scotland had shown him his own fundamental seriousness of vision. He could not find fulfilment in the life of a vagabond, or a literary hack. His ardent spirit craved for something more intellectually and spiritually demanding than any task he had hitherto applied himself to. Mistaken though he was in thinking that a Professorial Chair was the solution, he did rightly realize that his life had come to a turning-point—that he had to goad himself forward and harness his intelligence and creative imagination to worthwhile and challenging matters, otherwise his life could be permanently frustrating: he would slip into the existence of a penniless poetaster.

But despite the disappointment of the failure in the matter of the Edinburgh Chair, the year 1881 was far and away the richest so far in achievement.

Kinnaird Cottage, near Pitlochry, turned out to be a lovely place, only a few yards from 'a little green glen with a burn, a wonderful burn, gold and green and snow-white, singing loud and low in different steps of its career, now pouring over miniature crags, now fretting itself to death in a maze of rocky stairs and pots; never was so sweet a little river. Behind, great purple moorlands . . .' But alas! the weather was extremely wet, and few of the outdoor pleasures dreamt of could take place. The family was thrust in on itself, and Fanny and Louis decided to try their hands at stories of the supernatural. And so, to while away the time, Louis wrote *Thrawn Janet*, one of his strangest and most successful works.

The circumstances in which it was first read out are best told by Fanny:

'That evening is as clear in my memory as though it were yesterday,—the dim light of our one candle, with the acrid smell of the wick we forgot to snuff, the shadows in the corners of the "lang, laigh, mirk chalmer, perishing cauld," the driving rain on the roof close about our heads, and the gusts of wind that shook our windows. The very sound of the names— Murdoch Soulis, The Hangin' Shaw in the beild of the Black Hills, Balweary in the vale of Dule—sent a "cauld grue" along my bones. By the time the tale was finished, my husband had fairly frightened himself, and we crept down the stairs clinging hand in hand like two scared children.'

It is easy to understand why they were so frightened, for on each reading *Thrawn Janet* exerts a terrifying power. It takes us to a remote hill-village in early eighteenth-century Scotland, a community dark with superstition and with a grim, unrelenting religion, and centres on a woman who seems at first a harmless, cracked, once perhaps too free a creature, Janet; the story tells of her being ostracized by the members of the community, of her being befriended by the innocent, lonely young minister, and of her being possessed of the Devil. At least so it seems. For Stevenson does not explain his odd, disturbing story; the events are presented by one of the old villagers and are told in Scottish dialect. The teller believes his tale; he, like many a rural Scot in former days, accepts the existence of and goes in dread of the Devil. Stevenson's or the present-day reader's views on the Evil One seem beside the point as we read, horrified.

Thrawn Janet is Stevenson's first real excursion into the culture of his country. The story would be unthinkable without the pungent accents of the Lowland Scot, without the historical understanding of the beliefs of the period. It also shows an extension of Stevenson's powers of sympathy. Dotty and perhaps demon-dominated though she is, we feel pity for Janet and too for the poor young minister.

Here is the scene in which the minister first realizes what may be wrong with Janet:

'. . . he gaed to the window, an' stood glowrin' at Dule water. The trees are unco thick, an' the winter lies deep an' black under the manse; an' there was Janet washin' the cla'es wi' her coats kilted. She had her back to the minister, an' he, for his pairt, hardly kenned what he was lookin' at. Syne she turned round, an' shawed her face; Mr. Soulis had the same cauld grue as twice that day afore, an' it was borne in upon him what folk said, that

Janet was deid long syne, an' this was a bogie at her clay-cauld flesh. He drew back a pickle and he scanned her narrowly. She was tramp-trampin' in the cla'es croonin' to hersel'; and eh! Gude guide us, but it was a fearsome face. Whiles she sang louder, but there was nae man born o' woman that could tell the words o' her sang; an' whiles she lookit side-lang doun, but there was naething there for her to look at. There gaed a scunner through the flesh upon his banes; an' that was Heeven's advertisement.'

The summer continued wet. The Stevensons moved from Kinnaird to another cottage, some miles away, at Castleton of Braemar. The dramatic scenery surrounding the cottage (always known in the village as 'the late Miss M'Gregor's') could hardly be seen with the rain and mist. As Stevenson said in a letter to Mrs. Sitwell, 'the wind pipes, the rain comes down in squalls, great black clouds are continually overhead, and it is as cold as March. The country is delightful, more cannot be said; it is very beautiful, a perfect joy when we get a blink of sun to see it in!'

The weeks must have seemed to Louis' young stepson, Lloyd, to be passing very slowly. He was now twelve years old; a lively, energetic lad, with a taste for imaginative games and pursuits delightfully close to Louis' own. Throughout this particular summer of 1881, his stepfather, normally so good at improvising entertainment, had made Lloyd an audience for imaginary lectures to be delivered when he got the Chair at Edinburgh University. Poor Lloyd had had to sit while Louis paced up and down, delivering such rolling sentences as: 'Gentlemen, I hope none of you will make the fatal mistake of undervaluing the great share, the gigantic share that the Church, in spite of its defects. . .' Where was the organizer of fascinating 'war-games' which came to involve six hundred miniature lead soldiers, and was organized with the sort of elaborate plans Louis and Bob had so ardently rejoiced in when younger? Where was the painter of scenery for a toy theatre? Where was the inventive improviser of plays?

But Lloyd needn't have despaired. The boys' ideal companion was to return. The rain poured on; Louis had a cold and was forced to spend mornings in bed. One miserable morning in Braemar, Lloyd was amusing himself by touching up with a box of paints a map he had drawn of an imaginary island. His step-father came downstairs and leaned over his shoulder to see what the boy was doing. Before long he was joining in the elaboration of the map, and making up names for places on it. Lloyd felt a thrill of intense excitement as Louis wrote the names 'Skeleton Island' and 'Spy-Glass Hill' on the chart, and marked it with three red crosses to indicate the spots where treasure had been buried. As Louis and Lloyd worked at the map of 'Treasure Island', as the older man insisted it was called, Louis told the boy stories about the pirates who had frequented it, and of how the treasure had come to be stowed there. It was no wonder Lloyd expressed a wish for a story about it. However, he wasn't prepared for Louis' reaction—which was to take the map, put it in his pocket, and leave the room. Lloyd felt a little sad, perhaps even a little annoyed, to see his map disappear. However, any feelings of disappointment he had were shortly to be assuaged, for at noon the following day, he was summoned to his stepfather's room. He entered to see Louis sitting up in bed, with the map spread out in front of him on the counterpane. Lloyd was asked to sit down and listen to the first chapter of a new story which involved the island depicted on the map—to listen, in other words, to the first chapter of *Treasure Island*.

Lloyd Osborne was all his life to remember the intense excitement with which he listened to the opening page of the story—surely the most capturing of any in fiction. Who can fail to experience an almost physical sensation of mystery and of adventure to come when he reads the masterly first sentence:

'Squire Trelawney, Dr. Livesey, and the rest of these gentlemen having asked me to write down the whole particulars about Treasure Island, from the beginning to the end, keeping nothing back but the bearings of the island, and that only because there is still treasure not yet lifted, I take up my pen in the year of grace 17—, and go back to the time when my father kept the "Admiral Benbow" inn, and the brown old seaman, with the sabre-cut, first took up his lodging under our roof.'

Already the listener or reader longs for elucidation of the fascinating details seemingly casually referred to; in fact, this is an immensely careful introduction, pregnant with all the later key incidents.

Lloyd was not to be the only listener. Each morning Stevenson stayed in his room, by a fire, forgetting his cough, his slightly inflamed lungs, and wrote a chapter. Never had creation come so easily to him; events, people, places flowed from his pen. He knew exactly too what was to come next; at last, he was engaged on the full-length story it had been his ambition ever since early boyhood to create. And after lunch, he would read his morning's work to an entranced family.

'I had counted on one boy,' Stevenson later wrote; 'I found I had two in my audience. My father caught fire at once with all the romance and childishness of his original nature. His own stories, that every night of his life he put himself to sleep with, dealt perpetually with ships, roadside inns, robbers, old sailors, and commercial travellers before the era of steam. He never finished one of these romances: the lucky man did not require to! But in *Treasure Island* he recognized something kindred to his own imagination, it was *his* kind of picturesque: and he not only heard with delight the daily chapter, but set himself actively to collaborate. When the time came for Billy Bones's chest to be ransacked, he must have passed the better part of a day preparing, on the back of a legal envelope, an inventory of its contents, which I exactly followed; and the same of "Flint's old ship", the *Walrus*, was given at his particular request.'

What a touching image of the reunion between the father and son: the older listening rapt to a story by his son which coincided with his own private boyish imaginings.

During the days when *Treasure Island* was being written in such a rash of inspiration, a visitor arrived at the house. His name was Dr. Alexander Japp; he was an authority on the American philosopher/writer, Thoreau, on whom Stevenson had written an essay, and he had come to discuss certain aspects of his work. Sitting down with the rest of the family to hear the next instalment of the story, he listened with the greatest interest and intentness. As it happened, Dr. Japp was a friend of the editor of a boys' magazine, *Young Folks* (James Henderson), and had been charged by him to look out for new contributors. Here was a find indeed, and when he left, he had the first chapters of *The Sea Cook*, as Stevenson had provisionally called the story, in his pocket.

It is as well to tell the story of the fortunes of *Treasure Island* now. The first instalment duly appeared in *Young Folks*, the author being called Captain George North, to suggest a nautical origin for the tale, on 1 October 1881, and continued for the next seventeen issues, to be resumed after an interval. Strange to say, the first boy readers did not take to it; reading a story in serial form is different from absorbing oneself in a whole book. The gradual build-up of tension which seems so impressive a feature of the work made no appeal to the buyers of *Young Folks* who found it slow. A lot was promised, yet never did one actually get to the blood-and-thunder with which the average magazine serial straightaway started. Some boys wrote in to complain about it.

Nor was the writing as smooth and pleasurable an affair as has up to now been suggested. Persevering with a work, taking it through a middle to an end, had always been a difficulty with Louis, and indeed was to continue to be so for the rest of his life. After Chapter Fifteen, Stevenson's inspiration deserted him as dramatically as it had arrived. 'My mouth was empty,' as he himself put it, 'there was not one word more of *Treasure Island* in my bosom.' He was not able to go on with it until he had got back to Davos for the winter. (The reader who knows this fact can see a break in the book: the moment when Jim is on the island and Doctor Livesey takes up the story for three chapters marks it.)

Treasure Island was first issued in book-form by Cassells in 1883. Its fate in this guise could hardly have been more different from that in its former. It was riotously successful, and made Stevenson famous almost overnight. Readers of all kinds were enthusiastic and could not be torn away from it; few books since Dickens' had had a more rapturous reception, from Mr. Gladstone and Lord Rosebery and Lord Balfour to preparatory schoolboys, from literary critics to army officers. One reviewer saw it as one of the most welcome events in the world of literature for many years; for the great Victorian novelists, beloved by so many sections of the reading-public, were all dead, and their loss was much felt.

'We are to look for . . . no more Thackerays, no more Dickens. The stories have all been told. Plots are exploded. Incident is over. In moods of dejection these dark sayings seemed only too true. . . . But the darkest watch of the night is the one before the dawn, and relief is often nearest to us when we least expect it. All this gloomy nonsense was suddenly dispelled, and the fact that really and truly, behind this philosophical arras, we were all inwardly ravening for stories, was most satisfactorily established by the incontinent manner in which we flung ourselves into the arms of Mr. Robert Louis Stevenson to whom we could almost have raised a statue in the market-place for having written *Treasure Island*.'

Treasure Island made Stevenson's name, and even now is one of the most widely read books in our language, known to almost every sector of society.

So well-known is it that the admirer of Stevenson has a certain grudge against it—as indeed the author himself came to have; he could never re-read it. Being the book of Stevenson's encountered first in life, it has eclipsed his other productions. Educated people can all too often be met who only knowing *Treasure Island* dismiss Stevenson, judging him by it. It is a compelling book, admirably executed and full of invention, but utterly lacking in the richness and intensity of Louis' later works. It is nowhere near the same category of achievement as, say, *The Master of Ballantrae*. It is a one-dimensional work; the English background (largely unfamiliar to Stevenson), the unspecific eighteenth-century setting, the essentially preposterous nature of the story, the unindividualized tone of the boy-narrator (deliberate device though this is), all contribute to its being so. We may wonder what is going to happen next, our spines may pleasantly tingle, but we are never drawn into the thick of the people and events, as we are in the best of Stevenson's other books. It is, in point of fact, a work more or less devoid of emotion.

Yet provided that judgements of the author and of his work are not based on it, it is a book to value, and one which, moreover, occupies a most important place in literary history. Adventure-stories were, before that, the works of very indifferent writers indeed, ones who cared nothing for style and form. Stevenson's writing is always fresh and yet considered, highly articulate and highly economical. He brought to the tall story of piracy and buried treasure the craftsmanship of the French writers he admired—Flaubert or de Maupassant. He also freed the boys' story from the moralizing, muscular Christian elements which had weighed it down. Though the hero is a good boy, though virtue is triumphant, the author lets his imagination rip; he does not avoid violence, he does not pretend to whitewash the pirates and even refuses wholly to brand them as villains. He finds them fascinating, and the curious figure of Long John Silver, whom Stevenson based on Henley (like Henley, he is lame), has exerted a strange power over all readers. Indeed he is the book's most memorable character; shown as duplicitous and treacherous, seen in the act of murder, he reveals himself as capable of affection, as possessing both courage and dignity. And he is allowed to escape retribution. He is the first of the divided personalities which are to be so marked a feature of Stevenson's work; both evil and goodness exist inside him, not at warfare in his case, but living side by side. Such a figure would have been unthinkable in the stories of Ballantyne and Captain Mayne Reid.

Perhaps because the first chapters were written in a rush of creative fervour, they form the most impressive and individual part of the book. The feeling of the menace brought to the quiet Devonshire village by the arrival of the old sea-dog is marvellously conveyed; the opening section of the story has indeed a mythic quality—the forces of destruction appeal to our deepest fears of being threatened, preserved from childhood, and also to our excitement at the idea of confronting alien elements and eventually defeating them.

And the book possesses a strange sort of poetry. We can feel it at moments when Long John Silver speaks of his piratical career; we can feel it in such passages as the musical close:

'The bar silver and the arms still lie, for all that I know, where Flint buried them; and certainly they shall lie there for me. Oxen and wain-ropes would not bring me back again to that accursed island; and the worst dreams that ever I have are when I hear the surf booming about its coasts, or start upright in bed, with the sharp voice of Captain Flint still ringing in my ears: "Pieces of eight! Pieces of eight!" '

Chapter 11

During his first winter in Davos, Stevenson was much distressed by a tragedy which befell his old friend, Mrs. Sitwell; her son, the same boy who had taken to Louis so promptly after his arrival at Cockfield Rectory, had fallen dangerously ill with consumption, had been taken to hospital at Davos and died there. Stevenson was moved to write two verses on the subject. And the episode, bringing back memories of his landlady's son at San Francisco and of himself as a sick child, reminded him of his own condition, and in a letter to Sidney Colvin (who was later to marry Mrs. Sitwell), he wrote movingly and honestly about his own physical health.

'As to F.A.S., [Mrs. Sitwell's son] I believe I am no sound authority; I alternate between a stiff disregard and a kind of horror . . . It has helped to make me more conscious of the wolverine on my own shoulders, and that also makes me a poor judge and poor adviser. Perhaps, if we were all marched out in a row, and a piece of platoon firing to the drums performed, it would be well for us . . .'

'The wolverine' on his shoulders was to prove hideously troublesome in the following years. If Davos had brought slight improvement to Louis, summers in Scotland, while full of joy, saw such a serious worsening of his condition that he was forced to the conclusion that he would be scarcely ever able to stay in his own country again. And with this realization, came of course a burst of literary energy in portraying it.

What Louis had to put up with in the way of physical pain and degradation, of false recoveries and of cruel plunges back into the morass of consumptive fevers, scarcely bears thinking about. The next six years are a record of struggling against and bearing with the assaults and inroads of a disease which he and everyone who knew and loved him were perfectly aware would kill him long before he reached a respectable middle-age. Louis' courage and good spirits rarely failed him. Nor did those of Fanny—or those of Lloyd, Bob, Sidney Colvin, or Charles Baxter, all of whom saw their own emotional destinies intertwined with Louis'.

British winters being obviously too harsh for Louis and the prospect of yet another winter in Davos filling the family with gloom, the South of France was decided upon as a kindly and compatible place in which to live. In September 1882, Bob—still as intimate and beloved a companion as ever—escorted Louis to Provence, to help him look for a new home. But in Montpellier Louis collapsed, his state frightening even his cousin; the doctor told Louis to return to Marseilles, Fanny joined him. They found a house, a charming one, the Campagne Defli, in the country just outside Marseilles, and here, after a superficial return to health, Louis knew a torturing winter of haemorrhages, high temperatures, and bouts of utter exhaustion. Indeed there must have been times when Louis and his family felt themselves under a malignant curse. But the fortitude with which they bore their sufferings is both remarkable and impressive. Listen to this touching and agonizing letter from Fanny to John Addington Symonds (January 1883):

'Louis has been very ill again. I hasten to say that he is now better. But I thought at one time he would never be better again. He had continual haemorrhages and became so weak that he was twice insensible on one day, and was for a long time like one dead. At the worst, fever broke out in this village, typhus, I think, and all day the death-bells rang, and we could hear the chanting whilst the wretched villagers carried about the dead lying bare to the sun on their coffin-lids, so spreading the contagion through the streets. The evening of the day when Louis was so long insensible, the weather changed, becoming very clear and fine and greatly refreshing and reviving him. Then I said if it held good he should start in the morning for Nice and try what a change might do. Just at that time there was not money enough for the two of us, so he had to start alone, though I expected soon to be able to follow him. During the night, a peasant-man died in a house in our garden, and in the morning the corpse, hideously swollen in the stomach, was lying on its coffin-lid at our gates . . .

'I was to have a despatch from Toulon where Louis was to pass the night, two hours from St. Marcel, and another from Nice, some few hours farther, the next day. I waited, one, two, three, four days, and no word came. Neither telegram nor letter. The evening of the fourth day I went to Marseilles and telegraphed to the Toulon and Nice stations and to the bureau of police. I had been pouring out letters to every place I could think of. The people at Marseilles were very kind and advised me to take no farther steps to find my husband. He was certainly dead, they said. It was plain that he stopped at some little station on the road, speechless and dying, and it was now too late to do anything; I had much better return at once to my friends. . . . I waited all night at Marseilles and got no answer, all the next day and got no answer, then I went back to St. Marcel and there was nothing there. At eight I started on the train with Lloyd who had come for his holidays, but it only took us to Toulon where again I telegraphed. At last I got an answer the next day at noon. I waited at Toulon for the train I had reason to believe Louis travelled by, intending to stop at every station and inquire for him until I got to Nice. Imagine what those days were to me. I never received any of the letters Louis had written to me, and he was reading the first he had received from me when I knocked at his door. A week afterwards I had an answer from the police. Louis was much better: the change and the doctor, who seems very clever, have done wonderful things for him. . . .'

After this nerve-shattering episode, Louis' health picked up somewhat, and, a little later, the Stevensons were established at Hyères, where they lived for sixteen months, later described by Louis as the happiest period of his life. For the first time ever Louis had a proper home of his very own, and a very charming one too, the Chalet La Solitude. 'We all dwell together,' as Louis said to Mrs. Sitwell, 'and make fortunes in the loveliest house you ever saw, with a garden like a fairy story, and a view like a classical landscape.' The longer he lived there, the more he loved it—nor does he seem to have been unduly troubled with homesickness.

'This spot, our garden and our view, are sub-celestial. I sing daily with my Bunyan, that great bard,

"I dwell already the next door to Heaven!"

If you could see my roses, and my aloes, and my fig-marigolds, and my olives, and my view over a plain, and my view of certain mountains as graceful as Apollo, as severe as Zeus, you would not think the phrase exaggerated.'

Delight in his surroundings and the balm of the southern French air enabled Louis to live a peaceful yet busy life, and for his ill-health to recede a little from the foreground of the drama, for the wolverine to slink somewhat from his shoulders. Louis' daily routine now was one which filled him with satisfaction. He worked all morning at his desk. Then came lunch with a good local wine and a fresh salad. In the afternoon he went for a walk, during the course of which he would drop in on some new friends—a politically minded local wine-merchant, an eccentric upper-class Englishman who had decided to devote his energy to the raising of vegetables. Back at home he would attend to his correspondence—then dinner and conversation, in both of which a prominent part was played by their French maid, Valentine Roch, who followed them to England later, and afterwards wrote with great affection about the delightful atmosphere of the Stevenson household.

And at the desk, Louis wrote some of his best work—numerous essays, the charming verses that later became *The Child's Garden of Verses* but to begin with were called *Penny Whistles* (a nicer title), and *Prince Otto*. Lloyd Osbourne was of the opinion that of all his fiction, none save *The Master of Ballantrae* and *Weir of Hermiston* was closer to Louis' heart than this last book, though, as we shall see later, he had especial regard for the two David Balfour novels. Of all his full-length works, *Prince Otto* is, I think, the one least likely to find favour with a reader of today. It is set in an imaginary German principality, the forested land-scape of which is richly but somewhat over-picturesquely evoked; in character, it is something of a romance, something, almost, of an allegory, and it lacks the sense of reality, the imaginative integrity, and the excitement of Stevenson's other productions. Nevertheless, it is well worth reading, having, as it does, a touching and well-drawn central figure, and many moments of both charm and wistful beauty. Moreover, both story and main character reflect the themes and preoccupations of the author's past life as he now looked back over it. Otto—originally modelled on Bob, though in fact he possesses just as many similarities to Louis himself—prefers a life of following his own inclinations (which are towards gentle adventuring and contemplation) to succumbing to the demands, tedious and indeed often repugnant, of his position as hereditary ruler of the state of Grünewald. His doing so results in the government falling into the hands of unscrupulous people. As Otto's is essentially a good and kindly nature, he comes, while still maintaining his belief in the personal, in the imaginative pursuit rather than the public task, to realize that he has behaved wrongly, that one cannot both abdicate from responsibility and live at peace with oneself. It seems to me that in *Prince Otto*, Louis is working through some of his feelings about his own refusal to join his father's engineering business, about his rejection of the lot of the professional class man. For Louis' guilt over this decision—seemingly far back in the past now—was not by any means over; perhaps the reconciliation with his father had indeed renewed the uncomfortable emotion. For with increased regard for the embodiment of the values that he had spurned must have come some doubts as to whether his dismissal of them had been as fully justified as at the time he had thought. Furthermore, with a very important part of himself, Louis believed in self-fulfilment through hard work. Indeed, he had been devoting his energies to the pursuit of his chosen career and striving after excellence in it with a single-mindedness and a disregard for difficulty and inflictions to self that would have satisfied the most ascetic Scottish professional man. Now this strange similarity could be more openly acknowledged by him. Lloyd, writing of his stepfather at this time of his life, says:

'It must be remembered that he was one of the most pre-possessed men that ever lived . . . it was his work that always came first, that animated all his thoughts, that was the consuming joy and passion of his life . . . Stevenson offers the fascinating study of a man whose spiritual concentration kept him alive. He simply wouldn't die; refused to . . . In the light of modern psychology it is very plain what enabled him to hold death at bay till forty-four, while so many of his generation with the same disease and infinitely less impaired, succumbed long before him. First it was this tremendous prepossession for his work, and secondly, his invincible refusal to become an invalid.'

And though while at Hyères, Louis tasted success in the form of the reception of *Treasure Island*, dealt with in the previous chapter, he must have known that he had not yet given the world the best expression of what he had in him.

While he was in Hyères, friends came out to stay—Bob, talking as gaily and brilliantly as ever, Colvin, Charles Baxter, Henley. Affectionate letters went backwards and forwards between the young Stevensons and the older couple in Edinburgh. The contradictory elements in Thomas Stevenson's character have already been mentioned: the melancholia that had always troubled him from time to time now returned in more frequent and more protracted bursts. This man of steely faith would know shuddering fears of death, deep glooms about the whole nature of the universe. It became more necessary to him to involve himself in subjects outside himself, the very contemplation of which would cheer him up—such as the doings of his son. And Louis for his part became filled with a tenderness, a solicitousness for his father that lasted until the latter's death.

It has already been mentioned in discussing Louis' friends and fellow-members of the L.J.R. how the most dissolute but perhaps most talented of them, James Walter Ferrier, died young of consumption aggravated by dissipation. The sad event happened while Louis was at Hyères, and he took it very, very badly—in fact, Fanny begged other friends not to mention Ferrier's name so upset did Louis instantly become. His essay on Ferrier has already been quoted; very revealing of Louis' cast of mind at this stage of his life is his letter to Henley written shortly after hearing the news of Ferrier's death:

'It is strange . . . I was thinking in my bed, when I knew you I had six friends—Bob I had by nature; then came the good James Walter—with all his failings—the *gentleman* of the lot, alas to sink so low, alas to do so little, but now, thank God, in his quiet rest; next I found Baxter . . . fourth came Simpson; somewhere about the same time, I began to get intimate with Jenkin; last came Colvin. Then, one black winter afternoon, long Leslie Stephen, in his velvet jacket, met me in the Spec. by appointment, took me over to the infirmary, and in the crackling, blighting gaslight showed me that old head whose excellent representation I see before me in the photograph. [i.e. Henley's]. Now when a man has six friends, to introduce a seventh is usually hopeless. Yet when you were presented, you took to them and they to you upon the nail . . . I don't know if it is good Latin, most probably not: but this is enscrolled before my eyes for Walter: *Tandem e nubibus in apricum properat.* ["At last from out of the clouds he hastens towards the sunshine."] Rest, I suppose, I know, was all that remained; but O to look back, to remember all the mirth, all the kindness, all the humorous limitations and loved defects of that character; to think that he was young with me, sharing that weather-beaten, Fergussonian youth, looking forward through the clouds to the sunburst; and now clean gone from my path, silent—well, well. This has been a strange awakening. Last night, when I was alone in the house, with the window open on the lovely still night, I could have sworn he was in the room with me; I could show you the spot; and, what was very curious, heard his rich laughter, a thing I had not called to mind for I know not how long.'

He enclosed in this letter a tribute to Ferrier, later written up as the 'Old Mortality' essay previously quoted, begging Henley to pass this on to Ferrier's sister. 'It would let her know,' he said, 'how entirely, in the mind of (I suppose) his oldest friend, the good, true Ferrier obliterates the memory of the other, who was only his "lunatic brother".'

Stevenson's letter reveals, of course, if one needed any proof, the extent of his affection for his friends. But Ferrier's death brought forward in his mind other obsessions; in memorable phraseology, he evokes the wild youth he had spent, the ghost of which he had by no means laid; the way in which Ferrier, like the poet Fergusson before him, had misspent his life, achieving nothing, and the untimely nature of his death must have made Louis very mindful of the fact that as yet he had not completely vindicated himself and that he desperately wished to do so before his disease conquered him. Ferrier's death set his mind too back towards the psychological consequences of Edinburgh upper-class upbringings, though he wasn't properly to come to terms with this subject for some years. And the last sentence quoted suggests Stevenson's awareness of the opposing elements existing inside the same person. In the phrase that speaks of Ferrier's 'lunatic brother', we have a glimpse of the interest in the duality of personality which was to haunt Stevenson's later work. We can also note from his reaction to Ferrier's death the beginning too of a concern with the dark consequence of vice. And even more perhaps than at his own coming so near the 'grey ferry' Stevenson's vision of life underwent a transformation; indeed the death of a loved one always has this power, to make one aware of the transitory nature of life.

'It needs a blow like this,' he wrote to Ferrier's sister—all his letters of this period are intensely preoccupied with the theme of his friend's death—'to convict a man of mortality and its burthen. I always thought I should go by myself; not to survive. But now I feel as if the earth were undermined, and all my friends have lost a thickness of reality since that one passed. Those are happy who can take it otherwise; with that I found things all beginning to dislimn. Here we have no abiding city, and one felt as though he had—and O too much acted.'

Perhaps this is the beginning of Stevenson's turning his mind to the perennial questions of religion and the meaning of existence. But the shadow of mortality was to fall over him more nearly presently. After a visit to Nice made with four of his old friends, Louis caught a cold which developed into yet another attack of congestion of the lungs. On hearing of the gravity of his cousin's illness, Bob came over to France to help Fanny nurse him and to cheer him up; Fanny later declared that she didn't know what she would have done without him. This illness was in fact the prelude to another extended period of chronic ill-health, at the end of which he left France for England, to receive further examination from doctors. For May 1884 saw the worst hae-morrhage he had up till then endured. Incapable of speech, choked with a flow of blood, he managed, during its direst moments, to write on a piece of paper a message to Fanny: 'Don't be frightened; if this is death, it is an easy one.' Stevenson was forbidden by his doctors to speak, or even to move. Hour after hour, day after day, he had to lie still, enduring a great deal of pain. At times Fanny could scarcely find it in her to accept the suffering inflicted on her husband; it all seemed too much! She sat with him in darkened rooms with admirable patience, however, beguiling the time with ghost stories she made up on the spot (later written up as the stories in *The Dynamiter*). When the doctor at last pronounced him able to make the journey back to this country, Fanny wrote to Margaret Stevenson:

'The doctor says, "Keep him alive till he is forty, and then, although a winged bird, he may live to ninety". But, between now and forty, he must live as though he were walking on eggs, and for the next two years, no matter how well he feels, he must live the life of an invalid. He must be perfectly tranquil, troubled about nothing, have no shocks or surprises, not even pleasant ones; must not eat too much, drink too much, laugh too much; may write a little, but not too much; talk *very* little, and walk no more than can be helped.'

Sad though these restrictions were, at least there was a chance of a reasonable span of years lying ahead of him. Back in Britain, the Stevensons decided on Bournemouth as the place perhaps most conducive to the gentle brand of life now to be led; and the resort of pine-trees, sand banks, rhododendrons and chines at first appealed to Stevenson who always anyway liked being near the sea. After some months of hotels and lodgings, the Stevensons went to live in a house which Thomas Stevenson, acting on a characteristic impulse of generosity, bought as a present for Fanny. The house was named Skerryvore after perhaps the most significant lighthouse achievement of the Stevenson firm; it had a large garden with a stream and a ravine choked with lovely rhododendron bushes and from the top of the turret which graced the house a view of the sea could be had. Though Louis was afterwards to speak of his life at Bournemouth (almost three years in all) as that of a 'weevil in a biscuit', he was happy after a fashion here. Certainly, as we shall see, his time in Bournemouth formed one of his greatest creative periods. But its limitations on his life were frightful. There would be weeks now, instead of hours or days, when he had to lie motionless. Never was the sword of Damocles of another—and perhaps fatal—haemorrage not dangling above him. He hardly ever left the house; barbers had to call, for instance, to cut his hair.

How did Louis view his predicament? Increasingly he was having to fit his illness into his imaginative picture of life. Sometimes, as in this letter to Cummy to wish her a happy birthday, he tried a jauntily stoic approach to his troubles:

'. . . a diet is a beastly thing. I doubt, however, if it be as bad as not being allowed to speak, which I have tried fully, and do not like.' A more heart-felt note is struck in his letter to a Miss Monroe (in June 1886):

'I have bad health, am often condemned to silence for days together—was so once for six weeks, so that my voice was awful to hear when I first used it, like the whisper of a shadow—have outlived all my chief pleasures, which was active and adventurous, and ran in the open air; and being a person who prefers life to art, and who knows it is a far finer thing to be in love, or to risk a danger, than to paint the finest picture or write the noblest book, I begin to regard what remains to me of my life as very shadowy.'

Some of the very greatest writers have all their lives suffered from appalling ill-health and the imminence of death: Keats, Charlotte and Emily Brontë, Chekhov, Proust, D. H. Lawrence. Indeed, a tubercular condition seems often to heighten the sufferer's responses to life and to develop an intense ability to 'seize the moment'—it also, of course, forces the patient to develop his imagination, and to live vicariously in order to cope with living at all.

At this time of his life, Stevenson seems often, understandably, to have had at the same time at least three different imaginative ways of coping with his lot. The first is a regression to his boyhood fantasies of deeds of high adventure. He projected himself into the sort of escapades that in a more naive form he had given such vivid treatment to in *Treasure Island*. We can hear Stevenson in this vein in a letter written to a Savile Club friend—from Hyères, in fact.

'Seriously, do you like to repose? Ye Gods, I hate it. I never rest with any acceptation; I do not know what people mean who say they like sleep and that damned bedtime which, since long ere I was breeched, has rung a knell to all my day's doings and beings. And when a man, seemingly sane, tells me he has "fallen in love with stagnation", I can only say to him, "You will never be a Pirate!" . . . think of it! Never! After all boyhood's inspirations and youth's immortal day-dreams, you are condemned to sit down, grossly draw in your chair to the fat board, and be a beastly Burgess till you die. Can it be? Is there not some escape, some furlough from the Moral Law, some holiday jaunt contrivable into a Better Land? Shall we never shed blood? This prospect is too grey.

> Here lies a man who never did
> Anything but what he was bid;
> Who lived his life in paltry ease,
> And died of commonplace disease.

'To confess plainly, I had intended to spend my life (or any leisure I might have from Piracy upon the high seas) as the leader of a great horde of irregular cavalry, devastating whole valleys. I can still, looking back, see myself in many favourite attitudes; signalling for a boat from my pirate ship with a pocket handkerchief, I at the jetty end, and one or two of my bold blades keeping the crowd at bay; or else turning in the saddle to look back at my whole command (some five thousand strong) following me at the hand-gallop up the road out of the burning valley: this last by moonlight.'

In many ways this is a silly and affected letter. The words 'Shall we never shed blood? This prospect is too grey', indicate a cast of mind that is indeed one of the gravest casualties of peace, betokening an inability to see violence and strife in their true colours, as involving real sufferings for real people. Theatricality creeps in in the sort of situations Louis would have liked to be in; but on the other hand, when he rails against repose and sleep and bedtime, it must be remembered that these are the words of a man forced to lie on his bed for many weeks. Nor were his fantasies of high adventure a bad thing for mankind— since these provided part of the impulse for Stevenson's most characteristic fiction. Almost all his stories are adventure-stories —including many later ones which space will prevent me from dealing with: *The Wrecker* and *The Ebb-Tide*, for instance.

The second way of coping with his predicament is again one not uncommon; it is to dwell deliberately on the cheerful parts of life, to insist that these constitute indeed its strongest element. Practically, from the author's point of view, there is much to be said for it. Stevenson's essays of this period are full of a 'Yea-saying', life-affirming nature, pounding out views expressed in the works of two of his idols, Whitman and Meredith. Such a belief in life's glories, of course, does carry people through the darkest times, and can be justified—for it is the knowledge of the reality of human love, of beauty and of the constant interest to be found in life's objects that makes existence worth living or putting up with. But the trouble with optimism as a positive philosophy is that it can never go hand in hand with complete honesty, any more than extreme pessimism can. There is plainly something other than joy in a life which can involve someone lying in agony and in constant danger of a haemorrhage. In Louis' particular case it also took absolutely no heed of the emotional, the psychological sufferings he had undergone. So while he was no doubt right not to let his neuroses completely determine the plots, themes and structures of his work, it is the case that until he was able to face up to his miseries past and present, he could never achieve a work of adequate emotional breadth or depth.

He was attacked for his vaunted optimism by the well-known critic of the times William Archer, famous for his championship and translation of the great Norwegian dramatist, Henrik Ibsen (1828-1906) whose tragic and eminently credible dramas seemed to penetrate all the numerous façades conventional society had put up to disguise the complex emotions that lurked beneath. To Archer there was something almost dishonest in Stevenson's dwelling on the more picturesque, romantic features of life; Stevenson's personal reply to Archer is interesting, presenting as it does his position and his attitude towards that position with bravery and panache. (Archer doesn't seem to have realized Stevenson's invalid condition.)

'If you knew I was a chronic invalid, why say that my philosophy was unsuitable to such a case? . . . The fact is, consciously or not, you doubt my honesty; you think I am making faces, and at heart disbelieve my utterances. And this I am disposed to think must spring from your having not enough of pain, sorrow, and trouble, in your existence. It is easy to have too much; easy also or possible to have too little; enough is required that a man may appreciate what elements of consolation and joy there are in everything but absolutely overpowering physical pain or disgrace, and how in almost all circumstances the human soul can also play a fair part . . . not only do I believe that literature should give joy, but I see a universe, I suppose, eternally different from yours; a solemn, a terrible, but a very joyous and noble universe, where suffering is not at least wantonly inflicted, though it falls with dispassionate partiality, but where it may be, and generally is nobly borne; where, above all . . . *any brave man may make* out a life which shall be happy for himself, and, by so being, beneficient to those about him. And if he fails, why should I hear him weeping? I mean if I fail, why should I weep? Why should *you* hear *me*? Then to me, morals, the conscience, the affections, and the passions are, I will own frankly and sweepingly, so infinitely more important than the other parts of life, that I conceive men rather triflers who become immersed in the latter; and I will always think the man who keeps his lip stiff, and makes "a happy fireside chime," and carries a pleasant face about to friends and neighbours, infinitely greater (in the abstract) than an atrabilious Shakespeare or a backbiting Kant or Darwin. . . . To me, the medicine bottles on my chimney and the blood on my handkerchief are accidents; they do not colour my view of life, as you would know, I think, if you had experience of sickness; they do not exist in my prospect; I would as soon drag them under the eyes of my readers as I would mention a pimple I might chance to have. . . .'

This attitude indeed was to prevail for some time in Stevenson and to some extent condition his writing. As I have suggested, it is an inadequate one, and it did not in fact correspond to Stevenson's most serious thinking. Almost at the same time as he was boosting his militant belief in dwelling on the cheerful in life, he was writing to Edmund Gosse—the letters to whom always show him at his most sensible—'Nor is happiness, whether eternal or temporal, the reward that mankind seeks. Happinesses are but his wayside campings; his soul is in the journey; he was born for the struggle, and only tastes his life in effort and on the condition that he is opposed. How, then, is such a creature, so fiery, so pugnacious, so made up of discontent and aspiration, and such noble and uneasy passions—how can he be rewarded but by rest? . . . But the truth is, we must fight until we die; and when we die there can be no quiet for mankind but complete resumption into—what?—God, let us say—when all these desperate tricks will lie spellbound at last.' But it wasn't until the works of the end of his life that Stevenson was able to give literary embodiment to this deeper, fuller vision of existence; in *The Master of Ballantrae*, in *Catriona* and *The Beach of Falesá*, and above all, in *Weir of Hermiston*.

But this isn't to disparage the achievement of 1886. The privations of his health, the love of his family, his reconciliation with his parents, and through them with Scotland, enabled him to produce two works of major quality.

Stevenson had, throughout his life, experienced interesting and absorbing dreams in which dramas of varying kinds were enacted before his closed eyes. He called the agencies of these distorted but near-complete stories 'The Brownies' and one night they supplied him with a horrifying sequence of scenes reflecting his waking preoccupations with the essentially divided self of man. His wife heard him screaming while asleep and was— understandably—moved to wake him up. Whereupon he re-proached her with the words: 'I was dreaming a fine bogey tale.' He then told her the outline of what had come to him while asleep. From dawn the next day he was hard at work trying to turn his dream into a story. Louis read it aloud to Fanny who, though interested, criticized Louis for not bringing out the all-important allegorical element. Louis' first reaction was fury—he lost his temper and tore up what he had written, throwing it on the fire. But he must have respected Fanny's opinion for he began all over again. Despite his physical condition, he produced sixty thousand words in six days—an amazing rate! Despite the set-back in health it occasioned, it was worth it—*The Strange Case of Dr. Jekyll and Mr. Hyde* was an enormous and unprecedented success. Before long it was even being quoted by clergymen from pulpits, and 'Jekyll and Hyde' have become household words in English.

It is, of course, of the greatest significance that the idea came first into Louis' unconscious life; dream-life takes no notice of time, and Stevenson was back again in the world of his Scottish Calvinist upbringing, reliving the conflicts between his better nature and his desire to experiment with the forbidden that had caused him so much trouble as a child. The story as it now stands suggests Stevenson's agonized difficulty in coming to terms with what seemed like the promptings towards evil for its own sake. The picture of the world presented by Calvinism allows for them; it is the non-believer that finds them so hard to accommodate. *Jekyll and Hyde* is a far more tormented and guilt-ridden work than it is generally believed to be; too long has it been thought of as a horror-story. The hero (Jekyll) cannot cope with his evil impulses. He discovers a drug that can make him become another person for periods of time, and decides to use this second body for the isolation of the worst parts of his nature. Unfortunately the scheme goes wrong; he cannot escape from the evil body, the evil turns against itself, and Hyde consequently destroys himself. So the fable suggests the self-destructive nature of evil. No Puritan Christian could but agree with this. It is an uncomfortable work, challenging any easy theories of good and evil, though, and strange indeed for a man who claimed he had no desire to deal with the unpleasant sides of life.

The second important work of 1886 is *Kidnapped*. Like *Treasure Island*, it was conceived as a boys' book. But it is an infinitely greater work than its predecessor; it is one of the perennial classics of boyhood, and also a book to which we can return again and again throughout life. Indeed, it can be considered Stevenson's most perfect finished performance. And the two real reasons for its success are firstly that it has flesh-and-blood people for its characters—above all, the narrator, David Balfour, and Alan Breck, and secondly that it has a Scottish setting, it takes place among people and places the author loved and knew intimately. Indeed, the second reason is inextricably linked to the first—it is because they are Scots that the people come over so vividly to us. An author is nearly always best writing of the world he experienced in his boyhood and youth, the world that he took for granted and yet explored when his senses and intellect were developing.

Kidnapped has indeed many roots in Stevenson's early life. The story of a boy's wanderings round Scotland, it moves from the Lowlands, along the Scottish coasts Stevenson had known in his engineering-student days, takes in the isle of Earraid, which it will be remembered had made so magical an impression on Stevenson, and then through the wildest regions of the Highlands back to Edinburgh and the east of Scotland. And the boy himself is supposedly a member of Louis' mother's family, bearing their surname of Balfour. He is a marvellous creation; as he tells his enthralling tale we learn to know him well; his shrewd, puritanical, reserved yet passionate, high-minded Lowland Scot's personality is lovingly and accurately unfolded before us. For most of the book's duration he is thrust in the company of Highlanders, in particular, Alan Breck, in many ways the antithesis of himself—rash, proud, openly emotional, vain, extravagant, yet noble—whom he comes eventually both to regard and to love. And this at a time when Highlander-Lowlander relations were at their worst, their most tense: the difficult years after the '45.

Kidnapped and its sequel, *Catriona*, are the fruit of Louis' new-found interest in Highland history, and give a lively and rich picture of Scotland after the second Jacobite uprising, their sympathies being generously extended to both parties. The two books are based, indeed their central action springs, from one of the most mysterious and intriguing events in Scottish history: the Appin Murder. Both Louis and his father had in the past visited the site of the murder—a very romantic one near Ballachulish, where the Highlands rise wonderfully from Loch Linnhe —and eager reading of the procedure of the trials had renewed Louis' desire to make a story out of it. *Kidnapped* only gives us half the story, the tragic later events being unfolded in the more complex though less perfect *Catriona*. Something of the curious Appin Murder story and its significance for Stevenson should be told here.

It has already been related how the British Government sought to quell the Highlands after the '45 and made illegal many of the old customs and practices of its people. Inside Scotland enormous power was bestowed on the wily and staunchly Hanoverian Duke of Argyll, who was determined to stamp out any lingering Jacobite sympathies; he also had, greatly to his own advantage, confiscated the land of the rebel clans. In 1752, Colin Campbell of Glenure, whose unpopular task was to be factor to the Duke's family for the forfeited estates, was shot—presumably by a Stewart sympathizer; the Government felt it essential that immediate action should be taken to prevent any further insurrection. There were, indeed are, two principal suspects for the crime: James Stewart of the Glens and Alan Breck Stewart. James Stewart, though widely believed to be innocent, was tried for the crime and hanged, by order of Lord Prestongrange, who had previously behaved well towards the Highlanders. Alan Breck Stewart, whom tradition has branded the murderer, escaped and spent the remainder of his life in uneasy exile on the Continent. In *Kidnapped*, David Balfour—in a marvellously realized and thrilling scene—witnesses the murder in Appin of Campbell and sees the culprit to be neither James nor

Alan Breck Stewart. *Catriona* resolves round his attempt, doomed to failure, to clear both men of suspicion. Whether Stevenson's interpretation of the events is correct cannot as yet be ascertained; while it seems certain that poor, mean, frightened James Stewart was not guilty, the identity of the murderer, known to this day to certain members of the Scottish aristocracy, has not at this moment, even after over two hundred years have gone by, been disclosed. What one can admire without qualification is Stevenson's insight into the dangers and moral complications present in the murky episode, and the deftness with which he presents them.

The story of the Appin Murder is interwoven with David Balfour's personal history; he has been cheated of his rightful inheritance by his wicked, cracked old uncle, and at the end of the book comes into his own. This theme is as powerfully treated as the other. Who, once having read it, can forget David's arrival at the sinister benighted House of Shaws, or his uncle's attempts on his life? Or the deeply satisfying routing of Uncle Ebenezer by Alan?

There are other things to praise in *Kidnapped* too—the subtly and movingly drawn shifting relationships between David and Alan. Their quarrel during the flight in the heather is for me one of the most touching scenes in English literature. And David's confrontations with various Highland characters have a richly symbolic significance; they crystallize aspects of Scottish culture in memorable form. A particularly poetic example is the scene in which David and Alan witness Robin Oig (whom neither likes much) playing the pipes.

'But Robin only held out his hand as if to ask for silence, and struck into the slow measure of a pibroch. It was a fine piece of music in itself, and nobly played; but it seems, besides, it was a piece peculiar to the Appin Stewarts and a chief favourite with Alan. The first notes were scarce out, before there came a change in his face; when the time quickened, he seemed to grow restless in his seat; and long before that piece was at an end, the last signs of his anger died from him, and he had no thought but for the music.

' "Robin Oig," he said, when it was done, "ye are a great piper, I'm not fit to blow in the same kingdom with ye. Body of me! Ye have mair music in your sporran than I have in my head! And though it sticks in my mind that I could maybe show ye another of it with the cold steel, I warn ye beforehand—it'll no be fair! It would go against my heart to haggle a man that can blow the pipes as you can!"

'Thereupon the quarrel was made up; all night long the brose was going and the pipes changing hands; and the day had come pretty bright, and the three men were none the better for what they had been taking, before Robin as much as thought upon the road.'

In the face of such a little masterpiece as *Kidnapped*, one feels almost tempted to be grateful to the illness for forcing Louis to utilize his imaginative and creative resources as never before. Almost! because one cannot but be ultimately depressed by the dismal restrictedness of his existence. His pleasures when better, were not such as to satisfy so restless and vital a nature. Always fond of music, Louis bought himself a flageolet and played the treble clef lines of piano music by Schumann, Chopin, Lully and Rameau. The usual friends came down—Bob's friendship was as important as always, but the rift with Henley dated from this period. Collaborating on unsuccessful plays had contributed to this, and Henley of all his friends got on worst with Fanny, who may indeed have engineered the breach.

Another man of letters, however, became a friend—Henry James (1843-1916) one of the giants of our literature. American-born, with a wide experience of Continental culture, he wrote novels which have the intricate and deliberate artistry Stevenson so admired in the French writers, and which he himself brought to fiction, together with an insight into social and psychological issues which Stevenson only achieved in his last books. Henry James was perceptive and generous enough to see the true genius which had found its first real expression in *Kidnapped*, and wrote some of the earliest and perhaps best literary appreciation of Stevenson's art. With James' interest in his work, one can say that Stevenson came of age as a literary figure. The friendship between these two very different men is movingly recorded in their collected correspondence, edited by Janet Adam Smith, a book which all interested in either writer should read.

A sad event had occurred in 1885, one which contributed to the increasing deepening of Louis' awareness of life. His old friend, Professor Fleeming Jenkin, in whose Edinburgh house so many delightful evenings had been passed in his youth, who had been the oldest, the wisest of Louis' friends, died, and his death—the second one he had known within his circle of intimates—upset Louis and cast his mind back once more to Edinburgh days. But in this case it wasn't to what he had referred to after Ferrier's death as his 'Fergussonian' youth, but to the cultured, informed, sensitive yet solid, infinitely dependable life of the Edinburgh intelligentsia. This would occasion, of course, further reappreciation of his parents, and of their brand of Scottish civilization, and account for his increasing admiration for the Scottish characters he now so frequently drew. When he heard of Jenkin's death, Stevenson's immediate concern was with comforting his widow, and warmer, more loving letters than he wrote to Mrs. Jenkin cannot be imagined.

'Dear me, what happiness I owe to both of you!' he wrote as a postscript to one of these. And, at Mrs. Jenkin's request, he agreed to write a memorial biography of her husband. And unlike so many of his other non-fictional works, this was completed—a moving and substantial tribute to both his friend and to the merits of burgher Edinburgh.

For, I hope it has been made clear, Stevenson was throughout his life very much its product. Its narrower creeds he may have detested, he may have been through periods when Bohemianism seemed infinitely preferable to a life spent with qualified engineers and lawyers—but in so many important respects he was the child of his parents' culture. High-minded, attentive to the smallest detail of the requirements of his chosen profession, intensely loyal, he was as different from the amoral, pleasure-seeking, drifting people whom he often found so fascinating as can be—far more like Thomas Stevenson in both temperament and outlook than he was like most of the Barbizonians or the journalists of San Francisco.

He was to realize this more and more as his father's failing condition became monthly more obvious. As has been said, Thomas' declining years were blighted by an intensification of the melancholia which had been always a feature of his emotional life. Increasingly did he fall frequent prey to appalling self-doubts, when he felt chastised by a sense of his own unworthiness and inadequacy. How he must have been cheered by his son's letters, which took an interest in so many sides of life—from his scientific theories to his re-reading of Scott.

Now and again Louis would strike a more intimate note, as in this letter:

'I was delighted to hear you were keeping better; . . . Goodbye to all of you, with my best love. We had a dreadful overhauling of my conduct as a son the other night; and my wife stripped me of my illusions and made me admit I had been a detestable bad one. Of one thing in particular she convicted me in my own eyes: I mean, a most unkind reticence, which hung on me then, and I confess still hangs on me now, when I try to assure you that I do love you. Ever your bad son,

ROBERT LOUIS STEVENSON.'

After a while, the deterioration of Thomas' condition was such that it was obvious to all that his life was drawing to an end. Because of his own health, Louis had kept away from Scotland; now he made the last journey he was ever to make to his beloved native country. In the house where he had been affectionately watched over by his father when he was a sick little boy in bed, where he had discussed Covenanting history with him, and where he had fought a grim battle with him for his own independence and right to think for himself, he saw the most important person in his life lying mortally ill, in acute pain, and for long periods not in full possession of his mind. For two days Louis watched him dying—the end came on 8 May 1887. For months afterwards, Louis would be tormented day and night by 'ugly images of sickness, decline, and impaired reason'.

Louis was never to go to Edinburgh again, and he must have known this. What sorrow he must have felt as he left behind him the city which was increasingly to haunt his imagination. There lay buried he whom he had loved and hated, hated and then loved, more than any other person in the world. And there lay— irretrievably in the past, but somehow preserved in the tall black houses, the Adam squares, the Old Town's wynds and the pink rock of the Salisbury Crags—the joys and sorrows of his early life, which had united to make him the person he was.

And were to make him the writer he became. From now on— destined never to see Edinburgh again, never able to set eyes on his father—Thomas' character, his own struggle against him and his deep love for him were to dominate his work, at first covertly and then more fully and honestly.

171

Chapter 12

It had been his father's obviously waning health that had kept Louis in this country—a prisoner in Skerryvore. Many times his spirit had cried out in protestation and this had frequently taken the form of violent and often quixotic yearnings for action. Of late, Louis' interest in politics had increased—he now took a Tory rather than a Radical line, but his standpoint was as basically romantic as ever. He had identified himself with Gordon at his tragic end at Khartoum. Then he became emotionally involved in an Irish case. Though sympathetic to the subjugated position of the Irish, he was outraged by their acts of violence against the English and the English supporters within Ireland. In 1885 Curtin, a farmer in County Kerry, had been murdered by a group known as the 'moonlighters' (Irish extremists). His family had defended themselves against the rebels, indeed shooting one of them. As a result of this the family were boycotted by all their neighbours. Stevenson—with great passion and all sincerity—proposed going over to Ireland to live with his own family in the Curtins' farmhouse to champion and protect them. It is a tribute to Fanny's loyalty that though she thought the scheme mistaken, she was prepared to follow Louis to Ireland. The plan strikes one today as cranky, ill-judged and doomed to failure as well, but what of course it reveals is the frustrated capacity for heroic action within Louis. He wrote to Mrs. Fleeming Jenkin:

'I do not love this health-tending, house-keeping life of mine.

I have a taste for danger, which is human, like the fear of it. Here is a fair cause; a just cause; no knight ever set lance in rest for a juster.'

Because of Thomas' illness, the plan came to nothing. But after his father had died, Louis was free to leave his orderly, sequestered life in Bournemouth, and satisfy some of the gnawing longings for a richer more active life. Now his uncle, Dr. George Balfour, insisted that he had a change of climate; he recommended either Colorado or the hill-stations of India. Stevenson, it will come as no surprise, chose America. It was decided that Margaret Stevenson should accompany Louis, Fanny and Lloyd on their journeys. One has always suspected a basic unconventionality in Margaret Stevenson, which she transmitted to her son; this surely is revealed in her decision to follow her son to America, and, later, beyond that to the South Seas, hardly an expected place of residence for an elderly Scotswoman who had previously known little but Edinburgh. Stevenson never spoke much of his mother in his writings; one can presume, however, that they enjoyed a deep and natural understanding of each other, and shared a constant curiosity and a lack of received opinions about things and people.

Did Louis guess that he would never see Britain again? Did he know on 20 August 1887, as he received a succession of his friends in Armfield's Hotel in London, that he was looking on them for the last time? I think the thought must have crossed his mind and probably theirs too. Admittedly he kept up a lively and voluminous correspondence with all of them. But letters, however intimate and gossipy, are not the same as proximity. Louis must have missed these people who meant so much to him bitterly. How often cruising round the Pacific waters, or sitting in his Samoan home, he must have longed to see the faces of Bob, Sidney Colvin, Edmund Gosse, Henry James, Charles Baxter, even Henley with whom such sad tensions had arisen. They were often in his mind, that we know. Time and time again from a distance of many thousand miles, he would cast his mind back to the good times he had had with them, and as the years went by, he returned repeatedly to the Edinburgh days:

Do you remember—can we e'er forget?—
How, in the coiled perplexities of youth,

In our wild climate, in our scowling town,
We gloomed and shivered, sorrowed, sobbed and feared?
The belching winter wind, the missile rain,
The rare and welcome silence of the snows,
The laggard morn, the haggard day, the night,
The grimy spell of the nocturnal town,
Do you remember?—Ah, could one forget!

As when the fevered sick that all night long
Listed the wind intone, and hear at last
The ever-welcome voice of chanticleer
Sing in the bitter hour before the dawn,
With sudden ardour, these desire the day:
So sang in the gloom of youth the bird of hope;
So we, exulting, hearkened and desired.
For lo! as in the palace porch of life
We huddled with chimeras, from within—
How sweet to hear!—the music swelled and fell,
And through the breach of the revolving doors
What dreams of splendour blinded us and fled!

I have since then contended and rejoiced;
Amid the glories of the house of life
Profoundly entered, and the shrine beheld:
Yet when the lamp from my expiring eyes
Shall dwindle and recede, the voice of love
Fall insignificant on my closing ears,
What sound shall come but the old cry of the wind
In our inclement city? what return
But the image of the emptiness of youth,
Filled with the sound of footsteps and that voice
Of discontent and rapture and despair?
So, as in darkness, from the magic lamp,
The momentary pictures gleam and fade
And perish, and the night resurges—these
Shall I remember, and then all forget.

Certainly when in exile in the South Seas, he remembered Edinburgh as never before in his life, and explored in depth and with feeling the many aspects of his life there. If only because the

174

novels *Catriona* and *Weir of Hermiston* came out of his time there, we cannot regret that Stevenson left his own country for ever.

But he was right to go for other reasons. In the damp, foggy climates of Scotland and England he could only lead a half-life, could only endure the unbearable suffocation of invalidism. At least—far away from what he knew though he was—he could, in America, and to a far greater extent in the Pacific islands, lead a fairly normal existence. This made up for much. And those he most loved—his mother, his wife, his stepson—were with him.

The Stevensons left for America on 21 August 1887. The voyage Louis enjoyed very much, even though they turned out to be on a cargo-boat carrying animals. Sidney Colvin saw them to the docks; Henry James had a crate of champagne delivered to the ship. Stevenson's mind must have inevitably turned back to that other fateful voyage to the States. He was very different now from then—he knew security in his family life, he was successful in his chosen career as an author, and he had, of a very personal nature, a religious faith which was to deepen and to sustain him to the end.

During the Bournemouth years, Stevenson had become very influenced by the writings of Tolstoy. The great Russian novelist, to outlive Stevenson by sixteen years, had converted himself and many others to a Back-to-the-Gospel brand of Christianity, putting trust in the actual words of Christ rather than in any of the sacraments or dogmas of the Church. Stevenson had throughout his life had a peculiarly personal admiration for Christ, and though the particular interpretations accorded to his teachings by Tolstoy didn't remain ones Stevenson stuck to, they left their mark on him—he was to continue an undogmatic Christian who admired charity in action above all else. And besides, as he entered what, though only in his late thirties, he knew to be the declining years of his life, he returned to some of the abiding preoccupations of the Scottish religion of his childhood. The existence of evil, the need for a sense of sin, even for one of guilt, the battle put up by goodness against the forces of adversity, the uses of suffering, the virtues of a strict morality (though always it must allow for human frailty and variety), these are themes he turned to more and more.

I would like to quote in this context a strange and haunting fable that Louis wrote when in Samoa: *The House of Eld*. It says in succinct and allegorical form that one can never wholly escape from the creeds of one's childhood, that if they are narrow and restrictive, why so are others! Calvinism may have seemed at times in Louis' life a hideous and repressive thing, but was any other single faith—that of the Bohemians, that of the Socialists, that of the Tolstoyans—any less limited? Moreover, the fable implies that relationships with parents, striven against though they may have to be, endure always.

The House of Eld

'So soon as the child began to speak, the gyve was riveted; and the boys and girls limped about their play like convicts. Doubtless it was more pitiable to see and more painful to bear in youth; but even the grown folk, besides being very unhandy on their feet, were often sick with ulcers.

'About the time when Jack was ten years old, many strangers began to journey through that country. These he beheld going lightly by on the long roads, and the thing amazed him. "I wonder how it comes," he asked, "that all these strangers are so quick afoot, and we must drag about our fetter?"

' "My dear boy," said his uncle, the catechist, "do not complain about your fetter, for it is the only thing that makes life worth living. None are happy, none are good, none are respectable, that are not gyved like us. And I must tell you, besides, it is very dangerous talk. If you grumble of your iron, you will have no luck; if ever you take it off, you will be instantly smitten by a thunderbolt."

' "Are there no thunderbolts for these strangers?" asked Jack.

' "Jupiter is long suffering to the benighted," returned the catechist.

' "Upon my word, I could wish I had been less fortunate," said Jack. "For if I had been born benighted, I might now be going free; and it cannot be denied the iron is inconvenient, and the ulcer hurts."

' "Ah! cried his uncle, "do not envy the heathen! Theirs is a sad lot! Ah, poor souls, if they but knew the joys of being fettered! Poor souls, my heart yearns for them. But the truth is they are vile, odious, insolent, ill-conditioned, stinking brutes, not truly human—for what is a man without a fetter?—and you cannot be too particular not to touch or speak with them."

'After this talk, the child would never pass one of the unfettered on the road but what he spat at him and called him names, which was the practice of the children in that part.

'It chanced one day, when he was fifteen, he went into the woods, and the ulcer pained him. It was a fair day, with a blue sky; all the birds were singing; but Jack nursed his foot. Presently, another song began; it sounded like the singing of a person, only far more gay; at the same time there was a beating on the earth. Jack put aside the leaves; and there was a lad of his own village, leaping and dancing and singing to himself in a green dell; and on the grass beside him lay the dancer's iron.

' "Oh!" cried Jack, "you have your fetter off!"

' "For God's sake, don't tell your uncle!" cried the lad.

' "If you fear my uncle," returned Jack, "why do you not fear the thunderbolt?"

' "That is only an old wives' tale," said the other. "It is only told to children. Scores of us come here among the woods and dance for nights together, and are none the worse."

'This put Jack in a thousand new thoughts. He was a grave lad; he had no mind to dance himself; he wore his fetter manfully, and tended his ulcer without complaint. But he loved the less to be deceived or to see others cheated. He began to lie in wait for heathen travellers, at covert parts of the road, and in the dusk of the day, so that he might speak with them unseen; and these were greatly taken with their wayside questioner, and told him things of weight. The wearing of gyves (they said) was no command of Jupiter's. It was the contrivance of a white-faced thing, a sorcerer, that dwelt in that country in the Wood of Eld. He was one like Glaucus that could change his shape, yet he could always be told; for when he was crossed, he gobbled like a turkey. He had three lives; but the third smiting would make an end of him indeed; and with that his house of sorcery would vanish, the gyves fall, and the villagers take hands and dance like children.

' "And in your country?" Jack would ask.

'But at this the travellers, with one accord, would put him off; until Jack began to suppose there was no land entirely happy. Or, if there were, it must be one that kept its folks at home; which was natural enough.

'But the case of the gyves weighed upon him. The sight of

the children limping stuck in his eyes; the groans of such as dressed their ulcers haunted him. And it came at last in his mind that he was born to free them.

'There was in that village a sword of heavenly forgery, beaten upon Vulcan's anvil. It was never used but in the temple, and then the flat of it only; and it hung on a nail by the catechist's chimney. Early one night, Jack rose, and took the sword, and was gone out of the house and the village in the darkness.

'All night he walked at a venture; and when day came, he met strangers going to the fields. Then he asked after the Wood of Eld and the house of sorcery; and one said north, and one south; until Jack saw that they deceived him. So then, when he asked his way of any man, he showed the bright sword naked; and at that the gyve on the man's ankle rang, and answered in his stead; and the word was still *Straight on*. But the man, when his gyve spoke, spat and struck at Jack, and threw stones at him as he went away; so that his head was broken.

'So he came to that wood, and entered in, and he was aware of a house in a low place, where funguses grew, and the trees met, and the steaming of the marsh arose about it like a smoke. It was a fine house, and a very rambling; some parts of it were ancient like the hills, and some but of yesterday, and none finished; and all the ends of it were open, so that you could go in from every side. Yet it was in good repair, and all the chimneys smoked.

'Jack went in through the gable; and there was one room after another, all bare, but all furnished in part, so that a man could dwell there; and in each there was a fire burning, where a man could warm himself, and a table spread where he might eat. But Jack saw nowhere any living creature; only the bodies of some stuffed.

' "This is a hospitable house," said Jack; "but the ground must be quaggy underneath, for at every step the building quakes."

'He had gone some time in the house, when he began to be hungry. Then he looked at the food, and at first he was afraid; but he bared the sword, and by the shining of the sword, it seemed the food was honest. So he took the courage to sit down and eat, and he was refreshed in mind and body.

' "This is strange," thought he, "that in the house of sorcery there should be food so wholesome "

'As he was yet eating, there came into that room the appearance of his uncle, and Jack was afraid because he had taken the sword. But his uncle was never more kind, and sat down to meat with him, and praised him because he had taken the sword. Never had these two been more pleasantly together, and Jack was full of love to the man.

' "It was very well done," said his uncle, "to take the sword and come yourself into the House of Eld; a good thought and a brave deed. But now you are satisfied; and we may go home to dinner arm in arm."

' "Oh dear, no!" said Jack. "I am not satisfied yet."

' "How!" cried his uncle. "Are you not warmed by the fire? Does not this food sustain you?"

' "I see the food to be wholesome," said Jack; "and still it is no proof that a man should wear a gyve on his right leg."

'Now at this the appearance of his uncle gobbled like a turkey.

' "Jupiter!" cried Jack. "Is this the sorcerer?"

'His hand held back and his heart failed him for the love he bore his uncle; but he heaved up the sword and smote the appearance on the head; and it cried out aloud with the voice of his uncle; and fell to the ground; and a little bloodless white thing fled from the room.

'The cry rang in Jack's ears, and his knees smote together, and conscience cried upon him; and yet he was strengthened, and there woke in his bones the lust of that enchanter's blood. "If the gyves are to fall," said he, "I must go through with this, and when I get home I shall find my uncle dancing."

'So he went on after the bloodless thing. In the way, he met the appearance of his father; and his father was incensed and railed upon him, and called to him upon his duty, and bade him be home, while there was yet time. "For you can still," said he, "be home by sunset; and then all will be forgiven."

' "God knows," said Jack, "I fear your anger; but yet your anger does not prove that a man should wear a gyve on his right leg."

'And at that the appearance of his father gobbled like a turkey.

' "Ah, heaven," cried Jack, "the sorcerer again!"

'The blood ran backward in his body and his joints rebelled against him for the love he bore his father; but he heaved up the sword, and plunged it in the heart of the appearance; and the appearance cried out aloud with the voice of his father; and fell to the ground; and a little bloodless white thing fled from the room.

'The cry rang in Jack's ears, and his soul was darkened; but courage came to him. "I have done what I dare not think upon," said he. "I will go to an end with it, or perish. And when I get home, I pray God this may be a dream, and I may find my father dancing."

'So he went on after the bloodless thing that had escaped; and in the way he met the appearance of his mother, and she wept. "What have you done?" she cried. "What is this that you have done? Oh, come home (where you may be by bedtime) ere you do more ill to me and mine; for it is enough to smite my brother and your father."

' "Dear mother, it is not these that I have smitten," said Jack; "it was but the enchanter in their shape. And even if I had, it would not prove that a man should wear a gyve on his right leg."

'And at this the appearance gobbled like a turkey.

'He never knew how he did that; but he swung the sword on the one side, and clove the appearance through the midst; and it cried out aloud with the voice of his mother; and fell to the ground; and with the fall of it, the house was gone from over Jack's head, and he stood alone in the woods, and the gyve was loosened from his leg.

' "Well," said he, "the enchanter is now dead, and the fetter gone." But the cries rang in his soul, and the day was like night to him. "This has been a sore business," said he. "Let me get forth out of the wood, and see the good that I have done to others."

'He thought to leave the fetter where it lay, but when he turned to go, his mind was otherwise. So he stooped and put the gyve in his bosom; and the rough iron galled him as he went, and his bosom bled.

'Now when he was forth of the wood upon the highway, he met folk returning from the field; and those he met had no fetter on the right leg, but behold! they had one upon the left. Jack asked them what it signified; and they said, "that was the new wear, for the old was found to be a superstition". Then he looked at them nearly; and there was a new ulcer on the left ankle, and the old one on the right was not yet healed.

' "Now, may God forgive me!" cried Jack. "I would I were well home."

'And when he was home, there lay his uncle smitten on the head, and his father pierced through the heart, and his mother cloven through the midst. And he sat in the lone house and wept beside the bodies.

Moral

'Old is the tree and the fruit good,
Very old and thick the wood.
Woodman, is your courage stout?
Beware! the root is wrapped about
Your mother's heart, your father's bones;
And like the mandrake comes with groans.'

Calvinism, the Scottish burgher morality—these had sustained generations of his own people. Louis had been compelled by honesty to rebel against them, yet now he knew they contained truth as well as falsehood. Certainly the Scottish faith haunts Louis' later books. And the presence of 'the mother's heart, the father's bones' gives them their great emotional power.

America turned out to have been far more generally admiring of Stevenson's writings than Britain, and Stevenson was accorded the treatment of a celebrity. Indeed, throughout the remainder of his life, his reputation and sales in America were very high; some Americans, in fact, regard him even today as their own author, and some of the most appreciative writing about him has come from the States.

Louis proved too weak to make the proposed journey to Colorado; instead, Saranac Lake in the Adirondack Mountains (in upper New York State) was chosen—here a tuberculosis sanatorium had been recently established.

The Stevensons spent the winter of 1887-1888 there. The weather was bitterly cold, with an Arctic coldness—blizzards, thick fog, thaws which were followed by treacherous freezes so that a film of glossy ice lay over everything. However, the cold did not disagree with Louis, perhaps because of the altitude where the house was situated, and he was able to walk, to skate, to work. One intensely dark and cold winter's night, he was pacing the verandah of his house, gazing at the forest-land below him and at the clear starless sky above him, and listening to the noises of the river, which was carrying ice and huge boulders along in its spate. Suddenly the idea of a story with a setting in this vast forest-area came to him; at least, it was part of a story, the end in fact. This was it: an evil genius of a man had disappeared and then turned up in a remote spot to persecute the remainder of his suffering family. In this 'icy American wilderness' he would die, but before his death he would have been buried alive for several days. (This curious and terrifying tale had been told him by one of his uncles who had heard it in India.) But who were the family and the central character to be? And within a matter of minutes, exciting ones, Stevenson remembered a situation and a group of characters that had come into his head years before, when he had been making a journey across the East Highlands towards Blair Atholl.

'Here, thinking of quite other things, I had stumbled on the solution, or perhaps I should say (in stagewright phrase) the Curtain or final Tableau of a story conceived long before on the moors between Pitlochry and Strathairdle, conceived in Highland rain, in the blend of the smell of heather and bog-plants . . . So long ago, so far away it was, that I had first evoked the faces and the mutual tragic situation of the men of Durisdeer.'

The writing of this book—*The Master of Ballantrae*—caused him more difficulty and yet was a more intense and thrilling experience than had been the case with any of its predecessors. The problem, which was not, I think, wholly successfully solved, was how to join up these different elements so that they became one. Louis wrote about the hardness of his literary task in a letter to Henry James dated, Saranac Lake, March 1888.

'My novel is a tragedy; . . . Five parts of it are bound, human tragedy; the last one or two, I regret to say, not so soundly designed; I almost hesitate to write them; they are very picturesque, but they are fantastic; they shame, perhaps degrade, the beginning. I wish I knew; that was how the tale came to me, however. I got the situation; it was an old taste of mine: The older brother goes out in the '45, the younger stays; the younger, of course, gets title and estate and marries the bride designate of the elder— a family match, but he (the younger) had always loved her, and she had really loved the elder. Do you see the situation? Then the devil and Saranac suggested this *dénouement*, and I joined the two ends in a day or two of constant feverish thought, and began to write. And now—I wonder if I have not gone too far with the fantastic? The elder brother is an INCUBUS: supposed to be killed at Culloden, he turns up again and bleeds the family of money; on that stopping he comes and lives with them, whence flows the real tragedy, the nocturnal duel of the brothers (very naturally, and indeed, I think, inevitably arising), and second supposed death of the elder. Husband and wife now really make up, and then the cloven hoof appears. For the third supposed death and the manner of the third reappearance is steep; steep, sir. . . . I fear it shames the honest stuff so far; but then it is highly pictorial, and it leads up to the death of the elder brother at the hands of the younger in a perfectly cold-blooded murder, of which I wish (and mean) the reader to approve. You see how daring is the design. There are really but six characters, and one of these episodic, and yet it covers eighteen years, and will be, I imagine, the longest of my works.'

This letter shows that Stevenson felt himself to have embarked on his most challenging and bold work of fiction so far. He was right: *The Master of Ballantrae* is a complex and disturbing book and of a far more ambitious nature than *Kidnapped*, admirable though that is. It comes near to greatness, I think, but is very badly let down by its last part; the story of the live body in the coffin is an intriguing one, suitable perhaps for a tale of horror by the fireside, but it is not a fitting climax to the tense, psychological drama of a serious novel. And it does not seem to me particularly well done. Nor are any of the overseas parts of the book a success; the Master's piratical activities, especially as told by his Irish companion, are less convincing than the comparable scenes in *Treasure Island*, a book meant to be just light entertainment. Stevenson still hadn't learned only to listen to the deepest, truest voices of his imagination. Technically he matured early; in judgement less so, and only perhaps in *Weir of Hermiston* did he concentrate on what most truly aroused his creative fire.

But those chapters of *The Master of Ballantrae* which are set in Scotland—they do in fact constitute by far the larger section of the book—are intensely alive, and arouse deeper responses in the reader than do any of Stevenson's earlier writings.

The story itself has something of the folk-tale or the Border Ballad about it—there is a stark inevitability about the unfolding of the story, and a tragic simplicity too in its concentration on the theme of the conflict between the two brothers. It gains enormously from its narrative method; the strange events are presented as if literal historical truth by someone at once involved in the affairs of the central family, yet not directly participant. Mr. Mackellar's dry, fussy personality is the ideal one to be chosen as intermediary between the reading public and the obsessed emotion-driven people whose relationships form the novel's story. From such a man and from such a manner the complete authenticity of the curious facts presented can surely, one feels, be trusted. This feeling is generated by the very opening of the book:

'The full truth of this odd matter is what the world has long been looking for, and public curiosity is sure to welcome. It so befell that I was intimately mingled with the last years and history of the house; and there does not live one man so able as myself to make these matters plain, or so desirous to narrate them faithfully. I knew the Master; on many secret steps of his career I have an authentic memoir in my hand; I sailed with him on his last voyage almost alone; I made one upon that winter's journey of which so many tales have gone abroad; and I was there at the man's death.'

Straight away our credulity is satisfied—and we prepare ourselves for a narrative at once scrupulously accurate and intriguingly extraordinary.

The central theme—the struggle between the elder and the younger brothers—is one rich in implications, rich too in its relationship to Stevenson's own inner preoccupations. The Master is an embodiment of evil; it is he, however, of the two brothers who has charm, good looks, vitality—he is the more widely loved of the two, he certainly has far stronger appeal for women (his sexual charisma is constantly stressed), and during the course of his life, he knows much more adventure and excitement. Yet ultimately his evil nature is shown as being self-destructive. (Here we can see its link with *Jekyll and Hyde*.) Loving nobody, not even, in the deepest sense, himself, he is shown up as inwardly barren, and this sterility—symbolically emphasized by the fact that he has no heir, his only attendant being a sinister almost sexless Indian servant—not only shows him up badly against less attractive persons, but also involves inner unhappiness. He is incapable of any fulfilment because he has no positive desires, only negative ones; this vision of an evil man brings Stevenson close to much traditional Christian thinking on the subject of the Devil and of wickedness. The Devil is an angel perverted through pride—but he is non-creative, all he wishes for is the destruction of the virtuous, and all he can create is the antithesis of what is already created. So it is with the Master. He dreams of glory for himself, yet lacks the ability, the inventiveness, ever to attain it.

But, tragically, he does achieve the destruction of the good man, his brother. Henry Durie is a thrifty, gentle, hard-working man, lacking in charm or the ability to compel the attention or the love of others. (He does, however, earn the unflinching loyalty and affection of Mr. Mackellar the narrator; but it is the sad truth that both his father and his wife prefer the Master.) Though largely unhonoured in his own country, Henry preserves his fineness of nature until the Master's return—from then on, however, hatred makes devastating inroads into his soul. But the turning-point in his life that sets him on the downward path is the duel in which he believes himself to have killed his brother. The guilt is too much for him to bear; it is as if he has killed something inside himself. He descends into a state of simple-mindedness, the only psychological way of coping with what he has done. And his actions after he knows the truth—that the Master is not dead—are those of someone whose wits are not intact.

The above summary cannot, of course, do full justice to the complexities and fascinating ambiguities of the work. The fact that there are contradictions within the book is an indication that there were confusions within Stevenson's own mind about the nature of good and evil as external forces operating in this world. But they show too the level on which much of *The Master of Ballantrae* operates. Behind its story elemental forces lurk.

It was the first full-length work of fiction Stevenson wrote whose plot revolved on the characters' emotional relations with each other, and as a consequence of this, it turned out his most powerful so far. The Master's return, the duel by candle-light on the sands, the flight of Henry and Alison, the tempestuous cross-ing of the Atlantic, these are haunting, dramatic scenes presented with a poetic intensity that Stevenson had not hitherto achieved; once read they stay in the mind for ever.

Chapter 13

The Stevensons left Saranac late on 16 April 1888. After a spell
on the East Coast of America, during which he met some
celebrities of American literary life, notably Mark Twain, but
in which his health suffered a slight deterioration, Stevenson
came to the conclusion that a protracted voyage on the Pacific
would be the best thing for him psychologically and physically.
Fanny, who was in California visiting relations, found a yacht,
the *Casco*, that would serve their purpose. On 26 June the party
embarked on the ship, a ninety-five-foot-long schooner, luxuri-
ously fitted out (though the cockpit wasn't particularly safe) and
the sails were more intended for racing than for cruising. On 28
June, they left San Francisco harbour. And though Stevenson
was to live another six years, he was never to return to the
American mainland, never to leave the Pacific waters.

'The first experience,' Stevenson wrote of the Pacific Islands,
'can never be repeated. The first love, the first sunrise, the first
South Sea island, are memories apart, and touched a virginity of
sense. On the 28th of July 1888, the moon was an hour down by
four in the morning. In the east a radiating centre of brightness
told of the day; and beneath, on the skyline, the morning bank
was already building, black as ink. We have all read of the swift-
ness of the day's coming and departure in low latitudes; . . .
Although the dawn was thus preparing by four, the sun was not
up till six; and it was half-past five before we could distinguish

our expected islands from the clouds on the horizon. Eight degrees south, and the day two hours a-coming. The interval was passed on deck in the silence of expectation, the customary thrill of landfall heightened by the strangeness of the shores that we were then approaching. Slowly they took shape in the attenuating darkness. Ua-huna, piling up to a truncated summit, appeared the first upon the starboard bow; almost abeam arose our destination, Nuka-hiva, whelmed in cloud; and betwixt and to the southward, the first rays of the sun displayed the needles of Ua-pu. These pricked about the line of the horizon; like the pinnacles of some ornate and monstrous church, they stood there, in the sparkling brightness of the morning, the fit signboard of a world of wonders.'

And a world of wonders was indeed opened up to Stevenson in the Pacific, a world too in which he could at times feel well and capable of proper manly activity. The Stevensons visited the Marquesas, the Paumotus, Tahiti, Hawaii (where they stayed nearly six months)—then the Gilberts and Samoa. In this last Stevenson felt an immediate rapport with both scenery and people, so much so that he bought an estate on a wooded mountain-side. This he intended as a resting-place, a sort of anchor in the Pacific. In February 1890, he visited Sydney, to review his situation, and also to pick up mail, but here he fell ill. Haemorrhages and fevers once more descended, and it was apparent that only in the tropical islands could Stevenson find any real measure of health and consequent happiness. So the party boarded a steamer, the *Janet Nicoll*, which took them via many lesser islands back to the Gilberts and thence to the Marshalls, the return journey being made via the remote, wild island of New Caledonia. Following this voyage, Stevenson spent four or five weeks more in Sydney and then returned to Samoa. Here the business of building a home on the estate he had bought had been going on.

Almost three years were thus concerned in cruising round the Pacific, three years in which Stevenson's natural zest for life was able to find an outlet, for the tropical climate and sea air restored his energies, and his capacity for imaginative appreciation and enjoyment of the varieties of nature and men could be exercised. His voyages must have given his aesthetic sensibility the intensest satisfaction; his letters and journals are full of attempts to express the ravishing effects upon him of sun and water, of atoll and beach, of feathery palms and conical mountains rising to cloudy heights direct from the water. He has left accounts of his experiences in his extensive travelogue *In the South Seas*. Even more important as regards his development as a person was his coming into contact with the various peoples of the Pacific. Stevenson had never from his earliest thinking days been one to see the word 'primitive' as a term of condemnation; his studies of Highland culture had led him to realize the complexities and often beauties of the beliefs governing societies that enjoyed a lower material level and an earlier organizational structure. Indeed he was for ever and delightedly seeing parallels between the various Polynesian peoples and the Scottish Highlanders. The tribes that warred on the mountain islands of the Pacific struck him as remarkably similar in important respects to the clans of the Hebrides and the Western Islands; this aroused his interest and admiration the more.

'The Pacific is a strange place; the nineteenth century only exists in spots; all round, it is a no man's land of all ages, a stir-about of epochs and races, barbarisms and civilizations, virtues and crimes.'

No one was better able to appreciate this than Stevenson; in a sense, with his instinctive curiosity, his immediate response to the mysterious and elemental, and his dislike of glib moral judgements being passed on behaviour or ways of life, he was a natural anthropologist. He collected a mass of legends, made notes on customs and religious practices, and learned the past histories of the peoples he visited, and he not only met but made real friends with many of the chieftains and noble families of the islands. Out of this came certain historical writings and discussions of Polynesian culture, many larger works of this nature being projected. But the most significant effect of this contact with and absorption in Pacific ways was the ability it gave him to see his own Scottish culture in a more universal context, and therefore to see it in depth. *Catriona* and *Weir of Hermiston* are, among other things, studied and detailed surveys of the many facets of Scottish civilization at a particular time. And with this opened-up vision of his own society, Stevenson was able to view himself and the problems that had been his in a more objective light than ever before in his life.

Of course, in many respects he was unchanged. His natural

188

dislike of the bourgeoisie and of officialdom was confirmed on the whole by his Pacific experiences. He never got on very well with members of the civil service, there to govern and impose regulations on proud and ancient peoples, and they, for their part, didn't care much for him. He was quick to spot the hypocrisies, the power-lusts and the deceptions in both missionaries and traders. One of his finest stories, *The Beach of Falesá*, is a terrifying account of the cruelties and the callousnesses inflicted on the Polynesians by the white people—in this case, by the degenerate traders who, having failed in Europe and America, released their frustrations by easy dominance over the islanders. In this story an Englishman, who begins little different in his attitudes from his fellows, comes, through love of the girl he has bought and been farcically married to, to a newer and deeper understanding of humanity, more particularly the humanity of the Polynesian natives.

In 1889, Stevenson visited the island of Molokai (off the Hawaiian group), where there was the leper colony tended by Father Damien, a man of enormous courage and personal eccentricity who had died shortly before Stevenson's journey there. Stevenson wrote to Colvin:

'I am just home after twelve days' journey to Molokai, seven of them at the leper settlement, where I can only say that the sight of so much courage, cheerfulness, and devotion stung me too high to mind the infinite pity and horror of the sights . . . I have seen sights that cannot be told, and heard stories that cannot be repeated: yet I never admired my poor race so much, nor (strange as it may seem) loved life more than in the settlement. A horror of moral beauty broods over the place . . . it is the only way I can express the sense that lived with me all these days . . . Of old Damien, whose weaknesses and worse perhaps I heard fully, I think only the more. It was a European peasant: dirty, bigoted, untruthful, unwise, tricky, but superb with generosity, residual candour and fundamental good-humour . . . A man, with all the grime and paltriness of mankind, but a saint and hero all the more for that.'

Conceive Stevenson's anger when in 1889 he read a letter from a Honolulu Presbyterian clergyman (whom he had in fact met) attacking the idea that Father Damien was a 'most saintly philanthropist', and accusing him among many other vices of his having been 'not a pure man in his relations with women'. Stevenson's anti-bourgeois feeling was brought out to the full, and he wrote a vituperative reply in an open letter to Mr. Hyde, defending brave acts of self-sacrifice even if they are made at the expense of some of the nicer points of middle-class morality.

'You belong, sir, to a sect—I believe my sect, and that in which my ancestors laboured—which has enjoyed, and partly failed to utilise, an exceptional advantage in the islands of Hawaii . . . In the course of their evangelical calling, they . . . grew rich. It may be news to you that the houses of missionaries are a cause of mocking on the streets of Honolulu. It will at least be news to you, that when I returned your civil visit, the driver of my cab commented on the size, the taste, and the comfort of your home. It would have been news certainly to myself, had anyone told me that afternoon that I should live to drag such matter into print. But you see, sir, how you degrade better men to your own level; and it is needful that those who are to judge betwixt you and me, betwixt Damien and the devil's advocate, should understand your letter to have been penned in a house which could raise, and that very justly, the envy and the comments of the passers-by. I think (to employ a phrase of yours which I admired) it "should be attributed" to you that you have never visited the scene of Damien's life and death. If you had, and had recalled it, and looked about your pleasant rooms, even your pen perhaps would have been stayed. . . .'

This is the kind of Christ-like Christianity Stevenson admired—deeds of altruism made in the teeth of self regard and comfort. Though this letter reflects his dislike of smug Presbyterians, learnt in Scotland, it also shows an independence of judgement, a sternness of morality that is itself very Scottish.

And equally Scottish was his patriarchal delight in his new, and last, place of residence.

Chapter 14

Not Stevenson's most romantic dreams could have conjured up a more idyllic and beautiful home than that which was now his in Samoa. The estate was given by him a Samoan name—Vailima, the meeting of Five Waters. Though only three miles from the coast—the roll of surf could be heard from the higher points—it was situated at an altitude of six hundred feet. On some sides of the property was thick forest-land in which banyan trees grew and flying-foxes lived. The road that connected Vailima to the main centre of civilization in Samoa—the town of Apia—was steep and winding. When Stevenson first came to live at Vailima it was also rough and lined by densely matted trees; later, in gratitude for his kindness to them while they were in prison, some Samoan chiefs built what they called the Ala Loto Alofa, the Road of the Loving Hearts, a wider and less tortuous road bordered by a sweet-smelling lime hedge, and commanding from every turn a splendid view of the house.

The house was made of wood and painted a dark green. Along the front and round one side wall ran a large twelve-foot-deep verandah. The whole of the ground floor was taken up with a huge almost baronial hall. Various paintings and sculptures dominated it—a bust of Louis' grandfather, a portrait of Thomas Stevenson, a painting by the eminent English artist Sargent of Louis and Fanny, pictures executed by Bob, and a group in plaster by perhaps the greatest nineteenth-century sculptor, Auguste Rodin, with whom Stevenson had earlier made friends. Louis did most of his writing in a small and shadowy upstairs room with one window that looked out over pasture-lands and forest to the sea, and another that commanded a view of the steep slopes of Mount Vaea. This mountain had a magnetic fascination for Stevenson—from almost every point on the estate its majestic summit could be seen, and, alone of the family, he had scaled it. Not long after he had come to live in Vailima, he expressed a wish to be buried on the peak of Vaea, and his stepson has recorded that in the last year of his life, particularly at evening time, Louis would cast his eyes towards the mountain top. 'It was specially beautiful at dusk with the evening star shining above it, and it was then he would pause the longest in an abstraction that disturbed me.'

The garden and estate must have seemed a miracle, especially to one brought up in the intemperate climate of Scotland. There were banana trees, oranges, guavas, mangoes, and bread-fruit, there were coconut palms and several acres planted with particularly fine pineapples. Pawpaw and Cape gooseberries grew everywhere, limes formed the hedges dividing the various parts of the estate from one another, lemons and avocado pears, sweet potatoes and egg-plants abounded.

The climate of Samoa being so kindly a one, Stevenson was able to lead a more active life than it had been his fortune to lead for over ten years. He took the greatest interest in looking after the estate—interested himself in the livestock (pigs, cows, chickens), in the putting up of fences or sheds, even in some manual work on the land itself, to which he responded with a moving boyish ardour. He was able to ride, a pursuit he loved, though he had been frustrated in practising it for most of his life, and he could walk about his own land with all the pride of a monarch. As could be expected, he wrote copiously to all his friends until the last, and his letters are full of excited details about his life as plantation-runner, farmer and landlord. His ability to carry out the tasks necessary to these gave him a new sense of life, a new confidence in himself.

This sense of security given him by being master of a property that from the first he could love was enhanced by his having his family around him. Fanny and Lloyd took to the new life with an enthusiasm very nearly as keen as Louis' own; Margaret

Stevenson (who had left her son's family in Hawaii to return to Scotland) now rejoined them, and the family was added to by Fanny's daughter, Isobel Strong, accompanied by her husband Joe, and her little boy, Austin, whom Louis loved to play with and to teach. Isobel (Belle as she was usually called) was to prove a great asset to Louis for she acted as his amanuensis. For the effort of writing eventually became too great a strain for him and all his last work was dictated. Isobel, who had, so to speak, shared in his great upsurge of creative energy of the Samoan years, ones which saw Louis rising to unprecedented heights of literary achievement, recorded the following discussion with him:

'Our talk turned on Millet, to whom Louis takes off his hat. He made money for years doing ordinary popular work, and then, in spite of starvation and a large family, proceeded to paint what he thought was true art.

' "And yet," I said, "if I were one of the large family, I might not think it so fine. A painter might sacrifice his family to his art; would you? Would you go on writing things like *Will o' the Mill* if we were all starving . . . ?"

'Louis gave in. "You know well enough I would save my family if it carried me to the gallows' foot." ' '

Undoubtedly, then, having his family around him was a source of great comfort to Louis who celebrated them in a charming sequence of poems. But there must have been times when the atmosphere was somewhat claustrophobic, and isolation—even in so idyllic a setting as Vailima—cannot but heighten any difficulties in relationships.

Lloyd had given up a chance of studying at Cambridge to become a member of Louis' household. A graduate of Edinburgh University, and himself of literary ambitions (he and Louis collaborated on three stories of high adventure, *The Wrong Box*, *The Ebb-Tide* and *The Wrecker*), he was able to give Louis intellectual and imaginative companionship, but at the same time was for one his age, perhaps unduly dependent on the older man, and his involvement with a Samoan girl caused his stepfather some anxiety.

Fanny's devotion to Louis continued as strong as ever. She ran this strange household with great efficiency and energy. To the last, too, she interested herself in his literary projects, and *Weir of Hermiston* contains a moving verse dedication to her. But the loyal service she had unflaggingly given to her husband had always been accompanied by possessiveness and a jealous regard for his attention, and these last qualities increased. Moreover, the vein of hypochondria, which she had always possessed, became now more pronounced.

Nevertheless, the marriage was a real and living thing to the day of Louis' death and the family's continuous physical presence gave him an emotional kindly climate as important to his state of mind as the geographical one was to his bodily well-being. But as head of Vailima he was head of a larger family still: working on the estate and in the house were many Samoans. To Stevenson, they unanimously became members of a clan, with himself as chieftain, and he exercised a benevolent and concerned authority over them. The Samoans, accustomed to a patriarchal society, responded to this treatment—their love for Louis was expressed in many moving services and tributes. They took all their problems to him and expected him to arbitrate over them. Indeed, his fame in this direction spread beyond the confines of the estate, and Samoan nobles came to him to consult his opinion over legal and political matters.

This led Stevenson to dabble in Samoan politics; he wrote numerous letters to *The Times* and other papers on this subject, as well as involving himself in petitions, etc.; his participation made him an object of a not altogether kindly regard to the British authorities. It must be admitted that discretion and tact were not always in evidence in Stevenson's conduct, though ardent desire for humane and high-principled practice was. There is something touching, and almost, but not quite, incongruous in Louis, the former loafer and Bohemian, sitting in counsel over the legislative concerns of Polynesian chiefs; I say, not quite, because, as one has seen, there was always a strongly moral side to Louis, an unflinching pre-occupation with right-doing, even in his silliest days—and he had, of course, trained successfully as a lawyer.

Isobel Strong records, in her *Memories of Vailima*, some of Louis' methods of dealing with wrong-doers among his large, amorphous retinue of Samoans. A court was held, presided over by himself; the culprit could leave the Stevensons' service if he wished rather than face the hearing, and no fine was ever imposed without the culprit's agreeing to its justness. (The money went to either the Protestant or the Roman Catholic missionaries, depending on the 'criminal's' creed.) Then Stevenson would read a lecture of which the following is an example:

'Fiaali'i, you have confessed that you stole the cooked pigs, the taro, the palusamis, the breadfruit, and fish that fell to Vailima's portion at yesterday's feast. Your wish to eat was greater than your wish to be a gentleman. You have shown a bad heart and your sin is a great one, not alone for the pigs which count as naught, but because you have been false to your family . . . It is easy to say that you are sorry, that you wish you were dead: but that is no answer. We have lost far more than a few dozen baskets of food; we have lost our trust in you, which used to be so great, our confidence in your loyalty and high-chiefness. See how many bad things have resulted from your sin! . . . Fiaali'i, you are fined thirty dollars to be paid in weekly instalments. When the whole thirty-six dollars is ready, it will be handed you, and you will make us a great feast in Vailima by way of atonement, and for every pig stolen there shall be two pigs, and for every taro, two taro, and so on and more also. You shall be the host, but you shall call none of your friends to the feast . . . but the others shall invite *their* friends. Then you will be forgiven and this thing forgotten. We live only by the high-chief-will of God, nor must we be cruel to one another when the High-Chief-Son of God is so good to us all. One word must still be said. Let the story of this wicked business be buried in your hearts, lest strangers talk of it. Fiaali'i and the others have been tried and punished, and their penalties must not be increased by mockery or reproaches. Think of your own sins and hold your peace.'

At the end of the day, Vailima followed the custom of every Samoan household by having communal prayer and hymn-singing. This may have been started at the instigation of Louis' mother who took a great interest in the Samoans' religion. There is a certain irony in Louis, condemned in his youth as a scoffer against Christianity, presiding over his household—most of whom squatted on the floor, attending to their devotions by the light of many lamps. Lloyd would read from the Samoan transla-tion of the Bible, Louis would recite a prayer of his own com-position, then hymns would be sung and the Lord's Prayer said in Samoan. Sometimes bands of other Samoans would press their faces in curiosity against the windows of Vailima and see Stevenson sometimes wearing a tropical suit, sometimes dressed in the Stuart tartan, standing and reading such prayers as this— 'For the Family':

'Aid us, if it be Thy will, in our concerns. Have mercy on this land and innocent people. Help them who this day contend in disappointment with their frailties. Bless our family, bless our forest house, bless our island helpers. Thou who hast made for us this place of ease and hope, accept and inflame our gratitude; help us to repay, in service one to another, the debt of Thine unmerited benefits and mercies, so that when the period of our stewardship draws to a conclusion, when the windows begin to be darkened, when the bond of family is to be loosed, there shall be no bitterness of remorse in our farewells.'

Samoa was a popular stopping place in the Pacific, and the house saw a great deal of entertaining. Dinner-parties (the preparation for which would take at least a whole day, at the end of which the table would be groaning with tropical foods, English dishes and American ones) and balls were frequent occurrences; at the balls, people of all sorts would happily mingle. The Stevensons seem to have been quite remarkably unsnobbish: diplomats, traders, Samoan nobility, missionaries (in Samoa, Stevenson was on good terms with both the Catholic and the Protestant missionaries), would all join in the festivities together. Lloyd Osbourne said later that Stevenson could not resist offering hands of friendship to many who proved untrustworthy ne'er-do-wells; at the same time there is a boyish innocence about his willingness to extend hospitality to all manner of men. Moreover, even in his present position as dignitary of an estate, there still existed an emotional regard for the flotsam and jetsam of society: those outcasts, to whom he felt, but for his own talent, he might have belonged.

Letters constantly came to Vailima from England and Scotland and as frequently went back. Louis was as tireless a correspondent as ever, and in his letters he described almost all aspects of his life—from his dealings with the Samoan people to every stage of his work on his writings—and Louis, for his part, was familiar with the ins-and-outs of his friends' lives. Nevertheless, despite the fullness of his life, despite the fact that Louis was able to indulge in activities he had thought himself debarred from for

196

ever, he must have known sadness, a sense of the strangeness of destiny that had brought him to live and, as he knew full well, die in such a remote clime. Mountains tumbling down into the sea, waves breaking on beaches, all these took him back to the Scotland he would never see again. That is why in the two great novels he wrote in Samoa he recreates Scotland with such passion.

Catriona (1893) is the sequel to *Kidnapped*, though a very different book, one which should be looked on as a self-contained whole. *Kidnapped* has both a folk-tale quality and is a thrilling tale of adventure, an archetypal pursuit story. These elements are considerably diminished in *Catriona*, which concerns itself in the main with two themes very dominant in Stevenson's own life but which he had never allowed to enter his fiction before. The first is the difficulty of moral choice, particularly with regard to behaviour which one knows will have unfortunate effects on both oneself and on those dear to one, the second is romantic, sexual, love. In *Catriona* David Balfour tries to carry out—at considerable danger to himself—his intention of acquitting James of the Glens of the Appin Murder, a plan the more honourable since David in fact dislikes James and has reason to do so, for he has attempted to incriminate him with the Government authorities. As we have already seen in discussing *Kidnapped*, David's exertions were doomed to failure, since the Duke of Argyll intended a man to hang simply to illustrate the Government's severe policy towards rebels, and was not too concerned about the innocence or otherwise of the person made into this example. David is unswerving in his belief that real justice should be done and much of the novel's moving quality comes from his realization that in this world this is not always the way. And his sense of values is further disturbed in that the man who officially condemns James of the Glens to death, Lord Prestongrange (a real person), is someone for whom he feels both respect and affection. A good part of the novel is, in fact, taken up with David's relationship to Prestongrange; Stevenson's hand is always very sure when drawing relationships between younger and older men, perhaps springing from his own with both his father and Professor Fleeming Jenkin. And he comes to see, though not to agree, that good can come out of morally dubious, expedient deeds. Prestongrange had behind him an excellent record of just and kindly dealings with the Highlanders. And it is a matter of historical fact that the Appin Murder was the last explosion of violence in the troubled areas of Scotland. Indeed, the second half of the eighteenth century was a golden age of Scottish culture and saw a reconciliation between Lowland and Highland attitudes and practices. So in a way Prestongrange was right and sensible to act as he did.

At the same time, Stevenson obviously champions the individual moral strength of David—even against the sensible course of action in his world. There is a fine passage where David reflects on his behaviour after James has actually been hanged. This seems to me to have a depth of thought Stevenson had never reached before:

'. . . in the course of time, on November 8th, and in the midst of a prodigious storm of wind and rain, poor James of the Glens was duly hanged at Lettermore by Ballachulish.

'So there was the final upshot of my politics! Innocent men have perished before James, and are like to keep on perishing (in spite of all our wisdom) till the end of time. And till the end of time young folk (who are not yet used with the duplicity of life and men) will struggle as I did, and make heroical resolves and take long risks; and the course of events will push them upon the one side and go on like a marching army. James was hanged; and here was I dwelling in the house of Prestongrange, and grateful for his fatherly attention. . . . He had been hanged by fraud and violence, and the world tagged along, and there was not a pennyweight of difference; and the villains of that horrid plot were decent, kind, respectable fathers of families, who went to Kirk and took the sacrament!

'But I had my view of that detestable business they call politics —I had seen it from behind, when it is all bones and blackness; and I was cured for life of any temptations to take part in it again. A plain, quiet, private path was that which I was ambitious to walk in, when I might keep my head out of the way of dangers and my conscience out of the road of temptation. For, upon a retrospect, it appeared I had not done so grandly, after all; but with the greatest possible amount of big speech and preparation, had accomplished nothing.'

While this might have been written with some of his experiences in South Seas politics in the back of his mind, I think Stevenson is here voicing a distrust, felt from his adolescence onward, in society as a whole, in people in the mass. Only in private life could one's finest nature be satisfied. Stevenson himself had certainly found it so. And the rest of the novel after this passage is concerned with the growth of love between David and Catriona. Love had brought Stevenson his greatest happiness; it is to bring David his, too.

Not that Catriona resembles Fanny. With her grey eyes, proud bearing and soft musical Highland speech, she must surely be a presentation of Louis' happier, tender memories of 'Claire'. It is, of course, an edited picture—even now Louis found frankness in such matters hard in his fiction—and her story differs markedly from reality. For David marries Catriona, and their union is, we are told, to be successful and happy. It has, of course, symbolic undertones; it is the union of Lowland and Highland ways of life, of the two strains in Scottish national culture. And it is the union too of the two halves of Stevenson, the prudent man of conscience and thought, of moral intensity and intransigence, on the one hand, and the reckless, emotional man of instinct, the artist, on the other. David Balfour is brought before us in an even more sympathetic and intimate light than in *Kidnapped*. Myself I find him one of the most attractive central figures in the English novel. Stevenson himself thought so. He considered him 'as good a character as anybody has a right to ask for in a novel'.

After *Catriona*, Stevenson began work on several major projects: *Records of a Family of Engineers*, a history of the Stevensons, quoted from earlier in this book; *Sophia Scarlet*, a novel with a South Seas setting, three central female characters and a more overt treatment of sexual relations than was to be found in previous writings of his; *Heathercat*, a story of the Covenanters in the 'Killing-Time'—this was put aside because Stevenson found an increasing difficulty in identifying himself with them—and *St. Ives*. *St. Ives* Stevenson wrote a very great deal of; it has since been finished by Sir Arthur Quiller-Couch and therefore can be read as a complete book. It is the story of the adventures of a French prisoner from Napoleon's army in Scotland and England —full of many lively scenes and details, but ultimately rather lifeless. It was as well that Stevenson laid it aside to begin work on *Weir of Hermiston*.

For many years, Stevenson had been haunted by the curious and terrifying figure of Robert MacQueen, Lord Braxfield

(1722-1799) and had long intended to write a novel about this man who rose to the position of Lord Advocate. Like so many eminent Scots of his day, Braxfield had his portrait painted by the great Scottish artist Raeburn, on whom Stevenson in his youth, out of admiration, wrote an essay. In this he speaks of Braxfield and of Raeburn's attempts to capture his strange personality. (The portrait can be seen in the Scottish National Portrait Gallery.) Braxfield had 'left behind him, a reputation for rough and cruel speech; and to this day his name smacks of the gallows'. But Stevenson noted that he didn't seem from his picture a complete monster—he had a 'tart, wry, humorous look' about him, and 'a peculiarly subtle expression haunts the lower part of his face'. Then in Samoa, Stevenson re-read Lord Cockburn's *Memorials of his Time* in which another distinguished Scottish legal figure describes many of the leading people of Edinburgh at the end of the eighteenth and the early part of the nineteenth centuries. Braxfield's cruel and relentless treatment of prisoners in the dock, his coarseness and contemptuousness were once more revealed to him, as was his cleverness. Stories about Braxfield in court are many and frightening.

'Ye're a verra clever chiel, man,' he said to a prisoner in the dock, 'but ye wad be none the worse o' a hanging.'

At the same time, he was a man of enormous capability and legal knowledge. Stevenson's interest in the divided personality was thus most strongly aroused. He also seemed to embody some of the most forceful and aggressive qualities of the Scottish temperament.

Stevenson gives to Lord Justice Weir of Hermiston (as this fictional version of Braxfield is called) a son, Archie. Archie's mother has been a gentle, pious, foolish woman, based on Jean, Stevenson's great-grandmother—her tragic bewildered life is most movingly and economically described in the very first chapter of the novel. She has brought Archie up a religious, refined boy, as Cummy brought up Louis. Mrs. Weir dies when her son is quite young, and throughout his adolescence and youth, the only real significant feature in his emotional landscape is the 'Hanging Judge', his father. When Archie becomes a law student at Edinburgh University, his detestation of the harsh, callous, coarse side of his father's personality grows to important and intensely obsessive proportions. He is his mother's child in his sensitivity and his dislike of the worldly and the ruthless, his father's in his intransigence of viewpoint, his strength of character.

One day, Archie goes into the courtroom to hear his father try a case. Lord Hermiston's conduct is Braxfield's. He heaps jeers and insults at the criminal he condemns to death, a pathetic mean wretch, and his down-at-heel mistress. Archie watches the procedure aghast, noting the pathetic behaviour of the criminal who, while in the dock, is nursing his sore throat with a piece of grubby flannel. Later on, at the public execution, Archie is moved to denounce Jopp's death as a God-defying murder. His father in a terrifyingly well-done scene summons him to his presence to take him to task. Archie tells his father:

' "I was present while Jopp was tried. It was a hideous business. Father, it was a hideous thing! Grant he was vile, why should you hunt him with a vileness equal to his own? It was done with glee—that is the word—you did it with glee and I looked on, God help me! with horror." '

For his protests in public against his father's commands, Archie is exiled to the family's country estate.

It will be seen that while my Lord of Hermiston has very little in common with Thomas Stevenson, and the solemn, reserved, studious Archie bears only limited resemblances to Louis, the relationship between the father and son in the novel is an emotional parallel to the most important relationship of Stevenson's own life. It is described with white-hot power; one feels throughout that the author was intensely involved in what he was writing, with all his heart. For dreadful though much of my Lord Hermiston's views and behaviour were, yet Archie cannot dismiss him; he knows that in his distant and strange way, his father loves him, and that he himself in a secret and remote part of his being returns the emotion. The reader will not need to be told how close to Stevenson's deepest self this situation was, nor the complexities and agonies of mind and soul that inevitably ensue.

Releasing in fictional form the dominant emotional struggle of his life made Stevenson able to release other preoccupations and themes. In the country to which he is exiled, Archie falls in love with the fascinating Kirstie Elliot, in many ways a child of nature, who puts no conventional bridle on her passions. Archie's love for her is described with a lyrical sexuality that Louis—though it had been important in his feeling life—had not been able to give to his writing before. The scenes between Archie and Kirstie are at once both tender and stormy with contained physical desire. At last the rapture and guilt of the affair with 'Claire', which had been so decisive an event in his life, were, after over a quarter of a century, given honest and passionate expression.

Stevenson was aware on beginning *Weir*, the events of which were clearly and unifiedly worked out in his head, that he had embarked on a work different in stature, as it was in emotional texture, from anything he had ever attempted before. And the feeling was sustained as he wrote— concentrated, rich in implications, the writing encompasses a whole range of different feelings, and has an exactitude and a subtlety that elevates it into a totally other class of achievement from the rest of his work. The style suggests a complete authority, a total knowledge of the events and characters being dealt with and yet a sense of their ultimate mystery such as one finds and admires in Tolstoy or Dostoevsky.

Stevenson's health had been worsening for some time before he turned his attention to *Weir of Hermiston* and he composed it against considerable physical suffering. Moreover, as the book suggests, he was possessed with acute excitement and agitation of emotion as he worked at it. For even at his most active in Samoa—even as he climbed the slopes of Mount Vaea and plunged into island politics—he knew that his life was one doomed to end early. Even at his best, he was never free from physical discomforts and from the shadow of direct pains. As time went on, his health once more became the 'wolverine' of earlier years— and there seems now little doubt that *Weir of Hermiston* involved all and more of his tragically limited supply of energies. This is revealed by Lloyd Osbourne's account of Stevenson reading *Weir* to the Vailima household:

'One evening, after dinner, he read the first chapters of *Weir* aloud. I had my usual pencil and paper for the notes I always took on such occasions, but that night I made none. It was so superbly written that I listened to it in a sort of spell. It seemed absolutely beyond criticism; seemed the very zenith of anything he had ever accomplished; it flowed with such an inevitability and emotion, such a sureness and perfection, that the words seemed to strike against my heart. When he had finished, I sat dumb. I knew I

should have spoken, but I could not. The others praised it . . .
but I was in a dream from which I could not awake . . . Then
the party broke up and we dispersed on our different ways to
bed . . . I had hardly passed the threshold of the door, however,
when I heard Stevenson behind me. He was in a state of frightful
agitation; was trembling, breathless, almost beside himself. "My
God, you shall not go like that!" he cried out, seizing me by the
arm, and his thin fingers closing on it like a vice. "What! Not a
single note, not a single word, not even the courtesy of a lie!
You, the only one whose opinion I depend on, and all you can
say is 'Goodnight, Louis'! So that is your decision, is it? Just
'Goodnight, Louis'—like a blow in the face!"

'The bitterness and passion he put into these words is beyond
any power of mine to describe. . . .

'Then I tried to tell him the truth, but with difficulty, realising
how unpardonably I had hurt his pride . . . That it was a masterpiece; that never before had he written anything comparable
with *Weir*, that it promised to be the greatest novel in the English
language.

'We were in the dark. I could not see his face. But I believe he
listened with stupefaction. The reaction when it came was too
great for his sorely strained nerves; tears rained from his eyes—
and mine, too, streamed. Never had I known him to be so moved;
never had I been so moved myself; and in the all-pervading
darkness we were for once free to be ourselves, unashamed.
Thus we sat, with our arms about each other, talking far into the
night. Even after thirty years, I should not care to divulge
anything so sacred as those confidences; the revelation of that
tortured soul; the falterings of its Calvary . . . To me his heroism
took on new proportions, and I now was thankful I had refused an
important post to stay with him. "It will not be for long," he said.'

How this brings home to us the intensity of life which Stevenson
projected into *Weir*, and his feeling that he was producing his
masterpiece—also that in doing so he strained every nerve he
possessed because he was plundering his most secret and cherished
storehouse of memories, both joyous and tragic. *Weir* vindicates
Stevenson's lifelong faithfulness to his art, that 'heroism' his
stepson speaks of. While one might hesitate, especially as it is
unfinished, to call it 'the greatest novel in the English language',
it can most certainly take its place among our supreme master-

pieces of fiction. The great emotional force of the novel, its brooding tragic power have already been mentioned; it also recreates the Scotland of the early nineteenth century with both great solidity and deep feeling—from the New Town of Edinburgh and the Spec. Society up at the University to the wild Border world of the Four Black Brothers. Stevenson brings to life a wide range of different ways of life in a given country at a given time and in doing so extends our knowledge of humanity. His method of portrayal of character and events is the ultimate fruit of his practising the novelist's art, and also owes something to that long-ago legal training, suggesting the careful, compassionate balancing of information necessary to the fair judge. And the novel contains a whole gallery of wonderfully drawn people, of which my Lord Hermiston and his son are only two—all are flesh-and-blood beings with a life, it seems, of their own, the illusion always created by a great writer. The reader can have the pleasure of discovering them for himself, though I would advise him to look carefully at the sympathetic, touchingly painted Kirstie the elder and at the meretricious, hollow figure of treacherous Frank Innes.

Though *Weir* was never finished, we know what Stevenson intended to happen from the notes he left with Isobel Strong. Sidney Colvin has preserved them for us in his editorial afterword to the book. Whether the inspired quality of the nine chapters given to us could have been kept up cannot, of course, ever be known. Many have speculated on the matter. It seems to me unimportant. Incomplete in fact, it is complete in spirit, one of the richest and most fascinating books of English literature.

Alas! the strain of writing it was too great. Louis had spent the morning of Monday, 3 December 1894 dictating the powerful ninth chapter of *Weir*, dealing with the obstacles that come in the way of the love between Archie and Kirstie. In the afternoon he indulged in his favourite and psychologically necessary activity of writing letters to his friends back in Britain. At sunset he came downstairs to talk to Fanny. Helping her to prepare a salad for the evening meal he suddenly put his hands to his head, exclaiming, 'My head—oh, my head. What's that?' Then, saying, 'Do I look strange?' he collapsed to the floor. He never properly regained consciousness. The doctor was called—looking at the man insensible in the armchair, he realized that the brain haemorrhage Louis had had was fatal. The household were in what Lloyd later described as a 'frenzy of grief'. Their distress mounted as Louis' breathing became slower and more laborious. The Protestant minister who had been a close friend in recent years prayed by the dying man. At ten minutes past eight, Louis died.

The funeral was as romantic, as solemn and as informed by deep love as Louis could have hoped. Samoans cleared a trail through the thick forest up the steep slopes of Mount Vaea. On its beautiful lonely summit, commanding a view of rolling virginal green mountains and the vast expanses of the Pacific Ocean, his coffin was interred. Nineteen Europeans and sixty Samoans had made the hard ascent to pay their tribute to the man who had meant so much to them.

Indeed, perhaps Louis' most significant and singular quality was his ability to arouse love and in many different persons. He did it through his writings, as well as through his conversation and his acts. Even now in the second half of the twentieth century, his stories, his essays, his poems and his letters, for all their weaknesses, for all their flights of extravagant romanticism and egotism, have a capacity to make us love the writer and to love the people and places that he himself loved. For his was a great heart, and the best of the work that he gave to the world is the product of a great heart. It is this that gives him his unique stature in the culture of our country.

Stevenson had written an epitaph for himself, the lines of which were engraved on the tombstone above the Mount Vaea grave:

> Under the wide and starry sky,
> Dig the grave and let me lie.
> Glad did I live and gladly die,
>   And I laid me down with a will.
>
> This be the verse you grave for me:
> *Here he lies where he longed to be;*
> *Home is the sailor, home from sea,*
>   *And the hunter home from the hill.*

But I prefer the words of Edmund Gosse who, in his memorial essay, called Louis Stevenson, 'the most fascinating, the most inspiriting human being I have known'.

Principal Books Consulted

Sidney Colvin, edit.: TUSITALA EDITION OF ROBERT LOUIS STEVENSON'S WORKS 37 vols. (1923-1924)

Graham Balfour: THE LIFE OF ROBERT LOUIS STEVENSON (1901)
George Brown: A BOOK OF R.L.S. (1919)
David Daiches: STEVENSON AND THE ART OF FICTION (1951)
de Lancey Ferguson and Marshall Waingrow: STEVENSON'S LETTERS TO CHARLES BAXTER (1956)
J. C. Furnas: VOYAGE TO WINDWARD (1951)
Edmund Gosse: CRITICAL KIT-KATS (1913)
Lord Guthrie: ROBERT LOUIS STEVENSON: SOME PERSONAL RECOLLECTIONS (1920)
Robert Kiely: ROBERT LOUIS STEVENSON AND THE FICTION OF ADVENTURE (1964)
Andrew Lang: ADVENTURES AMONG BOOKS (1905)
Will H. Low: A CHRONICLE OF FRIENDSHIPS 1873-1900 (1908)
Rosaline Masson: I CAN REMEMBER R.L.S. (1922)
Rosaline Masson: THE LIFE OF ROBERT LOUIS STEVENSON (1923)
Lloyd Osbourne: AN INTIMATE PORTRAIT OF ROBERT LOUIS STEVENSON (1924)
Janet Adam Smith: HENRY JAMES AND ROBERT LOUIS STEVENSON: A RECORD OF A FRIENDSHIP AND CRITICISM (1948)
Janet Adam Smith: ROBERT LOUIS STEVENSON: COLLECTED POEMS (1971 revised edition)
J. A. Steuart: ROBERT LOUIS STEVENSON, MAN AND WRITER: A CRITICAL BIOGRAPHY (1924)
Isobel Strong and Lloyd Osbourne: MEMORIES OF VAILIMA (1903)